The Language Myth

Language is central to our lives, the cultural tool that arguably sets us apart from other species. Some scientists have argued that language is innate, a type of unique human 'instinct' pre-programmed in us from birth. In this book, Vyvyan Evans argues that this received wisdom is, in fact, a myth.

Debunking the notion of a language 'instinct', Evans demonstrates that language is related to other animal forms of communication; that languages exhibit staggering diversity; that we learn our mother tongue drawing on general properties and abilities of the human mind, rather than an inborn 'universal' grammar; that language is not autonomous but is closely related to other aspects of our mental lives; and that, ultimately, language and the mind reflect and draw upon the way we interact with others in the world.

Compellingly written and drawing on cutting-edge research, *The Language Myth* sets out a forceful alternative to the received wisdom, showing how language and the mind really work.

Vyvyan Evans is Professor of Linguistics in the School of Linguistics and English Language at Bangor University.

The Language Myth

Why Language Is Not an Instinct

VYVYAN EVANS

CAMBRIDGE
UNIVERSITY PRESS

CAMBRIDGE
UNIVERSITY PRESS

University Printing House, Cambridge CB2 8BS, United Kingdom

Cambridge University Press is part of the University of Cambridge.

It furthers the University's mission by disseminating knowledge in the pursuit of education, learning and research at the highest international levels of excellence.

www.cambridge.org
Information on this title: www.cambridge.org/9781107619753

© Vyvyan Evans 2014

This publication is in copyright. Subject to statutory exception and to the provisions of relevant collective licensing agreements, no reproduction of any part may take place without the written permission of Cambridge University Press.

First published 2014
4th printing 2019

Printed in the United Kingdom by TJ International Ltd. Padstow Cornwall

A catalogue record for this publication is available from the British Library

Library of Congress Cataloguing in Publication data
Evans, Vyvyan.
The language myth : why language is not an instinct / Vyvyan Evans.
    pages cm
ISBN 978-1-107-04396-1 (Hardback) – ISBN 978-1-107-61975-3 (Paperback)
1. Linguistic universals.   2. Cognitive grammar.   3. Innateness hypothesis (Linguistics)   4. Language and languages–Philosophy.   5. Psycholinguistics.   I. Title.
P204.E88 2014
401–dc23   2014014932

ISBN 978-1-107-04396-1 Hardback
ISBN 978-1-107-61975-3 Paperback

....

Every effort has been made to secure necessary permissions to reproduce copyright material in this work, though in some cases it has proved impossible to trace or contact copyright holders. If any omissions are brought to our notice, we will be happy to include appropriate acknowledgements on reprinting, or in any subsequent edition.

For Andrea Tyler

The great enemy of the truth is very often not the lie, deliberate, contrived and dishonest, but the myth, persistent, persuasive and unrealistic.

John F. Kennedy

Contents

Acknowledgements

I have wanted to write this book since I was a graduate student. But some things are better for the time it takes to grow, experience and learn. The specific impetus for this book was a challenge made to me by Stéphanie Pourcel, on Brighton pier, of all places. Her challenge, a number of years ago now, was to explain why the language-as-instinct thesis, the thesis associated with Noam Chomsky and his followers, is wrong. This book is my response to that challenge. I hope it does that job. More than that, I hope it fulfils the greater task of explaining how I think language works, how language relates to the mind, and what this reveals about what it means to be human.

A large number of colleagues have supported the research and the writing that has gone into this book. For logistical support, specific advice or simply responding to queries, I gratefully acknowledge Ben Bergen, Andy Clark, Ewa Dąbrowska, Adele Goldberg, George Lakoff, Ineke Mennen, Thora Tenbrink, Mike Tomasello, Mark Turner and Mike Wheeler. For detailed feedback on chapters, I am extremely indebted to Ben Ambridge, Mihailo Antović, Bastien Boutonnet, Vivien Mast, Svetoslava Antonova-Baumann and Alan Wallington. I am particularly indebted to Paul Ibbotson: Paul went *way* beyond the call of duty, and fearlessly read quite literally an entire draft of the book. His very extensive comments have shaped my presentation of various aspects of the book's content. I hope he approves of how I have responded to, and incorporated, his advice. I am also grateful for the immensely detailed and helpful advice provided by a number of anonymous reviewers for Cambridge University Press.

Finally, I gratefully acknowledge the support and care I have received from my editor at Cambridge University Press, Andrew Winnard. Andrew is a paragon of sound judgement and efficiency, and has provided extremely helpful advice on many aspects of the book. I hope to have done justice to the support he has afforded me.

This book is dedicated to my former Ph.D. supervisor, colleague, co-author and dear friend, Andrea Tyler. For a number of years, Ande and I have been intellectual co-conspirators in the language-as-use thesis – the thesis I present in the pages that follow. I hope she approves of what I have done in my part of the conspiracy.

1 Language and mind rethought

This is a book about language, and about its relationship with thought and the mind. It is also a book about how we acquire language, and why different languages are so diverse in their sound systems, vocabularies and grammars. Language is central to our lives, and is arguably the cultural tool that sets humans, us, apart from any other species. And on some accounts, language is *the* symbolic behaviour that allowed human singularities – art, religion and science – to occur.[1] In her Nobel Prize acceptance speech, the celebrated African-American writer, Toni Morrison, put things this way: "We die. That may be the meaning of life. But we do language. That may be the measure of our lives."[2] Language is clearly a big deal.

This book addresses a controversy that has raged in the behavioural and brain sciences since the middle of the last century: is language innate, something we are born with? Or does language emerge from use, based on more general mental skills and abilities? The dominant view, until recently, has been the former: we come into the world hard-wired with the rudiments of language. But this view now looks to be on increasingly shaky ground.

But what might it mean to claim that language is innate? Clearly our species, *Homo sapiens*, is biologically pre-prepared to acquire language in a way no other species is: we have evolved the articulatory capabilities to produce a complex set of distinct and discrete sound units – and these sound units vary from language to language; we have the musculature to control and facilitate the production of these sounds; we have the memory capabilities to produce and recall sequences of sounds in order to facilitate well-formed strings of sounds, making grammatically well-formed sentences; and we have complex statistical processing abilities allowing us both to perceive and to recognise sequences of

1

sounds. Crucially, we recognise fellow humans as being intentional agents, and, hence, are predisposed to interpret their sound sequences as meaningful. And, most significant of all, any given speech community has *agreed* a bewilderingly complex set of linguistic conventions – a language is nothing more than a set of linguistic conventions – allowing us to transmit and comprehend complex ideas: in English we agree that the sound units that make up the word *cat* represent the idea that is associated with the sound segments that in French are signalled orthographically as *chat*, or in Hindi as *billi*.

Conventional wisdom has maintained, over and above this physiological pre-preparedness for language, that we are born with a set of grammatical rules (universal knowledge structures), stored somewhere in our minds, that allow us to acquire grammar almost effortlessly. The idea is that the grammar that underlies all of the 7,000 or so of the world's languages is essentially the same. In short, our species has evolved a specialised grammar module, embedded in our brains, and genetically encoded. And this provides us with the ability to acquire language in the first place: our grammar faculty is in place at birth.

This idea is often referred to as Universal Grammar: all human languages, no matter the variety we happen to end up speaking, are essentially the same. Whether someone learns English, Japanese, Swahili, Tongan or whatever, when you get down to it, they are all alike. Sure, each of these languages has different vocabularies. And each language makes use of a different, although partially overlapping, set of sounds. But underneath it all, the essential ingredient of language – our grammar – is pre-programmed in the human genome: we are all born to produce language because of our common genetic heritage, our Universal Grammar. Just as all of us grow distinctively human organs – brains, livers, hearts and kidneys – so too we develop language: a consequence of our grammar organ, which grows in the human brain, and which no other species possesses. And it is this innately specified knowledge of grammar that underpins our ability to develop and acquire language – any language – in the first place.

This book, and the range of ideas I cover, are presented from the perspective of linguistics – the scientific study of language – my home discipline. While linguistics covers many more areas and sub-disciplines than are represented here, I've chosen the range of topics on show, in the chapters to follow, for a very specific reason. The majority of the evidence, viewed with objective eyes, now appears to show that language is not innate in the way just outlined.

In a nutshell, I aim to convince you of the following: language *doesn't* arise from innately programmed knowledge of human grammar, a so-called 'Universal Grammar'. I will argue that language reflects and builds upon general properties and abilities of the human mind – specifically our species-specific cultural intelligence; it reflects human pro-social inclinations for inter-subjective communication. I will seek to persuade you that when we acquire language in infancy, we do so by acquiring the language of our parents and caregivers, painstakingly, and by making many mistakes in the process. Language is not something that emerges automatically, and effortlessly. It arises primarily from the language input we are exposed to, from which we construct our mother tongue. Moreover, human infants, I will show, are not empty vessels that come empty-handed to the language learning process. We come ready-equipped with a battery of various general learning mechanisms that make us adept at acquiring our mother tongue(s).

But why should this discussion matter at all? Why should we care? The study of language, for perhaps obvious reasons, is central to a great many other disciplines; after all, if language is the hallmark of what it means to be human, if it is the measure of our lives, then this stands to reason. And because of the centrality of language to all else, it is crucial our understanding of it is accurate. It is also critical that we understand how language relates to other aspects of mental function and social life. And perhaps more than this: language is an index of our very humanity. What would Shakespeare be without his ability to invent, and re-invent the human psyche through language? Language is more than the paradigm example of cultural behaviour, one that sets us apart from any other species on the planet. We all have a vested interest in it: it makes us who we are, and allows us to explore ourselves: our emotional highs and lows. We should all care about language, even when we take it for granted, for without it we are barely human.

And here is the *really* important part. While I, and a great many other professional linguists, now think the old view is wrong, nevertheless, the old view – Universal Grammar: the eponymous 'language myth' – still lingers; despite being *completely* wrong, it is alive and kicking. I have written this book to demonstrate exactly why the old view is a myth; and to show what the reality is. This book is thus a users' manual for all language users, and for all thinking people. And, it is also, I hope, a reasonably accessible overview of the way language really works.

This book surveys discoveries from a broad array of disciplines; these include linguistics, psychology, philosophy, neurobiology, primatology, ethology and cognitive anthropology. And these discoveries – which have emerged since the mid-1980s – have thrown into relief long-held assumptions about the nature and structure of language, as well as the mind, and the way we acquire our native tongue(s). In this book, I present the emerging reality.

∾

Linguistics is a relatively new discipline compared to others, especially compared to long-established subjects such as philosophy and rhetoric, or even more recent sciences such as astronomy and medicine. Its founding father is often taken to be the eminent Swiss linguist, Ferdinand de Saussure, whose *Course in General Linguistics* (2013) was published posthumously in 1916. The Zeitgeist for much of the second half of the twentieth century, however, was an extreme form of rationalism, which assumed that language is an instinct, something wholly unrelated to any other form of non-human communication. This language myth assumed that all human languages are governed by a single set of universals buried in the recesses of the human mind, with which we are born.

The reasons for taking this sort of perspective were based on a number of assumptions about the nature of language, in most cases before actual detailed research had been carried out. But today, we now know a vast amount about the diversity exhibited by the languages of the world – although acknowledging that we still only know something about a fraction of the world's 7,000 or so languages. We also know a vast amount about how children acquire language, much more than we did when the *language-as-instinct thesis*, as I shall call the language myth, was formulated, originally in the 1950s and 1960s. Indeed, the preponderance of evidence now leads a great many linguists, myself included, to the incontrovertible conclusion that language reflects, in important ways, more general, and generalizable, properties of mind. And, importantly, we learn language from our parents and caregivers, through painstaking practice and use. This, for ease, I refer to as the *language-as-use thesis*. In contrast, the language-as-instinct thesis, I will seek to persuade you, is a myth; and, it is made up of a number of component sub-myths.

Taking stock of language

Before moving on, let's get a preliminary sense of what language is for, and how it is organised. Language is integral to our lives. We use it to buy groceries in the supermarket, to get a job, to hire or fire an employee, to buy train tickets, and to compose an email. We use it to make a telephone call, to flirt, to invite someone out on a date, to propose marriage, to get married, to quarrel, and to make up afterwards. Language allows us to make friends, and enemies, to pass the time of day, and so on. In our everyday lives, we produce and comprehend language with such apparent ease that we take it for granted. Yet the ease with which we use language belies a level of complexity of immense proportions. You might not know a preposition from an adverb, or the difference between the passive voice and the indicative, nor what the double object construction is. You might also be at a loss if I asked you how to conjugate the copula in English, or what perfective aspect is. Yet like around 400 million other native speakers of English around the world, you and I deploy the copula and successfully conjugate it countless times every day. In other words, our knowledge of language is implicit rather than explicit. While you might not be able to explain to a foreigner, should they ask, how to conjugate the copula without the aid of a book of English grammar, you can do it with your hands tied behind your back. Each of us carries around in our heads a 'mental grammar' far more impressive than any written grammar. In short, you or I don't have to know that the verb *be* is the copula to know how to use it.

Another sobering fact about spoken – and indeed signed – language is this: unlike other forms of cultural behaviour, it is blind to demographics, socioeconomics and ethnic difference.[3] I, you and every other cognitively normal human being in the world uses (or comes to use) language with the apparent ease that we take for granted. Put another way, it doesn't matter whether you are rich or poor, black or white or what the colour of your eyes are. You are destined to acquire at least one language – although the majority of the world's nearly 7 billion people grow up speaking two or more languages. In this, the pattern of monolingualism amongst English-speaking populations is not the norm. And, by around 4 years of age, each normally developing human child is a linguistic genius. Nevertheless, we carry on 'learning' our mother tongue, throughout our lives. This is the case not least because the language we speak changes and evolves, often in quite short periods of time.

In virtually all of the situations in which we find ourselves in our daily lives, language allows quick and effective expression, and provides a well-developed means of encoding and transmitting complex and subtle ideas. Language does this by fulfilling two key functions, functions that underpin linguistic communication.

The first is that language enables us to express our wishes, feelings, likes, dislikes and ideas. This language achieves by encoding and externalising our thoughts. To do this, language uses symbols. Symbols are meaningful bits of language. These include sub-parts of words, such as *un-* and *-ed* in *uninterested*, whole words like *walk*, *yesterday* and *knickers* or groups of words which form clauses, such as *behind the sofa*, and groups of clauses which form sentences, like *She left her knickers behind the sofa*.

The symbols that make up English, or any language, consist of two parts, a form and a meaning. Forms may be spoken, written or signed – as in British Sign Language, the sign language of the British deaf community – while the meanings are the ideas, or concepts, that are conventionally associated with them. For instance, in spoken English, the word *cat* is made up of the three distinct sound segments, technically known as phonemes /k/, /æ/ and /t/ which combine to give the form /kæt/. The meaning unit conventionally paired with this form constitutes the stable know-ledge that you and I have relating to cats: that they have four legs, whiskers, a tail, make sounds of particular sorts, exhibit quirky, cat-like behaviour of particular kinds, and so on.

However, for language to function effectively as a means of communication, it is not enough that it employs symbols in order to associate forms and meanings. In addition, these form-meaning pairings must be recognised by, and accessible to, others in our community. After all, we use language in order to get our ideas across: to communicate. This involves a process of transmission by the speaker, and decoding and interpretation by the hearer. In short, language fulfils a symbolic or communicative function.

But in addition, the messages we choose to encode symbolically in language invariably perform an interactive and hence social role – the second function of language. For instance, we can use language to change the way the world is. When a member of the clergy makes the utterance: *I now pronounce you husband and wife*, in an appropriate setting, and addressed to two consenting adults, the utterance changes an aspect of the world in a rather special way. From the moment the utterance has been made, the legal, social and moral status holding between the two individuals is irrevocably altered. The newly created husband and wife have obligations and potential claims towards and against each other that they didn't have prior to the utterance of these words. In some countries, even their tax status is altered. In short, language can be used to perform *actions* which have consequences in the real world.

But one doesn't need the special status of a member of the clergy, a Prime Minister or a sovereign to be able to alter aspects of the world through language. An everyday expression such as *Shut that door on the way out!* also represents an action performed through language – in this, language bestows complete equality: we can all do it. This expression is an attempt to have someone do something, thereby altering an aspect of the world to suit our own wishes or desires.

Another way in which language fulfils its interactive function is by enabling us to express our thoughts and feelings about the world. The expressions *terrorist* and *freedom fighter* might be used to describe the same individual by different people with different perspectives, and different agendas. Using language to speak of a *war on terror* or describing the campaign to criminalise abortion as *Pro-life* is more than mere wordplay. Language carries with it systems of ideas: words have concepts attached to them. Language use helps to frame, or reframe particular issues, and this framing can be both positive and negative.[4] Language has been described as a loaded weapon: it brings with it real-world consequences.[5]

Language also plays a role in how we affect other people, and how we make others feel, achieved just by our choice of words. Expressions such as *Shut up!* versus *I'm terribly sorry to interrupt you*, while ostensibly conveying the same meaning, affect our addressee in very different ways. This is because the way in which we present our public selves is conveyed, in large part, through language. The nature of the language we choose to use signals information about our attitudes towards others, ourselves and the situations in which we find ourselves.

I've already intimated that a key function of language is social interaction. For instance, we use language to engage in gossip, to get to know someone, to conduct business, to make a purchase in a shop, to attract members of the same or opposite sex, to declare undying love, and so forth. But how, exactly, do we make use of language in order to facilitate these social functions? We do so by engaging in culturally recognised activities in order to achieve (what are at least usually) mutually understood goals. Moreover, language use arises *in* these joint activities, which are often extremely difficult without it.

For example, imagine going to a shoe shop in order to purchase a pair of John Wayne cowboy boots. This involves a sales assistant approaching you and offering help, interacting with a sales assistant in order to have your feet measured, the assistant fetching the required cowboy boots from the stock room for you to try on, agreeing the purchase, making payment, and the assistant boxing or wrapping the boots. This service encounter is an example of a culturally recognised joint activity. And, crucially, it relies on language use in order to accomplish the desired outcome: the purchase of the boots.

But in addition to using language during the course of a service encounter of this kind, we have to build a mental representation of what is going on, in order to keep track of what stage we are at in proceedings. This involves integrating information we get from language, with information derived from other cues, such as seeing that the sales assistant has brought the wrong colour boots from the store room, or that uncomfortable feeling when the boots are too tight, as you try them on. The information which accumulates, during joint activities of this sort, is gleaned from our discourse – our use of language – and from the ongoing and ever-changing situation(s) in which we find ourselves.

~

Recall that I said that words consist of symbols: form–meaning pairings. Language encompasses a wide range of different types of knowledge which serve to support symbol use. One kind of knowledge concerns the individual sounds that make up a particular language, and the rules that govern the way these sounds can be combined. While there is a finite inventory of all the possible sounds a human being can make, different languages draw on different numbers of these in producing the words that make up a language. This is why a French speaker finds it difficult to pronounce the *th* sound in English, and why a Chinese speaker often cannot pronounce the *r* sound: *fried rice* becomes *flied lice*. These sounds simply don't exist in French, or Mandarin. Indeed, English speakers often sound equally absurd when speaking other languages, as I can attest from years of mangling the French language. A number of French sounds simply don't exist in English.

Standard English consists of twelve simple vowel sounds. These include the /ɪ/ in p̲i̲t and the /e/ in p̲e̲t. There are, in addition, a further eight two-vowel sound sequences, known as diphthongs, such as the /eɪ/ in d̲a̲y. English also has twenty-four consonants like the /z/ in z̲ip and the /ŋ/ in ri̲n̲g. This makes a total of forty-four distinct sound segments from which all English words are derived – at least in standard British Received Pronunciation (RP). This total may, on the face of it, be somewhat surprising, given that the alphabet consists of only twenty-six letters. Yet the English spelling system is, in fact, the Latin spelling system, and as applied to English is notoriously treacherous, as is made abundantly clear by the following poem by T. S. Watt:

> I take it you already know
> Of tough and bough and cough and dough?
> Others may stumble but not you
> On hiccough, thorough, slough and through.
> Well done! And now you wish perhaps,
> To learn of less familiar traps?
> Beware of heard, a dreadful word
> That looks like beard and sounds like bird.
> And dead, it's said like bed, not bead
> for goodness' sake don't call it 'deed'!
> Watch out for meat and great and threat
> (they rhyme with suite and straight and debt).[6]

A second type of knowledge involves word structure. Each of us intuitively knows how simple words are combined to make complex words – and the meanings associated with the parts of words involved. We know the difference between *teaching*, *teacher* and *teachable*. A teacher is a person who carries out the activity of teaching, while a subject is teachable (or not). We add the suffixes *-er*, *-ing* and *-able* to the verb stem *teach* at will in order to derive the requisite meaning. We also know that while a *teacher* is someone who teaches, we can't necessarily add *-er* willy nilly to create similar meanings. Much of our knowledge appears to be word-specific. For instance, a *villager* is not someone who 'villages' and a *bestseller* is not someone who 'bestsells'. In fact, a bestseller is not a person at all.

Another type of knowledge relates to the range of meanings associated with words and other linguistic expressions. Knowledge of this kind is not the restricted definitional kind that you might find given as concise definitions in a desk dictionary, for instance. The sort of meanings associated with words that you carry around in your head is better likened to an encyclopaedia. In fact, knowledge of this type is commonly referred to as encyclopaedic knowledge. For instance, consider everything you must know in order to understand what *open* means in the following expressions: *open a book, open your briefcase, open the curtains, open your mouth* and *open her blouse*. The kind of knowledge you must have access to, stuffed somewhere in your head, concerns the range of scenarios in which very different sorts of things can be 'opened'. After all, we apply 'open' to very different sorts of 'containers' such as a briefcase, a mouth and a blouse, with apertures of different kinds, whose opening is achieved in different ways and for different purposes. It is less clear that a book is a container, and it is not at all clear that there is a container that is opened by virtue of opening curtains. We conventionally use *open* in relation to these very different scenarios, and many others, including such things as 'opening' a bank account. The word meanings that are stuffed into our heads appear not to resemble the narrow, precise definitions of a dictionary at all. Rather, they relate to the sorts of things and situations with respect to which *open* can apply, the way the opening occurs, and the purposes for the 'opening' event.

Consider how you would go about opening a blouse versus a briefcase, the different sorts of entities you would be likely to find inside each (!), and the reasons for the 'opening' event.

Another kind of knowledge concerns our ability to combine words using knowledge of regular patterns in order to make a seemingly infinite number of novel sentences; we possess knowledge of the abstract rules that make up everything you and I know about English sentence structure. Part of this involves our knowledge regarding word order. We know, intuitively, that in the expression *The window cleaner nervously kissed the supermodel*, the window cleaner did the kissing. But if we reverse the window cleaner and the supermodel – *The supermodel confidently kissed the window cleaner* – now we have a different 'kisser' and 'kissee'. Part of what you, and I, know about a language, then, involves knowing the order in which words are positioned in a sentence. The order, after all, determines the role we attribute to the window cleaner and the supermodel in the kissing event. Of course, other languages vary in quite remarkable ways. Hungarian, for instance, has no fixed word order. Each language represents a unique system replete with its own conventions.

In addition, we possess a large inventory of idioms which are an essential part of any language, and which often pose problems for the language learner. For instance, try explaining to a foreign student why, in English, we can sleep *tight*, *soundly* and *deeply*, but we don't sleep *wide*! *To bend over backwards* means, somewhat bizarrely, to try very hard, rather than to bend over backwards, and *to jump down someone's throat* means something quite different from what it literally says. And *to kick the bucket*, which means 'to die', changes its meaning entirely even if we replace just one of the words. For instance, *to kick the mop* refers, presumably, to a frustrated janitor rather than death.

The final kind of knowledge that I'll touch on relates to what we might think of as contextualisation cues. These include the gestures which accompany our utterances, our facial expression, and cues relating to features of stress, intonation and pitch. For instance, whether the pitch of an utterance rises or falls can determine whether we interpret the utterance to be a question or a statement. Moreover, even a well-judged pause or glance can provide an effective means of signalling meaning; for instance, Marina Hyde, the journalist, writing in *The Guardian*, once noted that the appeal of Alistair Campbell – Tony Blair's once fearsome spin doctor – was "based entirely on the look he wore – a look which said: 'I'd like to shag you, if only I had the time.'"[7]

Myths and realities

In this book I present a number of myths, associated with the language-as-instinct thesis. I contrast these with what I suggest are the more plausible realities, given current knowledge. These realities suggest a wholly different thesis: language-as-use. Beginning with Chapter 2, each chapter commences with a succinct statement of the myth, and then presents the reasons for thinking that the reality lies away from the position maintained by it. The focus, then, is on debunking the myths, in part by presenting the evidence which supports the realities. And in so doing, I aim to show what contemporary research reveals about the nature of language, its function and organisation: how language is learned, and the way it reflects fundamental aspects of the human mind.

In view of this, a reasonable question to ask is: what exactly do I mean by a 'myth'? And, equally, what do I mean by a 'reality'? A myth, for my purposes, is an unproven account of a linguistic phenomenon that appears to be at odds with actual findings relating to language, the mind, and so on. The myth may derive from a best-guess attempt to account for an observed phenomenon. Moreover, what makes something a myth is that it relates to a speculative approach to understanding language. For instance, the basis for the language-as-instinct thesis derives from the proposals made by the famous (or perhaps infamous) American researcher Noam Chomsky, beginning in the 1950s and 1960s. Chomsky made a number of observations about the nature of language, and speculated that as language emerges apparently effortlessly, and all humans appear to be capable of acquiring language, then there must be an innately specified Universal Grammar that allows language to grow in the minds of humans, but no other species: language is an instinct.

But some readers may be surprised to learn that the language-as-instinct thesis is not based on actual findings. Nor is it based on detailed observations about how children appear to acquire language. Even today, over fifty years after it was first proposed, there is a paucity of cross-linguistic studies that have been conducted by Chomsky and his colleagues aiming to substantiate the claims of the language-as-instinct thesis. Chomsky's arguments were largely logical in nature, and to him (and his followers) self-evident: evidence was not required. And myths do have a tendency of becoming immune to evidence – that's what a myth is: plausible, institutionalised through ritual retelling, and the worst possible nightmare for 'truth'. But putting Chomsky's cult-status aside, progress in any field of science requires hard evidence, rather than the word of a 'great man'. Good theories, ultimately, ensure that reality bites, in the form of evidence for or against. And a good theory should, at least in principle, have a way of being proved wrong.[8] As the scientific findings have accrued, these increasingly make it very hard indeed to maintain the language-as-instinct thesis, as I hope to show you.

A reality, in contrast, consists of an account following detailed observations, data collection and analysis relating to the linguistic phenomenon. In other words, the realities I describe in this book follow from findings of fact, and analyses based on them, rather than being due to speculative arm-chair theorising.

My presentation of myths and realities focuses on some of the burning questions in the study of language and mind. These include the following.

Is human language unrelated to animal
communication systems?

The myth maintains that language is the preserve of humans, and humans alone; it cannot be compared to anything found amongst non-humans, and is unrelated to any non-human communicative capability. And the myth reinforces a view that there is an immense divide that separates human language from the communicative systems of other species. And more generally, it separates humans from all other species. But recent findings on the way other species communicate, from apes to whales, from vervets to starlings, increasingly suggest that such a view may overstate the divide that separates human language and non-human communicative systems. Indeed, many of the characteristics exhibited by human language are found, to varying degrees, across a broad spectrum of animal communication systems. In point of fact, we can learn more about human language, and what makes it special, by seeking to understand how it relates to and is derived from the communication systems of other species. This suggests that, although human language is qualitatively different, it is related to other non-human communication systems.

Are there language universals?

The language-as-instinct thesis claims that human babies enter the world pre-equipped to learn language. Language emerges effortlessly and automatically. And this is because we are all born with a Universal Grammar: a pre-specified listing of language universals – a universal being a feature of grammar that is shared by all languages. Moreover, as all languages are assumed to derive from this Universal Grammar, the study of a single language can reveal its design. In other words, despite having different sound systems and vocabularies, all languages are basically like English. Hence, we don't in fact need to learn or study any of the exotic languages out there – we need only focus on English, which contains the answers to how all other languages work. But, like the myth that language is unrelated to animal forms of communication, the myth of language universals is contradicted by the evidence. I argue that language emerges and diversifies, in and during specific instances of language use. Once I've reviewed some of the evidence for linguistic diversity, evidence that is incompatible with the language-as-instinct worldview, I present some of the usage-based pressures that collectively conspire to give rise to linguistic diversity.

Is language innate?

No one disputes that human children come into the world biologically prepared for language – from speech production apparatus, to information processing capacity, to memory storage, we are neurobiologically equipped to acquire spoken or signed language in a way no other species is. But the issue under the microscope is this: the language-as-instinct thesis proposes that a special kind of knowledge – grammatical knowledge – must be present at birth. Linguistic knowledge – a Universal Grammar that all humans are born with – is hard-wired into the microcircuitry of the human brain. The view that language is innate is, in a number of respects, highly attractive – at a stroke, it solves the problem of trying to account for how children acquire language without receiving negative feedback, from their parents and caregivers, when they make mistakes – it has been widely reported that parents, for the most part, don't systematically correct errors children make as they acquire language. And children can and do acquire their mother tongue without correction of any sort.[9] Moreover, children have acquired spoken language before they begin formal schooling: children are not *taught* spoken language, they just acquire it, seemingly automatically. But such a strong view eliminates the need for learning – apart from the relatively trivial task of learning the words of whatever language it is we end up speaking. The essentials of language, common to all languages, are present in our brains prior to birth, so the language myth contends. But we now know that these specific assumptions are incorrect, as I shall show.

Is language a distinct module in the mind?

In western thought there has been a venerable tradition in which the mind has been conceived in terms of distinct faculties. With the advent of cognitive science in the 1950s, the digital computer became the analogy of choice for the human mind. While the idea that the mind is a computer has been a central and highly influential heuristic in cognitive science, the radical proposal that the mind, like the computer, is also modular was made by philosopher of mind Jerry Fodor. In a now classic book, *Modularity of Mind*, published in 1983, whose reverberations are felt to this day, Fodor proposed that language is the paradigm example of a mental module. And this view, from the language-as-instinct perspective, makes perfect sense. According to Fodor, a mental module is realised in dedicated neural architecture. It copes with a specific and restricted type of information, and is impervious to the workings of other modules. As a consequence, a module can be selectively impaired, resulting in the breakdown in the behaviour associated with the module. And as a module deals with a specific type of information, the module will emerge at the particular point during the life cycle when it is needed. Hence, a mental module, in developmental terms, follows a characteristic schedule. The notion that the mind is modular might, on the face of it, make intuitive sense. In our everyday lives we associate component parts of artefacts with specific functions. The principle of modularity of design is both a practical and sensible approach to the manufacture not just of computers but of many, many aspects of everyday commodities, from cars to children's toys. However, the evidence, as will become clear, provides very little grounds for thinking that language is a module of mind, or indeed that the mind is modular.

Is there a universal Mentalese?

The language myth contends that meaning in natural languages, such as English or Japanese, derives, ultimately, from a universal language of thought: Mentalese. Mentalese is the mind's internal or private language, and makes thought possible. It is universal in the sense that all humans are born with it. It is language-like, consisting of symbols, which can be combined by rules of mental syntax. Without Mentalese we could not learn the meanings of words in any given language – spoken or signed. But as I shall show, Mentalese assumes a view of mind that is wrong-headed: it assumes that human minds are computer-like. It also suffers from a number of other difficulties, which make this supposition deeply problematic.

Is thought independent of language?

While everyone accepts that language affects thought in the sense that we use language to argue, persuade, convince and so on, according to the language myth, thought is, in principle, independent. The idea that systematic patterns in grammatical and semantic representations across languages (a.k.a. linguistic relativity) give rise to corresponding differences in patterns of thought across communities is utterly wrong. As we shall see, the language-as-instinct theorists mischaracterise the thesis of linguistic relativity. Moreover, there is also now a significant amount of scientific evidence suggesting that, in point of fact, the linguistic patterning of our native tongue(s) does indeed have indelible and habitual consequences for how we perceive the world.

∼

From this brief overview of the issues, one salient theme that emerges is, surely, the following. Language and rational thought – so the language-as-instinct myth contends – are too complex and arguably too mysterious to be accounted for without appeal to special knowledge. Such knowledge is 'special' in the sense that we simply don't know where it comes from. Experience, and general learning mechanisms, can't account for these unique features of the human mind. Thus, language must be hard-wired, part of our genetic endowment: enter Universal Grammar.

Richard Dawkins describes this type of explanation as an argument from incredulity,[10] while Daniel Everett notes that it boils down, essentially, to a lack of imagination.[11] It proceeds as follows: we (= the extremely clever, tenured professors) can't see how children could possibly learn something as complex as grammar – which underpins language. Therefore, they can't learn it. Thus, grammar must be innate.

The cognitive scientist Anthony Chemero[12] has described such a move as a Hegelian argument after the widely ridiculed 'proof' of Hegel. In 1801, Hegel claimed that the number of planets in the solar system was seven, based on premises which he provided, and had no evidence for. Indeed, we now know that there are eight major planets, and five dwarf planets, including Pluto. The language-as-instinct thesis is precisely this: a Hegelian argument.

But, speculation aside, we know, today, a vast amount about how language is learned, how languages differ, how concepts are formed, and how language interfaces with conceptual knowledge. While we certainly don't know everything there is to know, or even a fraction of everything, at this juncture we are in a position to do far better than the language-as-instinct thesis. In the pages that follow, I will present the case for a nearer approximation to the reality: the language-as-use thesis.

A straw man?

One of the objections, I anticipate, to this book is that I am attacking a straw man. Surely the 'myths' described above are not taken seriously? Indeed, one colleague has firmly censured me with the following reprimand: "These 'myths' are extreme views that barely anyone subscribes to."

Alas, this is not the case. The views that I classify as myths are presented as established fact in many of the linguistics textbooks currently in use in many of the stellar universities throughout the English-speaking world. I was trained using these textbooks, and they are still compulsory reading for today's undergraduate and graduate students – tomorrow's researchers, educators and language professionals – even at the university where I teach and work. University students are regularly told that there *is* a Universal Grammar, that language *is* innate, that language *is* incommensurable with non-human communication systems, and that all languages *are* essentially English-like.

For instance, the world's best-selling university textbook on language is *An Introduction to Language*, written by Professor Victoria Fromkin and colleagues. This book, now in its tenth revised edition, proclaims the following in its very first chapter:

> This business is just what the linguist attempts – to find out the laws of a language, and the laws of all languages. Those laws that pertain to all human languages, representing the universal properties of language, constitute a **Universal Grammar** ... To discover the nature of this Universal Grammar whose principles characterize all human languages is a major aim of linguistic theory...the more we investigate this question, the more evidence accumulates to support Chomsky's view that there is a universal grammar that is part of the human biologically endowed language faculty.[13]

A recently published textbook introduction to the English language, *The Structure of Modern English*, by Professor Laurel Brinton, makes the following claims in its introductory chapter:

> Language is rule-governed, creative, universal, innate and learned, all at the same time ... A more general set of constraints on language is known as **language universals**. These are features of language that are not language specific ... Inherent in the notion of universals is the belief that language is innate, that we are born with an inborn capacity for language acquisition.[14]

As we shall see, the claims made in both these representative textbooks are wrong – they fly in the face of, now, several decades of evidence-based research.

More worrying, the educated general public has been treated to a series of best-selling popular books on language by Professor Steven Pinker of Harvard University, no less. Pinker is talented, eloquent and erudite. He presents various views of language and mind adopting the language-as-instinct thesis that he has helped to develop. The educated general public who have read such pop-sci. bestsellers, including *The Language Instinct* (1994), *Words and Rules* (2001), *How the Mind Works* (1997), *The Blank Slate* (2002) and *The Stuff of Thought* (2007), might be forgiven, given Pinker's eloquence, for thinking that Pinker is right, and everything is settled. Far from it: don't be fooled! As we shall see, the language-as-instinct crowd don't always fight fair: ideas can be massaged to fit the claims, and often, too often, the facts are misrepresented, ridiculed or simply not presented at all. Moreover, since Pinker's first popular book appeared, back in 1994, science has moved on. And to end it all, Pinker is largely wrong, about language and about a number of other things too – as we shall see.

So here it is: I will be arguing that there is no Universal Grammar, and language is not innate: at least, not in the way supposed. More than that, the current generation of university students is still being systematically presented, at the very least, with controversial claims for which there is scant empirical evidence. And the general public deserve a proper exposure to the full facts, and the state of the art. This all matters because language is central to such a vast array of disciplines throughout the humanities as well as the cognitive and behavioural sciences. More than that, language is central to virtually everything we do: it *is* the measure of our lives. And, if for no other reason than that, it deserves to be correctly understood and appreciated.

I've written this book precisely because the myths I shall be refuting do not add up to a straw man. The language myth described and debunked in this book is very much alive. The component myths that make it up – that I tackle in each of the chapters to follow – relate to versions of the brand of speculative linguistics argued for by the linguist Noam Chomsky, and speculative psychology developed by his collaborator, the philosopher of mind Jerry Fodor – about whom we'll hear later. These myths are now widely believed to constitute established fact. More worryingly, these views are sanctioned by widely adopted textbooks. This all amounts to an object lesson in how retellings of a particular story, however erroneous, can become widely disseminated as established fact. The language-as-instinct thesis is plausible. But plausibility does not amount to reality. The language-as-instinct thesis is a Hegelian argument, without empirical basis, and, worse, a myth. And as J. F. Kennedy once observed, a myth "persistent, persuasive and unrealistic" poses the greatest harm to the quest for truth.

Lessons from evolution

In the mediaeval Great Chain of Being all life and matter was conceptualised as forming a hierarchy. In the Renaissance worldview, God sat at the pinnacle, with angels located below. Then came humans, followed by animals, vegetation and finally inanimate matter.

This view of existence was radically challenged in the nineteenth century by Darwin's dangerous idea: humans evolved from the Great Apes. The evolutionary picture Darwin presented did more than offend the Creationist myth provided by Christian dogma. It challenged a fundamental presumption that all sensible people held: humans are qualitatively different from all other animals. In fact, humans are so much more than animals that they are not animals at all – or so we often assume, even today. After all, the derogatory use of the term *animal* relates to a crazed beast, devoid of reason, and driven by blind emotion and bodily function. The story of evolution is dangerous not because it is an affront to the power of God, and even his very existence – although it is from the Creationist perspective – but because it challenges our own presumptions about our place in the world; it challenges our fundamental beliefs about our relation to the cats, dogs and horses we call pets and use to serve us in our everyday lives.

Today we know that our species, *Homo sapiens* (wise man), shared a common ancestor with modern chimpanzees and bonobos sometime around 6 million years ago. And all three species shared a common ancestor with gorillas and orang-utans around 15 million years ago. Anatomically modern humans – humans that look, more or less, like you and me – are only around 170,000 years old, give or take 30,000 years, the dating margin of error. We know this from carbon dating of fossils, and from genetic dating of mitochondrial DNA found in female humans.[15] And the evidence for evolution shows that the changes that paved the way for modern humans were gradual, and continuous.[16] We didn't evolve from *Homo erectus* (upright man) overnight – *Homo erectus* was one of the earliest species of the genus *Homo*. Around 1.8 million years of gradual change intervened.

That said, the nature of language, and its status as being 'unique', are emotive issues, *especially* for linguists. After all, professional linguists – scholars like me who study language(s) for a living – have gathered a vast amount of information about language. We know far more than any previous generation about how it works: its internal structure, the relation between form and meaning, how it is processed by the brain, and the socio-cultural status of the words and phrases we produce. For many professional linguists, language *is* unique *a priori*. And indeed, human language provides a richness that seemingly is not apparent anywhere else. As Bertrand Russell has pithily put it: "No matter how eloquently a dog may bark, he cannot tell you that his parents were poor but honest." And as George Carlin has joked: "'Meow' means 'woof' in cat." The point, of course, is that cats just have 'meow', and dogs 'woof' – and these vocalisations must serve all the possible mental states the lowly dog or cat seeks to express.

Humans, in contrast, can combine vast numbers of words, forming sentences of incredible grammatical complexity. And this enables us to talk about almost anything we choose, from the consequences of inflation for the national economy to the (decidedly odd) dress sense of Superman, who wears his underpants on the outside.

But the danger with emphasising the uniqueness of language is that it can seem to overstate the gap between human language and other forms of communication, such as animal systems of communication – an issue I shall address in the next chapter. After all, if language is unlike anything else, it is then but a small step – and a slippery slope – to claiming that language really must have emerged out of thin air. The language-as-instinct thesis proposes something very much like this. Its progenitor and most extreme proponent, Noam Chomsky, has claimed that language was most likely the result of a genetic mutation. On this account, language emerged all at once in a perfect or near-perfect state, in one lucky individual, who won the greatest linguistic jackpot of all time.[17]

But this account has been criticised by a wide range of scholars on evolutionary grounds. For instance, one prominent expert, the biological anthropologist Terrence Deacon, has described it as a hopeful monster story, after evolutionarily implausible and widely ridiculed claims made by the German geneticist Richard Goldenschmidt in the 1940s. A hopeful monster account of evolution proposes that evolution may involve a sudden very large change from one generation to the next, facilitating the emergence of a new feature.[18] According to Deacon, Chomsky explains away the origin-of-language problem by sleight of hand: like a white rabbit, it is pulled from out of evolution's magic hat. And consequently, this hopeful monster explanation – the language-as-instinct thesis – is completely at odds with the facts of evolution. Language, as we know it today, must have required many changes to the cognitive (re-)organisation, as well as the anatomy, of pre-linguistic hominins, in order to achieve its current level of sophistication. These would have both affected the primate brain plan inherited by ancestral humans, and changed the anatomy of the genus *Homo*. Moreover, the result would have facilitated an anatomy enabling the production of speech in *Homo neanderthalensis* (Neanderthal man) – now extinct, but who probably had some form of speech capability – as well as *Homo heidelber-gensis*, the common ancestor of both humans and Neanderthals.[19]

Such changes, at the very, very least, would have necessitated quantitative variations in the pre-human brain such as an expansion of the frontal part of the cortex – the outer layer of the human brain – relative to other regions. Greater direct control by the cortex over the mouth would also have been required, not least to produce the articulatory gestures to facilitate speech: speech is one of the most complex neuromuscular activities we accomplish, involving around an incredible seventy-eight distinct muscles.[20] A further change has been the lowering of the larynx (or voice box), compared even to our forebears, which has taken evolutionary time to accomplish. As I explain in the next chapter, this was required in order to facilitate speech production, but at the risk of death by choking – an unfortunate side effect of being able to talk. In the United Kingdom around 16,000 people are treated in hospitals each year for choking. And status is no barrier: US President George W. Bush hit the headlines in 2002 when he fainted for a few seconds and fell off a couch after choking on a pretzel. Other changes would have been required, such as an expansion of working-memory, required for composing and producing utterances. Increased memory would have been required for developing temporal sequencing skills, essential for human syntax – the ability to produce grammatically well-formed sentences.

In contrast, chimpanzees, for instance, only have a working-memory capability equivalent to that of a two-year-old human infant.[21] But a sophisticated working-memory is essential for human-like grammar, which requires recalling and sequencing strings of words in the correct order. In short, even if an ancestral human being had, by some chance mutation, developed a language gene, without a language-ready brain and body, the gene would have been useless.

Just as language had to be presaged by many other changes to the ancestral human genome, occurring gradually and incrementally, it is likely that language itself emerged gradually. Just as evolution teaches us that changes build upon one another incrementally, another lesson relates to the principle of evolutionary natural drift.[22]

Evolution as natural drift nuances the classic Darwinian formulation that evolution involves, more or less, progressive fitness. Evolution as natural drift presumes a co-determining relationship between organism and environment. An organism evolves in order to best obtain advantage from regularities in its environment. From this perspective, evolution involves co-evolution. For instance, honeybees see in the ultraviolet range of the colour spectrum. Flowers have co-evolved with honeybees so that those most likely to be pollinated are the species which provide greatest ultraviolet reflectance.

As ancestral humans were anatomically incapable of speech, it is highly plausible that proto-language emerged via other means. And this involved co-evolution of neuroanatomical changes ultimately resulting in spoken language.[23] A likely suspect is gesture, and as we shall see in the next chapter, chimpanzees and other primates make ready use of gestures for purposes of communication.[24] We thus gain insight into human language by looking for similarities with (and differences from) other forms of animal communication. To paraphrase the metaphysical poet John Donne, no species is an island. And language did not emerge out of thin air. It is grounded in the communicative tendencies apparent in our ancestral forebears.[25] And various forms of proto-language abound, to varying degrees, in many other extant species.

All that said, human language does, nevertheless, achieve the level of sophistication absent elsewhere. And this is because humans have evolved a special kind of intelligence – cultural intelligence – that harnesses the communicative abilities that are apparent elsewhere, about which I shall have more to say later, especially in the final chapter when I fully review the new synthesis: the language-as-use thesis. Nevertheless, this sceptred kind of intelligence facilitates a range of cooperative behaviours of which language is an example *par excellence*. This is the issue to which we now turn.

2 Is human language unrelated to animal communication systems?

Myth: Language is the preserve of humans, and humans alone; it cannot be compared to anything found amongst non-humans, and is unrelated to any non-human communicative capability.

Until relatively recently, it had been widely assumed that human language was unique: while some animals may have rudimentary forms of communication, these are limited, and relatively uninteresting. Moreover, so the myth goes, human language is unrelated to animal forms of communication. Even if it did derive from an evolutionarily earlier form of human proto-language, this bore no relation to the communication systems found, today, amongst other primates, mammals and countless other types of species in the animal kingdom. But the accumulation of research on the way other species communicate, from apes to whales, from vervets to starlings, increasingly suggests this may overstate the divide between human language and non-human communicative systems. Many of the characteristics exhibited by language are found, to varying degrees, across a broad spectrum of animal communication systems.

In key respects, many of our nearest primate cousins are so like us, from our DNA to our bad habits. In Disney's film *The Jungle Book*, King Louie – an orang-utan – famously desired the secret of man's red fire. And it has recently been reported that Tori the orang-utan has developed a smoking habit. Tori, a resident at a zoo in Indonesia, first acquired the habit by picking up cigarette butts that were tossed near her enclosure, and imitating humans by drawing on them.[1] Later she would beg for cigarettes from visitors, holding two fingers together to her mouth. Sadly, visitors too often obliged and Tori became a cigarette junkie. Her keepers were forced to move her to a more spacious and better-protected location. And which zoo visitor can fail to be struck by just how human-like young monkeys' faces are, how fragile, how like our new-borns' their tiny limbs, hands and fingers?

To be sure, human language stands out from the decidedly restricted vocalisations of monkeys and apes. Moreover, it exhibits a degree of sophistication that far exceeds any other form of animal communication. Even our closest primate cousins seem incapable of acquiring anything more than a rudimentary communicative system, even after intensive training over several years. The complexity that is language is surely a species-specific trait. That said, many species, while falling far short of human language, do nevertheless exhibit impressively complex communication systems in natural settings. And they can be taught far more complex systems in artificial contexts, as when raised alongside humans.

According to the language-as-instinct thesis, human language is a singularity, unrelated to any other form of animal communication. Chomsky is quite clear: sometime in the recent past language emerged all at once, in a near-perfect form, in one individual, as a sudden jump in evolution. Writing as recently as 2010, Chomsky explains that "roughly 100,000+ years ago . . . there were no languages . . . [but] . . . a rewiring of the brain took place in some individual, call him Prometheus".[2] And this led to language.

In this chapter, I will show that it is erroneous to think that human language is a singularity, and, in this sense, unrelated to the communication systems of other species.[3] In fact, we can learn more about human language, and what makes it special, by better understanding how it relates to, and is derived from, the communication systems of other species. For human language evolved from earlier systems of proto-language which abound today in nature. The sophistication exhibited by human language lies on a continuum, which takes in less sophisticated forms of animal communication.

From busy bees to startling starlings

What is language for? I said in the previous chapter that it fulfils two main functions: it tells us about things, *and* it allows us to interact, in various ways, with other members of our species – from service encounters in shops and banks, to interacting with friends, family and lovers. And in so doing, we attempt to influence the actions, thoughts and feelings of others. Both functions allow us to communicate with one another.

As a means of communication, language has much in common with a myriad others that abound in nature. The distinctive body-marking of some species provides a signal that is interpreted by would-be predators as a warning of danger. An example is the yellow and black stripes of wasps. This colouration succeeds either through hard-wired behaviour on the part of potential predators, or through learning that yellow and black stripes can leave a nasty sting in your mouth – quite literally. In this way, the distinct body-markings signal a message.

Of course, we wouldn't normally consider the *message* signalled by body colouration to be language-like. Communication systems are usually assumed to involve some level of intentionality – the signaller, to some degree, is consciously conveying a message, in a specific context, for some particular purpose. Moreover, communication systems found in the wild can be more or less complex, more or less individually learned, and more or less flexibly applied to a range of contexts. Some of the most significant complexity associated with non-human communication systems involves birdsong, and the song of Baleen whales. The greatest flexibility is associated with the naturally occurring gestures of apes, such as chimpanzees, which also appear to be individually learned. And arguably, all the features that some linguists have claimed make human language unique are manifested in animal communication systems.

A good example, and an important feature of human language syntax, is known as recursion. Recursion – the ability to embed grammatical phrases in other phrases – is crucial for the human ability to produce complex sentences, as I explain later. Chomsky and colleagues have claimed that this is unique to human language.[4] Yet it turns out that at least one other species has been shown to be capable of recognising recursion – and there may be others. Moreover, the linguistic anthropologist Daniel Everett has even claimed that at least one human language, Pirahã, spoken by a remote tribe in the Amazonian jungle, may not exhibit recursion.[5]

But first things first; let's begin by getting a sense of the sorts of communication systems that abound in the wild. I begin with the humble honeybee. Honeybees live in large colonies consisting of a queen bee, drones (male bees) and worker bees, which are the offspring of the queen and drones. In classic work, Karl von Frisch, the Austrian ethologist, was the first to figure out the significance of the waggle dance of the honeybee.[6] And not only did he later receive the Nobel Prize for his efforts, he demonstrated something quite remarkable. It had previously been assumed that the symbolic function of language was unique to humans. Indeed, when von Frisch first published his findings in the 1950s, his claims were treated with scepticism. But his studies of over 6,000 cases of honeybee dances have since been experimentally verified. We now know with certainty that honeybees, as well as other species, are indeed capable of communicating information about sources of food.

Once a worker has located a source of nectar, it returns to the hive in order to signal the location to the other forager bees. This is achieved via a sophisticated dance performed on a wall inside the hive. The dance indicates the distance of the food source from the hive, as well as its direction. For instance, in a species of bee from Italy, a circular dance indicates that the food source is relatively close, within 20 feet, a sickle dance – a crescent-shaped pattern – indicates the food source is between around 20 and 60 feet from the hive, while tail-wagging – or waggle dance – indicates a distance greater than 60 feet. The movement associated with circular and waggle dances look something like the diagrams below.

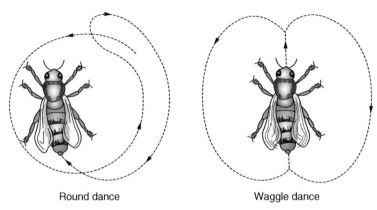

Round dance   Waggle dance

Von Frisch (1976: 70).

Finer distinctions are indicated by the frequency with which the dance is repeated. A slower repetition indicates a greater distance. This means of communication is much like some of the traits central to human language: it is symbolic – conveying a message using an arbitrary symbolic code to do so, e.g., a dance; it is inter-subjective – involving a signal between two or more individuals; and it is referential – involving reference to a third party, in this case a source of nectar. And, arguably, bee dances exhibit cultural differences: different species of bee have slightly different dances to convey much the same meaning.

While bees deploy dance to communicate, other species make use of vocalisations. A striking example is the alarm calls made by vervet monkeys. Vervets live in southern and eastern Africa. They make specific and distinct calls upon sight of different predators: a chutter when they see snakes, and different calls when they spot eagles or leopards. And, tellingly, other vervets take an appropriate form of evasive action, even if they haven't seen the predator.[7] For instance, upon hearing a leopard-call, other vervets run towards trees and begin climbing. Upon hearing an eagle alarm call, they look up into the air. And upon hearing a snake-call, they look down at the ground, often by standing on their two rear legs. While the vervet alarm calls appear to be innate – the calls emerge at a relatively fixed point in a vervet's development, and do not rely on having previously heard other vervet alarm calls – vervet parents nevertheless appear to positively reinforce the production of the correct alarm call in infants, by repeating the call. Moreover, there are reports of infant vervets being punished when providing an incorrect alarm call.

Clearly, while communicative systems such as these are interesting, they are highly restricted in terms of their communicative value. In the case of both busy bees and vocal vervets the symbolic systems used are limited to specific contexts of use. This is not, of course, to trivialise the importance of those contexts, and the value of the communicative systems for the well-being and survival of the species. But human language is much more flexible in the range of contexts that it can refer to – from declaring undying love to commenting on the weather – especially in the rain-sodden UK!

And, it is flexible in another way too – different communities of humans adopt different linguistic varieties: Swahili, Japanese and English are all quite distinct, in a range of ways. This is because the system itself is inherently flexible. Its flexibility arises from a process that allows us to combine otherwise meaningless symbols. Sounds and words can be combined in a range of ways, following the 'rules' of an abstract grammar, individually learned, that each human seems to carry around with them in their heads.

It has been claimed that *the* stand-out property that provides this degree of flexibility is recursion. This is the mechanism that allows us to 'embed' phrases within larger sentence structures. For instance, take the expression *Death is only the beginning*, uttered by Imhotep in the 1999 movie *The Mummy*. This phrase can be embedded in the grammatical frame *X said Y*, providing a more complex sentence: *Imhotep said that death is only the beginning*. This sentence can then be further embedded in the same frame recursively: *Evelyn said that Imhotep said that death is only the beginning*.

Relative clauses – clauses introduced by expressions like *who* or *which* – enable us to add information to a sentence. And again, this is an example of recursion: we are capable of building up highly complex sentences, recursively. An expression such as *Phoebe runs a lingerie shop* can be embellished with a relative clause *which sells frilly knickers*: *Phoebe runs a lingerie shop which sells frilly knickers.* And this process of recursion can occur, in principle, ad infinitum: *Phoebe runs a lingerie shop, which sells frilly knickers, which have purple sequins sewn down one side.* Chomsky and colleagues have suggested that not only is recursion unique to human language, it may be the definitional feature of language.[8]

However, recent research on European starlings provides evidence that these birds can also learn to recognise recursion.[9] Starlings sing long and relatively complicated songs, consisting of acoustic motifs. The motifs are made up of sequences of rattles and warbles. A team of researchers at the University of Chicago[10] designed motifs, featuring recordings of rattles (which I'll represent as A) and warbles (which I'll represent as B). These motifs were of two sorts. One sort included a basic AB pattern that could be extended: ABABAB, etc. A second pattern involved embedding elements recursively in the basic AB frame, like this: AnBn. In this frame, the 'n' represents an embedding of the preceding element, as in AABB, AAABBB, AAAABBBB, and so on. Now here's the crucial part: an AnBn pattern is a recursive pattern; the insertion of additional rattles (A) and warbles (B) in such a sequence, in principle ad infinitum, is a manifestation of recursive embedding, albeit a non-linguistic one. And if starlings are able to recognise, or can be trained to recognise, the difference between the two patterns, they could, in principle, be capable of recursion.

To test this, two groups of starlings were trained on each of the patterns. One group of birds was rewarded for recognising the non-recursive AB pattern. Another group was rewarded each time they recognised the recursive AnBn pattern. The researchers found that, following this training, the startling starlings did indeed learn to identify the recursive patterns.

But wait. The language-as-instinct crowd would no doubt chide that this is surely taking things too far. After all, recursive embedding in human language syntax, producing meaningful sentences, is one thing. It's quite another to suggest that starlings have anything like the same ability. Surely equating starling and human recursive abilities is stretching the point too far? But remember, I'm not *equating* anything. I'm not trying to show that the facility of starlings to recognise patterns of warbles and rattles amounts to anything like the complexity involved in human language syntax. My claim is simply this: recursion appears *not* to be a uniquely human trait; to maintain that human language is a singularity, totally unrelated to the abilities and communication systems of other species, incorrectly skews our view of language. And it impoverishes our study of it.

But while starlings seem able to learn to recognise recursion, what about the complexity of animal communication systems in the wild? Research using underwater hydrophones, and subsequent digital acoustic analysis, demonstrates that ethereal whale song exhibits a similar level of complexity to human musical traditions. Moreover, whale song appears to have a socio-communicative function.

Take, for instance, the song of humpback whales. Whale song is produced by male humpbacks during the mating season. While it is assumed it has a role in mating, its precise function is still not fully understood. It is still unclear whether the song of male humpbacks is designed to attract a female to mate, or whether it has some other social bonding function. What is clear, however, is that the song has a hierarchical structure, consisting of vocalisations of varying frequencies.[11] The base units of the song, the 'notes', consist of single uninterrupted emissions of sound which last for up to a few seconds at a time. Notes are integrated with between four and six other notes, on average, to form a sub-phrase. This lasts for around 10 seconds. Two sub-phrases are combined to produce a phrase, which is repeated for between 2 and 4 minutes, making a theme. The whale song consists of a series of themes, and can last from anything from 30 minutes to several days.

Communication in the wild

One of the striking features of some animal vocalisations – for instance, vervet alarm calls – is that they are not learned; they emerge in vervet development regardless of whether infant vervets are exposed to alarm calls by their parents or not. In contrast, human language is acquired through learning. And learning takes place in contexts of social interaction: a process of cultural transmission. This is most clearly evident in cases where language doesn't emerge, in the unfortunate cases of so-called 'feral children'. In some cases, children are lost by accident, as in the fictional story of the man-cub Mowgli, as depicted by Rudyard Kipling in his classic stories. Mowgli grew up in the Indian jungle, raised amongst wolves. Yet, eventually, he returned to a human village, becoming fully integrated back into human social life.

True-life cases tend not to be so heart-warming. In one well-documented case, a child dubbed the wild boy of Aveyron, and later named Victor, was found in the South of France in 1797. Victor was estimated to be around 12 years old when found, and, like Mowgli, had also been brought up amongst wolves. A French physician spent the best part of the next five years attempting to teach the boy to speak. But, although Victor learnt to recognise words such as his name, short phrases and commands, he never learned to speak properly.

Perhaps the most famous fictional feral child of all is Tarzan. In the books by Edgar Rice Borroughs, Tarzan is reared by apes from the age of one until he is a young adult. Despite this, he excelled at language. The reality is sadly different. Human language only emerges within a human socio-cultural setting. And, as in the case of Victor, once a child has reached a certain age – the so-called 'critical period' for language learning – then the ability to learn language appears to become significantly diminished. Unlike vervet alarms calls, then, without exposure to human language, a child will never be capable of speech. And from the early teens, the ability is typically dramatically diminished.

A related aspect of the socio-cultural basis of human language is that it varies, often markedly, across cultural contexts. Different languages are an obvious example of cultural variability. Even a single language, as realised by different cultures, makes this obvious. As George Bernard Shaw once famously observed: "England and America are two countries separated by a common language." For instance, the verb *to toss* shares a 'to throw' meaning in both American and British varieties. But while *a tosser* is someone who throws (in American English), in British English it additionally has a pejorative meaning which is probably more salient. An American colleague of mine, who was giving a lecture to a group of distinguished academics in the UK, came unstuck over exactly this. Unaware of the pejorative meaning, my colleague continued to refer to *tossing* and *tossers*, even innocently referring to one senior professor as a *tosser* while making his linguistic argument. Slowly, he realised, from the embarrassed faces of the members of the British academic establishment present, that something was amiss. But not knowing the 'other' meaning, he was at a loss to realise his *faux pas* – if you are an American, now go and look it up. The moral is that human language is shaped, transmitted and learned within a cultural context, by virtue of the social group(s) within which we as individuals live and are embedded.

But is there evidence that other animal communication systems exhibit this socio-cultural dimension? While baleen whales such as humpbacks produce song, there is another class of whale, the so-called 'toothed whales'. Toothed whales produce rapid bursts of clicks and whistles, rather than the long, low-frequency sounds of the Baleen whale song. They vocalise in a sonic spectrum between ten and twelve times as wide as that used by humans. The production of high-frequency whale whistles, which can travel for thousands of kilometres under the ocean, are used by toothed whales both for navigation, and for communication, such as for coordinating hunting. In water, both smell and sight are reduced, while sound travels four times faster than in air. Hence, sound can be used very effectively. To support this, whales have evolved acute hearing. The Beluga whale, for instance, which inhabits the dark, ice-covered waters of the Arctic, can hear in an especially wide range: 10Hz to 150kHz. This contrasts with the human ear which has a much narrower range: 10Hz to 20kHz.

Scientists now know that the whistles deployed by sperm whales, a species of toothed whale, are used by individual whales to identify themselves within a group, and to identify themselves as belonging to a particular group.[12] Strikingly, whales give themselves 'names': whistle combinations are used by whales to name themselves, and identify their group affiliation.

Sperm whales are highly sociable creatures, with, at 8 kg, the largest brain size of any known animal, living or extinct. Female sperm whales live in long-term 'sororities' that remain stable over decades – sperm whales live for around seventy years on average. Females and their young live separately from males, and the rearing of young is shared between members of the adult female unit. And the social units – the sororities – participate in looser affiliations with other female units, forming clans.

The series of clicks produced by whales, in their sororities, form a stereotyped pattern known as a coda. It had long been suspected by marine biologists that sperm whale codas have a social function; in particular, it was suspected that they may serve as vocal signatures to identify either the individual whale or the sorority to which it belongs. To test this, a recent survey of codas was conducted by scientists off the coast of the island of Dominica.[13] The recordings were analysed using specialised click-detection software. The findings revealed that the codas contained three levels of structural information, a consequence of variation in patterning of the clicks. A coda is unique to an individual sperm whale, providing a signature or 'name'. It also identifies the sorority to which the whale belongs. Finally, it additionally encodes which clan the sorority is part of. Sperm whales use this information when creating new groups: female sperm whales prefer to form groupings with whales whose coda belongs to their own clan, rather than whales from other clans. This finding is significant as it shows the communication system of sperm whales, like that of humans, has a socio-cultural motivation.[14]

Sperm whales are not alone in using vocalisations for identifying and establishing socio-cultural relations. The song of the Baleen humpback whales comes in different 'dialects'. While whale song evolves over time, whales from the same geographical area – which might be as wide as an ocean basin – sing similar songs. However, whales from non-overlapping regions sing markedly different songs.[15]

I now turn, finally, to the communicative strategies of our nearest primate cousin: the common chimpanzee (*Pan troglodyte*). Chimps use gestures to communicate in a qualitatively different way from their vocalisations. Chimp vocalisations, like those of vervet monkeys, are inflexible; in chimps they are used to coordinate foraging, to defend against aggressors, and to warn of danger. However, chimp gestures, in the wild, are used in much more varied situations and contexts, including more social and intimate ones. These include play, grooming, nursing and sexual encounters. Chimps use gestures intentionally, in order to attempt to influence the behaviour of other chimps – much like the interactional function of human language I discussed earlier. The gestures are learned individually – like human language – and can be used flexibly, also like human language.

For instance, just as a word such as *on* can be used to describe different spatial configurations – a fly can be *on* the table (horizontal top surface), *on* my nose (vertical surface) or *on* the ceiling (horizontal lower surface) – so chimps can use particular gestures to signal different meanings. For instance, an infant chimp touches the relevant part of their mother's anatomy to signal that it wants to suckle, or that it wants to ride on her back.

Similarly, different gestures can be used for the same goal: slapping the ground and bodybeating for play.[16] This mirrors the linguistic ability of humans to use different words to convey a similar meaning, such as when we describe a disreputable person as a 'crook', or a 'villain'. The flexibility evident in human language is, it seems, also apparent in the gestural communication of chimps.

Chimp gestures are of two types. The first involves an action that forms an integral part of an activity. The action is gestured, standing for the entire activity. For instance, an infant chimp will raise its arms – the initial action in play – in order to signal that it wishes to play.

Integral actions such as this, signalling a specific activity, are equivalent to human speech 'acts': where an utterance can have the 'force' of an action.[17] For example, on 3 September 1939, when Neville Chamberlain, the British Prime Minister, stated that "This country is at war with Germany" in a broadcast to the nation, a state of war came into effect. The utterance, by a designated authority, the Prime Minister, was to alter irrevocably the socio-political and legal status holding between the two countries. In this way, the utterance itself served to create a state of war; it was an action achieved through speech.[18] In related fashion, a chimp, by performing the raised arm gesture, brings play into effect. It does so by miming an action that is integral to it.

The second type of communicative gesture is an 'attention-getter', a means of getting other chimps to look. A stand-out example is leaf-clipping. This is performed typically by frisky adult males: the gesture makes a noise, the purpose being to draw the female attention to the male's erect sexual arousal. This type of gesture is similar to human 'attention-getters'. An example is a word like *hey*; in British English this expression draws attention, ensuring that the channel is open prior to proceeding with communication.

Talking animals

In Hugh Lofting's tales of Dr Dolittle, the good doctor from Puddleby-on-the-Marsh gives up on his human patients in Victorian England. He decides, instead, to care for animals; and, serendipitously, he has the special talent of being able to *talk* to other creatures in their own tongue. Talking animals have been a staple of human imagination since time immemorial. But can animals really learn to talk, and to communicate with humans?

In the twentieth century, a tradition of studies conducted by primatologists attempted to examine exactly this. In early work, from the 1930s on, scientists sought to teach chimps to recognise and produce spoken words. But alas, this wasn't very successful. In one notable case, a chimp named Viki was brought up as a human infant. Yet, after about six years, she could only produce a few words, 'mama', 'papa', 'up', and 'cup', and these were all produced as a guttural croak.[19]

The difficulty, it turned out, was that the vocal tract of chimps is not well suited to the production of speech. A speech-ready vocal tract evolved in the genus *Homo* – our lineage – in two stages. The first stage involved the lowering of the larynx – or voice box – relative to the hyoid bone. This enables airflow to be transmitted more easily through the mouth. The larynx descends over the first few years of life, and is one instance in which individual development reflects evolutionary development – the "ontogeny recapitulates phylogeny" slogan of the nineteenth-century German biologist Ernst Haeckel. Human infants are born with a much higher larynx, which only reaches its final resting place in the early teens.

The second stage involved the lowering of the hyoid bone relative to the skull. The hyoid bone is anchored by muscles to the mouth, and aids tongue movement and swallowing – and its lowering relative to the skull facilitates the movement of the tongue up and down, as well as from side to side, essential for speech production. In contrast to humans – and indeed other species of the genus *Homo*, including *Homo heidelbergensis*, the common ancestor of both *Homo sapiens* and *Homo neanderthalensis* who most likely had some form of speech capability[20] – while the larynx in chimps does descend relative to the hyoid bone, it doesn't do so to anything like the same extent.[21] And the chimp hyoid bone has barely shifted at all. What this means is that chimps cannot easily direct airflow through their mouths, nor can they control their tongue shapes to the degree found in humans. And both evolutionary adaptations are required to produce the range of sounds evident in human speech.[22] The acoustic consequences are that our species – *Homo sapiens* – can produce a formidable range and number of different sounds. The difference between chimpanzee (A) and human (B) vocal tracts is captured in the diagrams below.

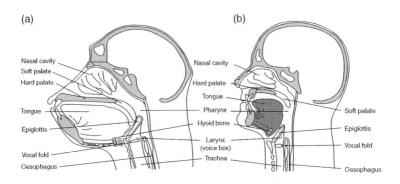

Beginning in the 1960s, various approaches were devised by comparative psychologists to teach chimps to communicate without using vocalisations. One approach involved teaching chimps a version of American Sign Language (ASL). Perhaps the most celebrated signing chimp is Washoe, captured in the wild at the age of about one. Thereafter, Washoe was raised as a human child by American psychologists Alan and Beatrice Gardner. The Gardners fed, clothed, played with and toilet-trained Washoe, just like any other human infant.

ASL is a language with its own vocabulary and grammar, used by the deaf community in the United States of America and much of Canada. By the age of four, Washoe could produce about 132 signs, and comprehended many more.[23] After a few more years, Washoe's active vocabulary had increased to around 200 signs.[24] In addition, Washoe could coin new words. For instance, upon seeing a duck she combined signs for *water* and *bird* to create a new word: *waterbird*. Moreover, she could combine signs in order to produce complex utterances of up to five words. Examples include: *Washoe sorry, baby down, go in, hug hurry, out open please hurry*. Washoe understood and could answer questions. She was particularly good at answering questions starting with *what, where* and *who*. However, she had more difficulty dealing with questions concerning *how, where* and *why*.

Washoe was also able to place words in the correct order to make a well-formed sentence. She was capable, for instance, of producing sentences with both subject and object in the correct position either side of the verb, as in the following attested examples: *You tickle me, I tickle you*. This demonstrates that Washoe had acquired, at the very least, a rudimentary understanding of syntax.

A further remarkable finding relates to a chimp named Loulis, whom Washoe 'adopted' as her son. The Gardners reported that Loulis spontaneously acquired signs from Washoe. Moreover, Washoe was seen actively teaching Loulis new signs.

As I observed in the previous chapter, chimps and other apes have relatively impoverished working-memories compared to adult humans. And human syntax depends on the ability to hold word sequences in memory as a sentence is being constructed. A second approach was developed to counter this. This was carried out by the psychologist David Premack, who worked most famously with another female chimpanzee, called Sarah.

Sarah was taught a language that involved plastic shapes which represented words. The plastic shapes varied, not only in shape, but in size and texture too.[25] The advantage of this approach was that the symbols could be arranged, following particular rules, to produce sentences. And as Sarah was able to produce an utterance by laying out the shapes in sentences on a surface in front of her, this reduced the load placed on her short-term memory.

Premack and his colleagues found that Sarah was able to understand and produce relatively sophisticated sentences, arguably more sophisticated than those exhibited by Washoe. For example, Sarah could produce sentences such as the following: *Randy give apple Sarah*. This sentence encodes a scene of transfer involving three participants either side of the verb. These are: 'Randy', the entity doing the transferring; 'the apple', which is the entity being transferred; and 'Sarah', the recipient of the transferred object.

In addition, Sarah could produce conditional sentences involving the *if . . . then . . .* construction. For instance, in the expression *If John eats his dinner then he gets ice cream*, not only does an event sequence have to be retained in memory, but also it relates to a hypothetical situation. This is actually a complex imaginative feat: to understand the hypothetical situation, we also have to create and hold in memory the parallel situation in which John doesn't eat his dinner and, alas, misses out on ice cream. This shows that Sarah, at least in this respect, comes close to the linguistic potential of humans.

The impressive ability of chimps to master some rudimentary aspects of language shouldn't, perhaps, be too surprising. After all, chimps are our closest living relatives. We now know that we share nearly 98 per cent of our DNA sequences with chimpanzees. According to the primate scientist Frans de Waal, who has worked on the Human Genome Project, "Darwin wasn't just provocative in saying that we descend from the apes – he didn't go far enough ... We are apes in every way, from our long arms and tailless bodies to our habits and temperament."[26]

The mental abilities of chimps are, in general terms, remarkably similar to those of humans.[27] For instance, both humans and chimps understand things in the here and now. Chimps, like humans, can recall and learn from the past. Moreover, they anticipate future events. And chimps, like humans, are able to make inferences about what other members of their species are thinking. Chimps understand and can read the intentions of others based on behaviour and other visual cues – a very human trait. This allows them to infer the decision-making strategies of other chimps.

Despite all of the above, some psychologists and linguists have fiercely disputed the claim that the communicative potential of chimps can approach anything like the potential of humans, however distantly. The psychologist Herbert Terrace set out to replicate the Gardners' Washoe project. He worked with a chimp named Nim Chimpsky (a pun on Noam Chomsky). Like Washoe, Nim was also taught a version of ASL. But, unlike Washoe, Nim failed to develop anything like the complex abilities shown in the earlier experiments. There are specific reasons why Nim may not have achieved the same success, not least the way he was treated by his keepers. But Terrace, and others, have used these findings to dismiss out of hand even the possibility that apes might have some rudimentary communicative potential.[28]

Steven Pinker, in his book *The Language Instinct*, ridicules the very idea that apes might be able to learn to communicate. He says:

> People who spend a lot of time with animals are prone to develop indulgent attitudes about their powers of communication. My great-aunt Bella insisted in all sincerity that her Siamese cat Rusty understood English.

Of the work on Washoe and other apes he continues:

> the apes did not "learn American Sign Language." This preposterous claim is based on the myth that ASL is a crude system of pantomimes and gestures rather than a full language with complex phonology, morphology, and syntax.

He later says:

> The chimps' abilities at anything one would want to call grammar were next to nil. Signs were not coordinated into the well-defined motion contours of ASL and were not inflected for aspect, agreement, and so on.[29]

But Pinker's criticisms are disingenuous. Setting aside dotty aunts, the Gardners were not claiming that Washoe had learned human-like grammar. To dismiss the accomplishments of an ape, because it falls (perhaps well) short of human grammar, is to miss the point by a mile. No one believes that apes can actually acquire human-like language. The point is whether there are precursors, which suggest that human language is continuous with other forms of animal communication. If so, then human language could have developed, ultimately, from evolutionarily earlier forms of primate communication. But then, Pinker believes in the language-as-instinct thesis as fact: humans are born with an innate Universal Grammar, which no other species has. Thus, human language is quite unlike, and unrelated to, any other form of communication found in any other species. And even to entertain the possibility of similarities would make you as dotty as his great-aunt Bella.

But, as we shall see below, there is now a large body of evidence that, many objective commentators believe, points to rudimentary precursors of human-like grammar in non-humans. The caveats are crucial, of course. What we are dealing with is rudimentary and a precursor. There is no evidence for full-blown linguistic abilities in any other species or anything close; and we don't expect to find any. Nevertheless, the linguist Jim Hurford, in his towering work on language development in the light of evolution, extensively details the seeds of human-like language in other species.[30] Hurford observes that, while many animal communication systems serve simply to enable the animals to do things to one another, such as threatening or submitting, some species do go further. Some animal communication systems involve the rudiments of referring to third parties, and of jointly attending to this third party referent. The waggle dance of the bee is one example, as is, arguably, the leaf clipping gesture of the male chimp, enticing the female to notice his erection. And with these systems "some of the deepest foundations of modern human language have been laid down."[31]

Design features for language

One way of getting to grips with the degree of divergence between human language and animal communication systems is to understand what is distinctive about human language. This, then, might provide a basis for distinguishing between the two. In 1960, the

American linguist Charles Hockett published a set of thirteen "design features" of language. Hockett later added a further three features to make sixteen in total. He confidently proclaimed that these features are universal to all human languages, and language communication systems of other species fail to exhibit some or all of these.[32] I summarise Hockett's design features in the table below.

Summary of Hockett's design features for language

1 Vocal–auditory channel	Language is transmitted via spoken sounds perceived by the auditory channel
2 Broadcast/directional	The sound is broadcast in all directions. But the receiver can tell which direction it is coming from
3 Rapid fading	The signal fades quickly
4 Total feedback	The speaker can hear/perceive what s/he is saying/communicating
5 Interchangeability	The same person can be both sender and receiver of the signal
6 Specialisation	Signals are produced primarily for communication rather than some other function (e.g., echo-location)
7 Semanticity	Signals have specific and stable meanings, in an inter-subjective way
8 Arbitrariness	Signals do not resemble their meanings, e.g., there is nothing in the combination of sounds resulting in the words *dog* (English), *chien* (French) or *perro* (Spanish) that could be construed as resembling the animal referred to by these terms
9 Cultural transmission	Language is passed on, from parent to child, and from generation to generation
10 Learnability	Humans speaking one can language can, in principle, learn any other: any language is learnable by any cognitively normal human
11 Discreteness	Language is divided into discrete units of sound, and information is encoded from the combination of these
12 Duality of patterning	Language is organised into a dual layer of patterns. On one level, meaningless sounds pattern into words. On another, words form grammatical patterns giving rise to sentences

13 Displacement	Language enables users to discuss entities that are displaced in space and time. Hence, I can talk about what I did yesterday, or about what I saw on my way to work earlier today
14 Productivity	Linguistic resources can be used to generate new sentences that have novel meanings
15 Prevarication	Language allows users to lie, and to talk about things that haven't happened, or are impossible
16 Reflexiveness	Language can be deployed to talk about language itself

It turns out, however, in another blow to Hegelian argumentation, that all of Hockett's design features are variously manifested in animal communication systems. And in a stunning reverse, at least two, possibly three, of Hockett's design features are not evident in all human languages. The delicious irony, of course – one that I will continue to repeat throughout this book – is that intuition, fanned by unsubstantiated speculation, can often lead to erroneous conclusions. When the actual research is carried out – and the results are in – it sometimes transpires that what we actually find is not what we expect – a salutary lesson indeed.

But wherefore 'design features'?

For many of us, when we think of language, it is the spoken variety we have in mind. But human language is remarkable: it is not tied to a specific medium of expression. Deaf communities, for instance, make use of sign languages that employ the same levels of complexity associated with spoken language, including, as we have begun to see, a sophisticated grammar. In the UK, British Sign Language, usually abbreviated to BSL, is used by an estimated 125,000 deaf adults and around 200,000 children as their native language. This means that BSL has the highest number of monolingual users of any indigenous minority language in the UK. Moreover, BSL is formally recognised as a language by the UK government, having achieved official status in 2003 – a distinction, ironically, that English has yet to achieve in England!

While sign languages are, now, recognised as being full-blown languages, on a par with spoken languages,[33] they are frequently subject to misunderstanding. While the English spoken in America and in Britain is mutually intelligible, a popular misconception is that signers of American Sign Language (ASL) can be understood by users of BSL – they cannot.

The study of sign language is still in its infancy. Although records exist of a sign language in Britain among a deaf community as early as 1570, research by academic linguists and others only began in a concerted way in the 1950s and 1960s. Today, *Ethnologue* – the Encyclopaedia of the World's Languages – lists 130 sign languages used in the world. However, the true figure is likely to be way higher.

But because sign languages such as BSL don't make use of the medium of sound, they necessarily fall foul of Hockett's vocal–auditory channel design feature. And as they are signalled in a directional fashion, they also fail to exhibit the broadcast aspect of Hockett's second design feature. Somewhat ironically, therefore, two of Hockett's universal design features of language turn out not to be universal after all.

In terms of animal communication systems, both of these design features are widely attested; examples include vervet warning calls, the song of Baleen whales, and the signature whistles of sperm whales. A further striking example is provided by an African Grey parrot, named Alex. The psychologist Irene Pepperberg taught Alex to use around fifty words correctly in appropriate contexts. This involved vocalisations using the vocal–auditory channel.[34]

Another controversial design feature is specialisation. While human speech is specialised for facilitating communication, the same cannot be said, for example, of the echo-location systems of toothed whales. Whales make use of echo-location primarily for navigation purposes. The communicative function of echo-location is a useful added bonus.

However, seen from an evolutionary perspective, this design feature is a misnomer. Spoken language makes use of systems that evolved for other purposes. Human speech, for instance, involves air expelled from the lungs, passing through the larynx, with discrete sounds produced by changing the shape of the mouth, tongue and lips. But lungs evolved for breathing, and the mouth and tongue evolved for tasting and ingesting food. Moreover, even the sound system of human language, which consists of vowels and consonants is based on the evolutionarily earlier pattern of open and closing for imbibing and chewing food – sonorous vowels involve an opening in the airflow, while the less sonorous consonants involve (at least partial) closure.[35] The only component which is specialised for sound production is the larynx.

But the larynx is something also shared with other species, including amphibians, reptiles, birds, and other mammals, including Baleen whales (although not toothed whales, who make use of different physiological apparatus for emitting their sonar through water). Its evolutionary function was to produce sound, deployed by many species in vocalisations relating to evolutionarily urgent activities, such as signalling danger, predation and so on. Hence, the larynx was not originally designed to facilitate speech production anyway. Of course, one of the changes that has come about, in modern humans, is that the larynx sits much lower than in other species.

My point, of course, is that human speech only looks as though it is specialised for communication if you ignore the evolutionary trajectory that led to it. And the design feature of specialisation looks more tenuous still in the case of sign languages, which are based on the manual-gestural medium. Indeed, an increasing body of opinion contends that spoken language may have evolved from gestural communication, the communication type practised by modern-day chimpanzees. Humans, like other apes, have mirror neurons:[36] neurons that fire when we see someone else perform a gesture. It is this mirroring that may cause you to wince, for instance, when you see a stranger painfully stub their toe, or have their hand trapped in a suddenly closing car door.

And mirror neurons plausibly provide us with the basis for imitation, which allows us to learn gestures, and to learn to communicate via gesture – I shall argue, in Chapter 5, that a region of the brain referred to as Broca's area, and closely associated with language, is also implicated in processing gestures and hand shadows.

One possibility, then, is that human language emerged through gestures, made possible by the existence of mirror neurons.[37] And once linguistic symbolisation had developed, the facility to represent these through the vocal–auditory medium evolved. From this perspective, language evolved from hand to mouth,[38] and, self-evidently, hands, fingers and presumably mirror neurons didn't evolve to facilitate language. After all, macaque monkeys have mirror neurons, yet they don't appear to have human-like language.[39]

That said, the languages taught to apes do conform to the design feature specialisation, in the sense that Hockett uses the term: these systems were all designed purely for communication. But apes are not the only animals to which comparative psychologists have sought to teach human-like language. In the 1980s, two distinct training programmes were initiated with dolphins.[40] In one, a dolphin named Akeakami was trained to recognise hand gestures made by a trainer. Following training, the dolphin was able to recognise novel 'sentences' made up of the gestures. In the second, a dolphin called Phoenix was trained in a language devised from sounds generated by a computer. While the dolphins could not produce the 'languages' they'd been taught – after all, dolphins don't have hands, or on-board sound-emitting computers – their comprehension demonstrated that, like apes, dolphins are capable of developing communication systems that exhibit specialisation.

Semanticity – words having meanings associated with them – is another design feature that animals cannot possibly exhibit, or so claim the naysayers. Yet some members of non-human species do indeed appear capable of associating symbols, such as specific gestures, with things in the world. In the case of Akeakami, the dolphin was able to follow instructions by fetching specific objects requested, or by carrying one object and depositing it at another. She could only have achieved this if she understood the relation between a gesture and its meaning.[41]

Similarly, Washoe the chimp was carefully tested to ensure she understood the relation between a symbol and its meaning: Washoe was prompted to make a sign by being shown a corresponding picture – for, say, a dog. But the experimenter who was holding the picture was positioned so that that they could not see the picture, but could see the sign Washoe made in response. And a second experimenter was positioned so as to see the picture but not the sign. This system was designed in order to prevent the psychologists from prompting the ape, no matter how unconsciously, to signal the correct symbol. In this 'double blind' scenario, Washoe got most cases correct. And when she didn't, the errors were not random; they arose when Washoe made mistakes within a specific category, such as signing cat when the picture was that of a dog.[42]

Another feature of language that has previously been considered beyond the ken of non-humans is cultural transmission. The language myth contends that humans are alone in passing on their language across generations, and between members of the same socio-cultural group. Dialects of the same language, for instance, provide evidence for the cultural variability of language. Yet whale song also comes in dialects, as in the song of humpback whales which varies from region to region. Locality is a predictor of whale song: groups from different geographical regions have markedly different types of song.

Further striking examples of cultural transmission exhibited by animals comes from work by primatologists. One such example is Kanzi, a bonobo – a species of pygmy chimpanzee. Kanzi did not receive formal training, involving reinforcement with food upon production of the correct symbol. Instead, he acquired symbols by observing the training of his mother Matata.[43] Moreover, Matata also interacted with him using the symbols she had been taught. He then used them in interaction with people in normal daily activities. Kanzi seemingly picked up the symbols his mother was being taught. He used them himself, often going beyond his mother in terms of the complexity of his symbol combinations.

Now I turn to the design feature of learnability: speakers of one language can, with appropriate effort and time, come to speak, more or less fluently, another language. Chimps, like humans, appear to be flexible in terms of the symbol systems they can acquire. Sarah and Washoe learned different communicative systems. Washoe's 'language' was a version of ASL while Sarah learned a system involving the plastic symbols I described earlier. The way in which the plastic symbols could be combined followed specific rules. And the 'language' that Sarah was taught – termed Yerkish after the Yerkes Primate Centre in Atlanta where Sarah was initially trained – was a completely different 'language' from the version of ASL that Washoe was taught. The fact that two chimps can learn unrelated 'languages' is good evidence that chimpanzee communication systems appear to exhibit the design feature of learnability.

Perhaps most telling of all, in terms of design features exhibited by animal communication systems, is that of duality of patterning. This arguably strikes at the heart of what is meant to be unique about humans. Human language makes use of symbols that on their own are meaningless – the sound segments that make up words, as in [t], [ɪ], and [p] – and that combine to produce different, meaningful words: *tip* versus *pit*. In addition, words can be combined to create sentences. This provides a dual layer of patterning, involving meaningless sound segments and meaningful combinations. And so, this design feature relates to one of the claims at the heart of the language-as-instinct thesis: the definitional quality of human language is the combinatorial power of language – the rule-based combination that allows a relatively small set of sounds or signs that, on their own are meaningless, to give rise to a vast semantic possibility.

But here's the problem. There is now good evidence that apes in natural settings can combine vocalisations to make more complex units of meaning. This is similar to what humans do when we add a verbal marker that, on its own, is meaningless, to change the meaning of a word. For instance, the sound segment [s], on its own, is meaningless. But when we add it to a word such as *apple*, this changes the meaning of a word: *apple* → *apples*.[44]

Campbell's monkeys are a case in point. In a recent study of Campbell's, from the Ivory Coast, it was discovered that male monkeys can modify the meaning of vocalisations by adding a suffix.[45] For instance, when the monkeys see a leopard, they use the *krak* call. But when they hear a leopard, but don't see it, they add an *-oo* suffix to give the new vocalisation *krak-oo*. Moreover, they use *krak-oo* when they hear the leopard warning call of a neighbouring primate, the Diana monkey. The *-oo* suffix seems to work like a marker signalling that something is learned through hearsay, rather than gleaned directly, sort of like: 'Hey, there *might* be leopards!' Similarly, the *hok* call is used to warn of crowned eagles. But the *hok-oo* call is used to refer to any disturbance in the canopy above the monkeys' heads. It was even once observed to refer to a flying squirrel. What this strikingly reveals is that the combinatorial power of human syntax can be found, albeit in vastly reduced form, in another species. Campbell's monkeys appear to have a rudimentary form of morphology – the ability to build complex words from simpler meaningful units. And the use of the *-oo* suffix seems to be working much like human languages that grammatically encode how reliable a piece of information is.

While English doesn't do this, many languages do. For instance, in Quechua, the most widely spoken indigenous language in South America with between 8 and 10 million native speakers, grammatical markers are added to sentences to indicate how confident the speaker is of a particular assertion, and how they learned of it. For instance, the sentence *Neil Armstrong walked on the moon* would require a suffix to indicate the assertion had been gleaned through hearsay, functioning much like the *-oo* suffix of Campbell's monkeys.

In settings where primates have been trained by humans, the evidence is even more impressive. A chimp named Lana studied by the primatologist Sue Rumbaugh-Savage – who also worked with Kanzi – was able to figure out the semantic significance of word order. For instance, Lana – who, like Sarah, was taught the language Yerkish – was able to understand the difference between sentences such as *X give Lana apple*, and *Lana give X apple*.[46] For humans this distinction is so obvious it barely needs pointing out: in the first sentence, it is Lana who receives the apple, whilst in the second it is Lana who does the giving. Lana's awareness of the distinction, between the giver and receiver, illustrated she had grasped a key function of word order – a staple of many human languages.[47] And, moreover, this demonstrates that Lana understands that words can be combined to produce complex meaning.

But while there is now strong evidence that primates, both in experimental and in natural settings, exhibit duality of patterning, it also turns out that this is not in fact universal to all human languages. A sign language used by the Al-Sayyid community in the Negev desert of southern Israel has existed for around seventy years or so. While the Al-Sayyid sign language has a stable grammar, the symbols it uses, especially when employed by the older members of the community, haven't yet settled into conventional signs.[48] This would be equivalent to English choosing different sounds each time a speaker wanted to form, say, the word *cat*. Rather than being restricted to [k], [æ] and [t], different sounds could be selected on each occasion of use. The reason this decidedly odd-sounding procedure works, in this instance, is because the hand shapes and gestures used by sign languages are often iconic – they represent the thing they stand for. This is much like the way the icon for the 'delete' command on a computer desktop looks like the real-world entity that is associated with getting rid of stuff: the recycle bin. With stable rules of combination, different hand shapes can be deployed on different occasions, in order to produce roughly the same meaning. The way a sign language can function is a consequence, in part, of the medium deployed: manual signed gestures and facial expressions.

The medium provides different sorts of constraints and possibilities, which individual language users take advantage of.

While duality of patterning appears to be emerging in the Al-Sayyid sign language – and it has taken almost three generations of speakers for it to emerge – the point is that this design feature is not necessary for a fully functional language. Around 150 members of the Al-Sayyid Bedouin tribe, and many more hearing members, are fully functional in it.

Duality of patterning is closely related to productivity: the ability to combine linguistic symbols to produce new meanings. But productivity is a design feature that apes also appear to be capable of. For her part, Washoe and her mate were able to combine the hundreds of signs that they learned into novel combinations, ones they had never been taught, but rather created themselves. For instance, when Washoe's mate Moja didn't know the word for *thermos* he referred to it as a *metal cup drink*.[49]

Finally, I touch on three design features which have implications for the cognitive potential of apes: displacement, prevarication and reflexiveness. While previous generations of researchers doubted whether any other species exhibited these, on-going findings continue to offer surprises. And, in the process, this challenges us to rethink our assumptions.

Turning firstly to displacement, it is true that many animals inhabit the here and now – and out of sight really is out of mind. However, there is now very good evidence that chimps can communicate about what is no longer present – displacement. Apes in the wild, *and* in lab-settings, can refer to objects that are no longer in view. Both bonobos and orang-utans can select, transport and save a tool for use the next day. This demonstrates that they have the ability to anticipate and prepare for future events. They can also keep track of how long it has been since a particular event occurred – they have the ability to perceive the elapse of time.[50] In terms of linguistic abilities, Washoe was able to ask for items that were no longer in view or hidden – a clear demonstration of the use of language to address displacement. And let's not forget the humble honey bee: the waggle dance, located far from the source of nectar, is a paradigm example of communicative displacement – for the honey bee, out of sight is *not* out of mind.

Next up, prevarication: before much comparative research had been conducted, it had been assumed that humans were alone in their ability to lie (or prevaricate), and to use language to do so. While perhaps morally suspect, the ability to lie implies a high level of cognitive sophistication: what has been referred to as Machiavellian intelligence.[51] It demonstrates an ability to manipulate reality for ulterior motives. However, chimps, we now know, have the ability to mislead intentionally. And they use communicative strategies to do so. Chimps can do this because they understand that fellow chimps have wishes and desires of their own – that other chimps are intentional agents. Chimps understand that other members of their species have minds of their own, with their own wishes, desires and beliefs.[52] An understanding that others have minds is a significant cognitive achievement.

A recent study of chimps living in a rain forest in Uganda found that chimps took account of whether other chimps had knowledge of upcoming dangers when making warning calls. Chimps ahead of others tended only to make repeated *hoos* to warn of venomous snakes – but only if the chimps behind hadn't already seen the snake. When the following chimps had seen the danger, the leading chimps didn't issue the warning. Observations such as this strongly imply that chimps make inferences about what others know. And they can only do so if they understand that other chimps have intentions and beliefs. This response, by the chimps, is not an instinctive impulse, but evidence of intelligent behaviour.[53]

Finally, there is clear evidence that apes taught language can use language reflexively, to refer to language itself, as in the old joke – *Constantinople is a very long word, how do you spell it?* The joke turns on our reflexive understanding: *it* refers to 'Constantinople'. But the punch-line goes: *No, "i-t", "it"*.

One example of ape reflexiveness involved two gorillas, Michael and Koko. Michael, a silverback gorilla, had a working vocabulary of around 600 signs, taught to him by Koko, an older gorilla. On one occasion, Michael was locked out of the caravan where he and Koko lived. Koko demonstrated the sign she wanted Michael to use through the window, before she would let him back in. When Michael eventually did so, Koko signed back 'good sign'.[54]

In the foregoing, I've been primarily focusing on apes; and there's a good reason for this. After all, apes are our nearest cousins in the animal kingdom. But many other species also exhibit some of the features that are supposed to be unique to language. For instance, scrub jays – a member of the crow family – cache food for future use, which is a form of displacement. Indeed, they will even recover perishable worms sooner than less perishable seeds. Moreover, they will re-cache food if pilferers can be seen or heard; jays will retrieve cached food if another scrub jay, that might have seen the caching, approaches the cache; but they do nothing if a scrub jay that had not been present at the time of caching approaches. Scrub jays have also been observed pretending to cache food, suggesting an ability to prevaricate.[55] Moreover, there is evidence that ravens also engage in deceptive caching.[56] While this relates to behaviour, rather than communication, the point is that human language exemplifies behaviours that exist elsewhere in nature. Language makes available behaviours, in an inter-subjective way, which are already widespread in the animal kingdom.

All in the mind of the beholder

The findings I've been discussing add up to a body of evidence that any objective person would find compelling. Non-human species acquire, learn and use communicative systems. And in some respects, these systems exhibit the germs, even the basis, of (human) language-like traits.

But the claim that apes such as Washoe, Lana and others might be potentially capable of syntax – however impoverished – has been hotly contested by Herbert Terrace of Nim Chimpsky fame.

While Nim Chimpsky was found to sign 19,000 multi-word utterances of over 5,000 different kinds during the period of investigation, Terrace nevertheless vehemently argued that this amounted to no more than Nim blindly repeating gestures in order to obtain a reward such as food, or his trainer's praise. And, according to Terrace, Washoe – taught by the Gardners – couldn't possibly have really *understood* that a particular ASL sign had a specific meaning associated with it. She was simply trained to respond to a particular picture by providing a specific sign. The response is learned through reinforcement. Moreover, unconscious prompting may have been taking place between researchers and chimp, which would explain the accuracy with which Washoe responded, so Terrace argued.[57] In the works of researchers such as Terrace, and even Pinker, you can also feel the indignant incredulity: "Chimps can communicate? Geddadehere! Washoe *knows* the signs she's using have *meanings* attached to them? You're yanking my chain."

Yet, the double blind tests employed by the Gardners address this very concern. Moreover, the Gardners, and their collaborator Roger Fouts, found that Washoe began to acquire new signs without being explicitly taught them after a period of time. She simply picked them up from interacting with her carers, as any human child might. This appears to demonstrate that Washoe did indeed exhibit the design feature of semanticity.

Some commentators have hinted that Terrace was simply determined to oppose the prospect that chimps might be capable of exhibiting traits that are in some way language-like.[58] And Terrace's interpretation of what level of evidence is required in order to be convinced of Washoe's abilities does indeed seem to be somewhat rigid. The clue, perhaps, is in the name he chose to give his protégé: Nim Chimpsky. It is tempting to conjecture that Terrace's agenda was, after all, not too distant from that that of Noam Chomsky. Terrace was motivated by the language-as-instinct thesis. He duly 'found' that apes couldn't produce anything vaguely approaching human-like language because that is what his hypotheses predicted, and what he assumed he would find. Unsurprisingly, then, he interpreted his results, and indeed the work of others, in the light of the theoretical assumptions he was working with.

Even such an important commentator as Steven Pinker comes out of this with little credit. He implied that the Gardners were not far removed from his dotty great-aunt Bella: fond of animals and therefore prone to indulgent and wishful thinking. He makes no attempt to challenge the science, but ridicules a finding that is inconvenient for the theory he seeks to promote: the language-as-instinct thesis.

The reality is that there is now extensive evidence from ethological studies on animal communication and behaviour in the wild, as well as a voluminous body of research on animals reared in artificial settings, relating to the communicative abilities of animals. Of course, and as I have reiterated, we are not talking about full-blown language, or anything that even comes remotely close. But there is evidence of precursors that provide clues as to the evolutionary bases for human language. The communicative abilities of non-human species are continuous, rather than discontinuous, with human language. And the cognitive abilities that support this communication potential are also continuous with human cognition.

In the final analysis, whether or not one believes this conjecture – that the communicative abilities of other primates, and other species, approach human language, no matter how distantly – is determined by underlying beliefs about the uniqueness of language. If one assumes, as the language-as-instinct thesis contends, that language is unrelated to any other form of animal communication – that it is a singularity – and even somewhat more extremely, as in the case of Chomsky, that it arises by virtue of an evolutionary miracle bestowed on the world's first speaking human, Prometheus, then here comes the bleak assessment: the communicative potential of other species, including chimpanzees, cannot, by definition, be even vaguely associated with human language.

But such an assumption largely dismisses the question in advance, and gives rise to a Hegelian argument. The myth contends that human language is unique. Therefore evidence for animal communication must be interpreted as being incommensurable with it, and dismissed (see Pinker, and Terrace). The situation, the naysayers contend, is a straightforward separation between language – evidenced in humans – and communicative abilities that are of a wholly different type – in other animals. In fact, the reality is rather different: "Human language ... is a special means of conveying information about objects and events which are removed in time and space ... totally contiguous with similar systems found in other species".[59]

Of chimps and men

I began this chapter by asking whether human language is related to non-human systems of communication. From an evolutionary perspective it has to be: it is continuous with the other systems of communication evident in other species. Most, and possibly all, of the features exhibited by language are in evidence in other animal communication systems, and some species can be trained to deploy some traits that approach human language. Indeed, the human brain contains few if any unique neuronal types, and few if any genes lack a significant ancestral precedent.[60]

However, in terms of the functions to which human language is put, it is qualitatively different from other animal communication systems from which it has evolved. For example, very few naturally occurring ape gestures are referential in quite the same way human language is.[61] Attention-getters, for instance, attract the attention of another to themselves, as in the leaf-clipping gesture used by male chimps to attract the attention of a female to their sexual arousal. In contrast, human language regularly makes reference to entities outside the two-party communicative situation. Very rarely do chimp gestures enable this.[62] Similarly, ape communication is typically imperative: apes issue commands and instructions. In contrast, human language often goes beyond the imperative. It is also declarative: it is used as a medium for expressing thoughts, feelings and observations, from unrequited love to declarations of loyalty. Even such a banal expression as 'It's fine again', referring to the weather, describes a state of affairs that goes way beyond the imperative interactive strategy adopted by apes. The expression might serve as a response to a question, providing information about the weather outside. However, it might serve no other purpose than as a banal comment when passing the time of day with a neighbour. I summarise, in the two tables below, the most important differences between human language and the naturally occurring communication of other primate species, and how different communicative systems match up, across species, in terms of Hockett's design features.

Summary of differences between human language and ape gestures

Human linguistic trait	Ape communicative trait
Linguistic symbols are socially learned – this takes place via imitation in a socio-cultural matrix	Ape gestures are individually learned through ritualising part of a gesture sequence, e.g., raising arms to initiate play
Linguistic symbols are used triadically – to get someone else to attend to something outside the immediate relationship between the speaker and hearer	Ape gestures are typically used dyadically – to regulate the social interaction between the two apes involved
Linguistic symbols can be used declaratively – with no requirement that the hearer provides a behavioural response – as well as imperatively	Ape gestures are solely/primarily used imperatively, to induce a behavioural response from another
Linguistic symbols are perspectival: they can frame the same entity or event from different perspectives, e.g., *freedom fighter* versus *terrorist* to refer to the same individual	Ape gestures appear not to be perspectival in this way

Summary of how the communicative systems of various species fare according to Hockett's design features

Feature	Frogs and toads[63]	Bee dancing	Humpback (toothed) whales	Baleen whale song	Vervet alarm calls	Signing chimps	Apes reared in human contexts	Alex, an African Grey	Human sign language	Human spoken language
Vocal–Auditory channel	✓	x	✓	✓	✓	x	x	✓	x	✓
Broadcast/direction	✓	✓	✓	✓	✓	x	x	✓	x	✓
Rapid fading	✓	✓	✓	✓	✓	✓	✓	✓	✓	✓
Total feedback	✓	✓	✓	✓	✓	✓	✓	✓	✓	✓
Interchangeability	✓	✓	✓	✓	✓	✓	✓	✓	✓	✓
Specialisation	✓	✓	✓	✓	Probably	✓	✓	✓	✓	✓
Semanticity	✓	✓	✓	✓	✓	✓	✓	✓	✓	✓
Arbitrariness	✓	✓	✓	✓	✓	Partly	✓	?	Largely	Largely
Cultural transmission	x	✓	✓	✓	Probably not	✓	✓	✓	✓	✓
Learnability	x	?	Probably	Probably	✓	✓	✓	✓	✓	✓
Discreteness	x	✓	✓	✓	✓	✓	✓	✓	✓	✓
Duality of patterning	x	✓	✓	✓	x	✓	✓	✓	Not always	✓
Displacement	x	✓	?	?	x	x	✓	x	✓	✓
Productivity	x	✓	✓	✓	x	✓	✓	?	✓	✓
Prevarication	x	x	x	x	x	✓	✓	x	✓	✓
Reflexiveness	x	x	x	x	x	?	✓	x	✓	✓

Despite the range of communicative systems evident in the animal kingdom, the complexity of human language, the nature and type of messages it allows us to signal, how it is acquired, and crucially the range of functions it facilitates, are of both a different quality and a different level of complexity from any other.[64] Human language, after all, is the only animal communication system that differs radically in form and meaning across social groups of the same species. In the next chapter, I explore why.

3   Are there language universals?

Myth: *A Universal Grammar underpins all human languages; this specifies the various features that are shared by the world's languages. On this basis it is possible to extract all the extant linguistic universals by studying a single language, for instance, English.*

The language-as-instinct thesis claims that human babies enter the world pre-equipped to learn language. Language emerges effortlessly and automatically. And this is because we are all born with a Universal Grammar: a pre-specified listing of language universals – a universal being a feature of grammar that is shared by all human languages. Moreover, as all languages are assumed to derive from this Universal Grammar, the study of a single language can reveal its design. In essence, all languages, despite having different sound systems and vocabularies, are basically English-like.[1]

But like the myth that language is unrelated to animal forms of communication, the myth of language universals is contradicted by the evidence. The myth of Universal Grammar was proposed by Chomsky as early as the 1950s, and formalised in the 1960s[2] before the study of cross-linguistic diversity was well established. And so, one would have expected, once the facts had become known, the myth would have disappeared. But the thesis of Universal Grammar has proved difficult to eradicate. One reason is that the language-as-instinct thesis provides a complex and self-supporting worldview consisting of a number of sub-theses: all the elements providing inter-dependent planks, supporting the others regardless of the facts. Another is that advocates of this view have found it difficult to let go of the underlying rationalist impulse that underpins the entire system of beliefs: human language is unique, and its genetic endowment is bequeathed by nature. This view, in certain respects, is very appealing. In a single move, it explains the hard questions of language, and the mind.

The spectre of Universal Grammar has cast a long shadow; the shadow falls not just over the scientific study of language, but also over related areas including cognitive science, and psychology. In this chapter I explore the evidence for linguistic diversity, and develop the language-as-use alternative, which better aligns with the facts.

If languages are really as diverse as we now know them to be, how do we explain such diversity? I will hope to persuade you that language emerges and diversifies in and during specific instances of language use. Once I've reviewed some of the evidence for linguistic diversity, evidence that is incompatible with the language-as-instinct worldview, I present some of the pressures that arise naturally when we use language, usage pressures that collectively conspire to give rise to linguistic diversity.

Linguistic diversity: a whistle-stop tour

Today there are between 6,000 and 8,000 languages spoken in the world.[3] It is difficult to say precisely how many. And this is because it is inherently tricky to determine whether a spoken variety counts as a dialect or a language in its own right. You might think that an obvious way to decide would be to rely on mutual intelligibility. A speaker of American English can (more or less) understand a speaker of British English. In contrast, a monolingual speaker of French cannot understand a speaker of English (of either variety). On this measure, American and British 'Englishes' are dialects of a single language, whilst English and French count as distinct languages.

However, cultural identity and socio-political concerns are wont to intervene. Serbian and Croatian are considered to be separate languages by the peoples of Serbia and Croatia, respectively. But they *are* mutually intelligible, and they differ *less* markedly than American and British varieties of English – a colleague from Niš in

Serbia has even told me that he finds it easier to understand speakers from the capital of Croatia, Zagreb, at a distance of some 650 km, than some Serbian dialects, 80–100 km from Niš, in the south-east of Serbia. In contrast, Mandarin and Cantonese are considered to be dialects of Chinese by the Chinese government, even though they are barely mutually intelligible.

A second reason for the difficulty is that nearly every week one of the world's languages dies out. This happens when the last speaker of a language dies, or, more accurately, when the penultimate speaker dies, and so the last speaker has no one to converse with.[4] And, of the world's languages, a great many are endangered. Of course, a language can be revitalised. The most extreme example is Hebrew: the only example in history of the total revival of a dead language. By around 200 CE, Hebrew had ceased to be a living language – it no longer had native speakers – and it survived into the Middle Ages purely as the language of Jewish liturgy – equivalent to the role of Latin in the Catholic church in mediaeval Europe. Yet today, Hebrew has several million first-language users, and is the official language of a nation state: Israel. But sadly, in the overwhelming majority of cases, when a language is gone, it's gone for good.[5]

The most accurate reference work on the world's languages is the *Ethnologue* encyclopaedia. At the time of writing, there are 6,909 distinct languages of the world, as recorded by *Ethnologue*. Of these, around 82 per cent are spoken by populations of less than 100,000 people, 39 per cent are spoken by less than 10,000 people, and 8 per cent of the world's languages are considered to be endangered. Prior to 1492, with Christopher Columbus' first voyage to the Americas marking the beginning of western imperialism by European kingdoms, there were probably twice as many languages as there are today. And projecting backwards through time, there have probably existed around half a million languages in total, since the advent of *Homo sapiens*, around 170,000 years ago.[6]

While the figure of around 7,000 languages sounds a large number, only around 10 per cent of these have been studied in *any* detail – resulting in dictionaries and written records of the languages' grammars. Nevertheless, the striking finding to emerge, even from this relatively small subset of the world's languages, is just how different they are. As linguists Nicholas Evans and Stephen Levinson observe, "it's a jungle out there: languages differ in fundamental ways – in their sound systems (even if they have one), in their grammar, and in their semantics".[7]

To give you a sense of this diversity, consider this: the sound systems deployed by the world's languages range from 11 to 144 distinctive sounds. And, of course, sign languages don't use sounds at all. Some languages, such as English, have fairly restricted word order – in this sentence, *The supermodel kissed the window cleaner*, we know that the subject is *the supermodel* as it precedes the verb. Moreover, the word orders exhibited by languages can be extremely diverse. Some languages even have completely free word order, indigenous Australian languages, such as Jiwarli and Thalanyji, being examples.[8] Such languages would permit the English sentence *This woman kissed that bald window cleaner* to be conveyed as follows: *That this bald kissed woman window cleaner*. Moreover, while a language like English can add prefixes and suffixes to words – for instance, the word *interesting* can be negated using *un-*, making *uninteresting*, or the noun *teacher* is derived from the verb *teach* by adding the agentive *-er* suffix – some languages, such as Mandarin, lack the ability to build words from smaller units altogether. Still others build whole sentences not from single words, but from prefixes and suffixes, creating giant words. Such an example is the Inuit language Inuktitut, spoken in Eastern Canada. The Inuktitut word-phrase *tawakiqutiqarpiit* roughly translates into English as the following sentence: *Do you have any tobacco for sale?*

Universal Grammar meets (linguistic) reality

According to the language-as-instinct thesis, human children are able to acquire any language because at a deep level, all languages are essentially the same. Obviously, a child growing up in Tokyo will acquire Japanese while a child living in London will acquire English – regardless of the ethnicity of their parents. But stripping away the relatively superficial surface matter of different words and sounds, all children have knowledge that specifies how a language – any language – is structured and organised. This is the Universal Grammar that allows us to acquire whichever language it is we happen to be exposed to as infants.

But the language-as-instinct thesis – that there are universals which underpin all languages – is a presumption. It follows not from careful observation and description of countless languages, but from a particular intellectual commitment. Chomsky assumed that our knowledge of language is an integral part of our genetic endowment. And because of this presumption, Chomsky's followers are, at least in principle, absolved from studying other languages. The irony of this is that the language-as-instinct thesis is thereby shielded from the full extent of the counter-evidence. The ideological commitment to universalism comes from the rationalist Zeitgeist that informed Chomsky's thinking as he was developing his ideas, from the middle part of the twentieth century. For the language-as-instinct thesis, "the conceptual architecture, the essential conceptual parameters, are, as Leibniz would have it, 'innate ideas' … [which] has led to the search for universals without parallel concern for language difference".[9]

But what do the 'universals' look like, that are supposed to comprise our Universal Grammar? Chomsky originally proposed that the universals are of two sorts.[10] One kind consists of what we might think of as the 'ingredients' of any language. These include parts of speech such as nouns, verbs and adjectives, or grammatical relations such as subject and object. Other ingredients might include different sorts of sounds, such as vowels and consonants. The second type of universal consists of the 'rules' that apply to the 'ingredients', in constructing a language. For instance, rules relate to the ability to build multi-word units from other words. As an example, the phrase, *the supermodel from Clapham*, is a noun phrase: a phrase centred upon a noun, *supermodel.* The overall function of the phrase is to identify a particular kind of entity – in this case: the supermodel. Other sorts of rules relate to recursion – the ability to embed phrases and clauses within other phrases and clauses ad infinitum, which we met in the previous chapter.

Steven Pinker puts things as follows:

> It is safe to say that the grammatical machinery we use for English . . . is used in all the world's languages. All languages have a vocabulary in the tens of thousands, sorted into part-of-speech categories including noun and verb. Words are organized into phrases according to the X-bar system [the system used in an earlier version of Chomsky's theoretical architecture to represent grammatical organization] . . . The higher levels of phrase structure include auxiliaries . . . which signify tense, modality, aspect and negation. Phrases can be moved from their deep structure positions . . . by a . . . movement rule, thereby forming questions, relative clauses, passives and other widespread constructions. New word structures can be created and modified by derivational and inflectional rules. Inflectional rules primarily mark nouns for case and number, and mark verbs for tense, aspect, mood, voice, negation, and agreement with subjects and objects in number, gender and person. The phonological forms of words are defined by metrical and syllable trees and separate tiers of features like voicing, tone, and manner and place of articulation, and are subsequently adjusted by ordered phonological rules . . . [This suggests] that a Universal Grammar, not reducible to history or cognition, underlies the human language instinct.[11]

In the years since Chomsky famously proposed the language-as-instinct thesis in 1965, and Pinker, later in 1994, popularised it, the emerging facts of linguistic diversity have demonstrated that the Universal Grammar proposal is just plain wrong.[12] Two prominent experts, reviewing the facts of linguistic diversity in 2009 provided a damning assessment: "languages differ so fundamentally from one another . . . that it is very hard to find any single structural property they share. The claims of

Universal Grammar . . . are either empirically false, unfalsifiable, or misleading".[13] So, let's see why.

Sound systems

The strong claim made by the language-as-instinct thesis is that all languages adhere to the set of putative universals. If just one language is found not to exhibit a specific language universal, then the 'universal' is shown not to be universal at all. And, in turn, each 'universal' that is falsified puts a further nail in the coffin of the language-as-instinct's sub-thesis of Universal Grammar. Let's consider first, then, universals in the areas of sound.

We visited, in the previous chapter, Charles Hockett's design features of language. These were, and remain, highly influential, particularly in the language-as-instinct worldview: Hockett's design features were an early attempt to provide universal characteristics for language. Yet the existence of sign languages invalidates two of Hockett's design features. And, as we have also seen, duality of patterning is not inevitably a design feature of language either – it is invalidated by the Al-Sayyid Bedouin sign language community in which it has yet to emerge fully.[14]

In terms of spoken languages, the human vocal tract and auditory system put strong constraints on the type and range of sounds it is possible to make and to perceive. This has led to the hypothesis that there is a fixed set of sound parameters from which languages draw their sound inventories.[15] For instance, sounds can be produced either by obstructing the airflow by closing the mouth, or by leaving the airflow unobstructed. This difference gives rise to more sonorous vowels (no obstruction), and the less sonorous consonants (with obstruction).

Hence, obstruction constitutes a parameter which has two variants: vowels and consonants. In terms of the class of consonants, these can be obstructed at various points in the vocal tract, giving rise to other parameters. For instance, airflow can be obstructed by the lips closing, by the teeth coming together, by the tongue being raised at various points in the mouth to obstruct the flow of air, and so on. The notion of a finite and universal set of parameters was highly influential for Chomsky, as he developed his approach to Universal Grammar.

However, as the true extent of the diversity of sound systems across the world's languages has come to light, it has become increasingly clear that languages are not comprised of a universal set of phonetic categories. For one thing, sounds that were thought to be impossible keep turning up. It was thought impossible to produce a consonant with obstruction to the airflow being made at two places in the vocal tract. Yet it turns out that quite a number of languages allow this, including Yélî Dnye, of Rossel Island, Papua New Guinea. The Yélî language produces a consonant by using two places in the mouth simultaneously: the lips (a [p] or [b] sound), and at the teeth (a [t] or [d] sound), producing a doubly articulated [bd] sound – we will see more of the Rossel Island language later, when it has a starring role in Chapter 7.[16] As one leading phonetician has put it: "Languages can differ systematically in arbitrarily fine phonetic detail. This means we do not want to think about universal phonetic categories but rather universal phonetic resources, which are organized and harnessed by the cognitive system."[17]

Languages also combine sounds using phonological rules forming larger units. One of the most important is the syllable, which is built from consonants and vowels. Until recently, it was assumed that syllables in all the world's languages were made up of a consonant followed by a more sonorous vowel. This is the so-called 'consonant–vowel', or CV, structure. However, it turns out that the Australian aboriginal language Arrernte organises its syllables the other way round, with a vowel first. This gives a VC structure.[18]

Parts of speech

The language-as-instinct thesis assumes that languages are made up of parts of speech (also known as lexical classes), including the big four: nouns, verbs, adjectives and adverbs. However, many languages lack adverbs, while some, such as Lao, lack adjectives.[19] This doesn't mean that a language without adjectives can't express property concepts, for instance, *red*, as in *a red nose*. Different languages adopt different linguistic strategies to express these ideas. In Lao, which is spoken in Laos in South-East Asia, verbs are used to do roughly the same job as adjectives do in English. Moreover, some linguists have even claimed that nouns and verbs are not universal. The native Canadian language, Straits Salish, spoken in Vancouver Island, British Columbia, is a case in point.[20] In English we know that something is a noun, rather than a verb or an adjective, from its morphology – the sorts of affixes it takes. For instance, a noun can be pluralised, *boy* → *boys*, while verbs and adjectives can't. A verb can take the past tense *-ed* marker, nouns and adjectives can't. And adjectives can take the *-est* affix to form superlatives: *clean* → *cleanest*. Moreover, nouns, verbs and adjectives differ in terms of their syntax – where in the sentence they occur. For instance, nouns occupy the subject and object slots, the verb relates to an event or action, while an adjective encodes a property of the noun. In the following, *The elegant supermodel is dancing*, *elegant* is the adjective, *supermodel* the noun and *dancing* the verb. That is, nouns occupy a different slot, *and* have a different semantic function from verbs, and adjectives differ again.

In Straits Salish, there is a single lexical class: a lexical stem. It is not distinct in terms of its morphology or syntax, regardless of whether it describes a thing, an event or a property. While the lexical stems used in Straits Salish can indeed relate to things, events and properties, they have to be combined with other affixes in order to produce the required meaning. For instance, the lexical stem with the equivalent meaning of *sing* is in effect placed in a relative clause to produce a thing (noun) meaning – 'the one who is a sing(er)' – or an event (verb) meaning: 'the ones who are singing'.

But for those of you who thought that English has it all sorted, think again. Even in English, nouns and verbs are not stable categories: some nouns and verbs are 'nounier' or 'verbier' than others.[21] A property of English verbs that have a direct object is that they can be turned into nouns. This is done by adding the *-er* suffix, as with the verb *to import*: *The window cleaner imports rugs in his spare time* → *The window cleaner is an importer of rugs in his spare* *time*. But a few verbs are unable to undergo this prototypical behaviour. A good example is the verb *to know*: *The supermodel knew that fact* → **The supermodel was the knower of that fact* (grammarians use an asterisk preceding a sentence to indicate that it is usually judged to be an ungrammatical sentence by native speakers; hence the second sentence is just plain weird-sounding). Another typical property of verbs is that they can be turned into passive sentences: *The supermodel kissed the window cleaner* → *The window cleaner was kissed by the supermodel*. But some verbs fail to exhibit this prototypical property. The verb *to owe* is in this respect less verb-like than *to kiss*: *The window cleaner owes two pounds* → **Two pounds are owed by the window cleaner*.[22] What this reveals is that, even in a language like English, one that does have the lexical classes nouns and verbs, some verbs are less verb-like than others. Not all verbs (or nouns for that matter) conform to the prototypical behaviour associated with their lexical class. Verbs and nouns can be wayward and delinquent.

Let's consider another example of diversity. Many non-European languages boast parts of speech that seem positively alien to speakers of English. One such lexical class is that of ideophones. These linguistic oddities describe a perceptual experience in which several distinct sensations are rolled into one. A particularly evocative example is *ribuy-tibuy*, from Mundari, a language spoken in eastern India, Bangladesh and Nepal. This word describes the sight, sound and motion of the buttocks of a fat person rubbing together as they move. Ideophones are inserted into narratives as independent syntactic units, in order to spice things up.

Morphology

In the quotation cited earlier, Steven Pinker claimed that new words can be created by derivational and inflectional processes – by morphology – as when we add –*er* to the English verb *teach*, or the third person singular inflection -*s* to the verb *sing*, to signal person agreement and present tense. But many languages lack morphology altogether. Mandarin and Vietnamese are two such languages. They lack systematic morphological processes that allow the creation of new words. Moreover, these languages lack inflectional affixes that signal person, number and tense. This doesn't mean that these languages can't communicate the equivalent of past tense meaning, or the English plural meaning. In Mandarin, these notions are either inferred from context, or signalled by independent words, not affixes. Languages diverge in their morphological systems, often in quite surprising ways.

Syntax

In addition to supposed universals for parts of speech and morphology, the language-as-instinct thesis assumes various rules that determine how sentences are formed – syntax – across the languages of the world. One such presumed universal is that all languages build up words into constituent units. These units are known as phrases. A phrase is a unit made up of words that cluster around a part of speech, such as a noun, or verb, and so on. A phrase that is headed by a noun is known as a noun phrase (NP), one that clusters around a verb, a verb phrase (VP), etc. Evidence for distinct phrase structures, such as NPs, comes from the fact that in a language like English, an NP can be replaced by another element, such as a pronoun, which replaces exactly that unit in the sentence and nothing else. For instance, the sentence *The elegant supermodel is dancing*, can be rephrased as *she is dancing*, where *she* replaces the NP *the elegant supermodel*.

That said, many languages scramble words, allowing completely free word order. Take the following line from Virgil's *Aeneid*, written in Classical Latin: "ultima Cumaei venit iam carminis aetas".[23] The sentence literally translates as "last Cumaean arrived now song age", which would be rendered in English as: "the last age of the Cumaean song [has] now arrived". Latin, unlike English, has a complex case system in which words are morphologically marked to show the relationship between them. Because of this, words that 'belong' to phrases don't have to be sequenced in adjacent fashion in order to signify the relations that hold; in fact, Latin didn't have phrase structure at all.

For instance, the English NP, *the last age*, is represented in Latin by the words *ultima* (last) and *aetas* (age), which appear at the beginning and end of the sentence respectively. This is possible because both are marked for nominative case, showing they both relate to the subject of the sentence and 'belong' together. Consequently they don't have to appear together either in spoken Latin or on the page. Similarly, the NP *the Cumaean song* is represented by the Latin words *Cumaei* and *carminis*, which both carry genitive case, demonstrating they are related. And a consequence of Latin, and many other languages, employing case markings is that they are not restricted to using word order to designate the grammatical relationships between words. While Latin is an extinct language – it no longer has any native speakers – many languages in the world happily do without phrase structure, exhibiting completely free word order, including a large number of indigenous Australian languages. *The World Atlas of Language Structures Online*, published in 2011,[24] demonstrates that a significant subset of the world's languages lack any word order at all.

In the table below, I illustrate word order patterns based on a sample of 1,377 of the world's languages.[25] 'S' stands for subject, 'V' for verb and 'O' for object. For instance, English has an SVO word order, as illustrated by the following sentence: *The supermodel (S) kissed (V) the window cleaner (O).*

Word order patterns for a sample of the world's languages

Word order pattern	No. of languages
SOV	565
SVO	488
VSO	95
VOS	25
OVS	11
OSV	4
No dominant word order	189
	Total sample: 1,377

While some languages such as Latin employ case to distinguish grammatical relations, many languages lack both word order and case marking. Malay is such an example. Spoken by about 40 million people in Indonesia, Malaysia, Brunei and Singapore, Malay doesn't have a grammatical subject of a sentence, in the way English does. When a sentence in Malay describes an action performed by an agent on an object, either the agent (A) or object (O) can be placed before the verb (V): AVO or OVA. Which is which is signalled by voice – e.g., active or passive – and marked on the verb. As voice indicates whether the action is being 'performed' or 'suffered', Malay speakers can figure out whether the entity preceding the verb is the agent or the object, based on which grammatical marker appears on the verb.

To get a sense of how voice does this, consider an example from English of grammatical voice, in this case, passive voice: *The window cleaner was kissed (by the supermodel)*. In this sentence, we know that the action is performed by the supermodel, who is the agent, and the kissing is 'suffered' (or not!) by the window cleaner. We know this because we understand that in the passive construction the entity who 'suffers' the action comes first.

But in Malay things can get even more complicated: Malay can also omit agents and objects altogether. In such cases, which is which is inferred from the discourse context. For instance, in service encounters such as a shop setting, the equivalents of *I* and *you* are often omitted: *Bisa dibantu?* (Can [I] help [you]?). But in such situations, the *I* and *you* are self-evident, so Malay speakers often don't bother saying them.

Now, let's look at another example of a proposed universal that has fallen by the wayside. One much-celebrated rule, hypothesised to be universal, was meant to account for the observation – in English – that a *wh-* word (such as *what, which, whether* and so on) could not intervene between two clauses in a question. First, let's consider a case where a word can intervene. In the following question, *that* can intervene: *Where did the supermodel say that the window cleaner had to get off the train to meet her?*

But, in the following, the *wh-* word *whether* can't intervene (recall that an asterisk preceding a sentence shows that it is ungrammatical): *Where did the supermodel say whether the window cleaner had to get off the train to meet her?*

But later, it turned out that this supposedly universal 'rule' did not to apply to other Indo-European languages such as Italian or Russian: in those languages, a *wh-* word can intervene between two clauses in a question.[26] In short, this constraint turns out not to be universal at all. And moreover, this further illustrates the sobering lesson that one cannot generalise from a single language, English, to all of the world's other languages.

Lessons from linguistic typology

Linguistic typology is the branch of linguistics that studies linguistic diversity. Typologists do the hard graft of going out and studying exotic languages, writing dictionaries and grammars to capture them, and describing their points of similarity and difference. The findings I've reported so far in this chapter derive from several decades of research produced by typologists. Around the same time as Chomsky was formulating his language-as-instinct approach, the linguist Joseph Greenberg was conducting pioneering research which, beginning in the late 1950s, founded the field of linguistic typology.

Like Chomsky, Greenberg was motivated by the desire to identify linguistic universals. But, unlike Chomsky, Greenberg's approach was empirical; in his early famous work on universals, Greenberg compared thirty languages – by current standards a relatively small number for a typologist. And, around the same time as Chomsky was declaring it sufficient to study a single language to uncover Universal Grammar, Greenberg took a strikingly different view: "Assuming that it was important to discover generalizations which were valid for all languages, would not such statements be few in number and on the whole quite banal? Examples would be that languages had nouns and verbs (although some linguists denied even that) or that all languages had sound systems and distinguished between phonetic vowels and consonants."[27]

Greenberg observed that, logically, it is possible to have two types of linguistic universals. The first, absolute universals, are the kind assumed by the language-as-instinct thesis. And these are what he refers to as "few in number and on the whole quite banal". Indeed, it is the near-absence of any truly exceptionless universals, the banal apart, that has led to the pointed observation that "the emperor of Universal Grammar [i.e., Chomsky] has no clothes",[28] and is completely embarrassed.

From a typological perspective, there is a further problem with seeking absolute universals. Since the 1980s, the language-as-instinct thesis has proposed, in the face of the emerging facts of linguistic diversity, that there may be more flexibility in terms of what 'universal' means than what had been claimed earlier. In 1981, Chomsky proposed that our innate Universal Grammar consists of mental switches, known as parameters, that can be set in different ways. Switch the parameter one way rather than another, and you get a cascade of effects that make a language like English look very different from, say, the Australian language Jiwarli. But underneath it all, the great variation between the two is simply due to flicking mental switches.[29] In a slightly different variant, proposed by linguist Ray Jackendoff, Universal Grammar constitutes a 'toolkit'.[30] A particular language can select from the range of 'universals', eschewing some.

However, these views of a 'pick 'n' mix' Universal Grammar fail what I call the 'good science' test. In effect, if Universal Grammar is a flexible set of universals, then testing this claim becomes unfalsifiable: it cannot be disproved.[31] Even if language X lacks universal Y, this does not count as counterevidence for Universal Grammar. In the Universal Grammar-as-toolkit perspective, a language is not required to include all 'universals' but can mix and match as it pleases. However, the acid test for any prediction in science is that it must potentially be falsifiable. Put another way, for a theory to be worth its price of entry, we must be able to test it.[32]

If a prediction cannot be tested, then we have no way of knowing whether it is correct or not. And this is precisely the problem we have with Universal Grammar – it's untestable. A further related difficulty for the language-as-instinct thesis is this. The testing ground for the existence (or not) of absolute universals extends beyond the 7,000 or so living languages. All languages must be included: both those now extinct and those that will exist in the future.[33] After all, it takes just one counter-example to invalidate a universal, and counter-examples are often vanishingly rare. It should, by now, be obvious that Universal Grammar is in fact impossible to invalidate. And in terms of the 'good science' test, it makes very bad science indeed.

While Universal Grammar is concerned with absolute universals, Greenberg pointed out that there is a second type of 'universal': a conditional universal. These are universals in the sense that if language X has a particular property Y, then it will also have property Z. However, Greenberg concluded that even this may be too strong. For the most part, Greenberg discovered that conditional universals are implicational: if language X has property Y, then it will *tend to* have property Z.

A case in point relates to the way languages mark the negative. For instance, it was hypothesised that when a language marks the negative, it does so by adding a morpheme, as in English, which adds the negative marker *not*. However, Classical Tamil marked the negative by deleting the tense morpheme found in the assertive version of the utterance, rather than adding a negation morpheme.[34] This demonstrates that any 'universal' must nearly always be thought of in terms of a tendency of the sort proposed by Greenberg, rather than being unrestricted in nature – universals of the type associated with the language-as-instinct thesis.

So, how and why does language change?

So in the absence of a Universal Grammar that dictates the structure of languages, why is there such diversity in the languages of the world? In Chapter 8, I will argue that what sets our species, *Homo sapiens*, apart from other species is a special kind of intelligence: cultural intelligence. The language-as-use thesis contends that our ability to develop sophisticated culture – our cultural intelligence – has given rise to cooperative behaviour, linguistic communication being a paradigm example. The cooperative nature of language involves the sharing of our desires, wishes and so on, in the common pursuit of achieving communicative goals.

For instance, in a service encounter in a lingerie shop, the customer – typically, although not inevitably, female – must convey what sort of lingerie she is looking for – thereby sharing intentionality. And, together, the shop assistant and customer engage in a negotiated linguistic interaction to achieve this goal. Language, then, is a form of social interaction. It is in this context, of language use, that language takes on meaning. And in the process of constructing meaning, and negotiating the fulfilment of communicative goals, usage-based pressures come to bear; and these can result in language change. Over time, small changes, in both form and meaning during ordinary language use, give rise to linguistic diversity.

It's been known since the 1960s, with the study of sociolinguistic variation, that the language we use – including the words and phrases we select, how we pronounce them and so on – varies from day to day, from situation to situation and even from individual to individual. Different linguistic communities, even of single languages, exhibit distinct geographical accents and dialects, often comprising startling differences. This variation leads to change, which is gradual, and in many cases imperceptible. Nevertheless, over time the results can be spectacular.

For instance, the English spoken in England around 1,200 years ago was markedly different from the English spoken today. A contemporary monolingual speaker of English today has as much chance of understanding Old English as they do double-Dutch. To illustrate, the Old English sentence *sēō cwēn geseah þone guman* means "The woman saw the man."

A less spectacular, but, nevertheless, still striking example is the change, over time, that has taken place in the Queen's English.

The annual Christmas address made by Elizabeth II, since 1952, to citizens of the Commonwealth – fifty-four member states that are mostly former territories of the British Empire – has been studied by researchers at MacQuarie University in Australia. It was found that significant changes have taken place in the Queen's accent, in common with the language spoken by her subjects, since this time. The Received Pronunciation (RP) spoken by the Queen today is no longer the same as in the 1950s. In common with speakers of RP at large, sometimes also referred to as BBC or Oxford English, the Queen's accent today demonstrates an incorporation of some features of Britain's southern Estuary English. For example, in the Queen's broadcasts from the 1950s, the word *had* almost rhymed with *bed*. But thirty years later, *had* had migrated much closer towards the standard southern English pronunciation, which rhymes with *bad*.

According to the linguist William Croft,[35] language change is produced by similar principles to those that give rise to biological diversity, as seen across evolutionary time. And we can better understand how language evolves by drawing on neo-Darwinian evolutionary theory.[36] In the neo-Darwinian story, an important idea is that of a replicator. A replicator is an entity whose structure can be passed on in successive replications. An example from biology is the gene, which contains material that is passed on to offspring through procreation. Crucially, however, the process of replication may introduce differences, which result in a slightly different structure from the original replicator. Changes introduced during on-going replication can build up, and result in a replicator that, through successive replications, can have quite different properties from the original replicator.

Changes occur during the replication process due to errors in the copying process. Genes are contained in DNA sequences. And the copying errors, known as mutations, give rise to 'new' DNA sequences being replicated, or actually created. These copying errors are known as altered replications, and contrast with normal replication, which copies the original replicator exactly.

Replicators are 'carried' by individuals – you and me. And we interact with our environment, and each other, in such a way that replication occurs. During our daily lives accidents can happen, and an individual can be snuffed out. This tragedy leads to the extinction of one individual. But others successfully procreate, and get to live on, via copies of their DNA in further rounds of replication, and altered replication. From the neo-Darwinian perspective, this process of extinction (death) and proliferation (procreation) is a form of selection. Survival involves particular genes being selected, while others are obliterated by bad luck, fate, poor judgement, and so on.

So what are the linguistic counterparts of these concepts from evolutionary theory? While in biology the gene represents a replicator, which is embedded in strands of DNA, a linguistic replicator is an element of language realised in a spoken utterance. The elements of language that count as replicators include words (e.g., *supermodel*), morphemes (e.g., *–er*, as in *lover*, and *-ed*, as in *loved*) and grammatical constructions (e.g., idioms such as *She jumped down my throat*), and fixed grammatical sentence-level structures such as the passive construction: Patient BE PAST PAR-TICIPLE by AGENT (as in: *The window cleaner was kissed uncon-scious by the supermodel*). Croft calls these linguistic replicators "linguemes". This term is pronounced so that it rhymes with *dream*, and indeed with the term 'meme' – an element of culture or behaviour that may also be replicated, as coined by Richard Dawkins.[37] A lingueme, then, is the hereditary material central to language change.

Normal replication occurs when linguemes are used in accord-ance with the conventions of a given language. Altered replication occurs when an utterance provides a meaning that breaks with those same conventions – as when the Queen began to use the form *had* rather than *hed* to convey the intended meaning. The consequence of an altered replication is that an innovation occurs. And it is these innovations that can lead to language change.

Of course, language change doesn't depend solely on a group of speakers dying, or being more successful at breeding – although language death can be caused by an entire speech community dying out, or being wiped out. More commonly, language users – you and me – play a role in the selection of utterances due to the various social and communication networks within which we interact – a point to which I'll return shortly. And, critically, language change involves not just altered replication – resulting in innovation – but also the spread of the innovation through a community. Once an innovation has taken hold, and become established as the new convention, the language can be said to have definitively changed. Indeed, the change of pronunciation, over time, exhibited by the Queen is the consequence of the propagation of a particular lingueme that has become established as convention – *had* replacing *hed*. Ironically, the Queen is likely to have been influenced by younger members of her entourage who are leading the change in the Queen's English.

So, language change involves an innovation, which results from an altered replication of a lingueme. This lingueme is then propagated through a linguistic community. And this occurs because the altered replication is repeatedly selected, over other linguemes, each time we use language. In time, this innovation becomes established as a new convention. And so language change has occurred.

But knowing that language changes, because linguemes are selected for during spoken interaction, still doesn't explain *why* language changes. What causes altered replications of linguemes? And what motivates the selection of some altered replications, and not others? What is the counterpart of a genetic mutation?

Linguistic behaviour is a form of social action.[38] After all, language is not merely a means of encoding information – its symbolic function. Language can self-evidently change social relationships, as when a rector pronounces a couple husband and wife, or when a Prime Minister declares that a state of war now exists between their own nation and another – thereby fulfilling its interactive function. More generally, of course, people use language to influence the mental states of others, when we persuade, are economical with the truth in order to present ourselves in a more flattering light, engage in discussions and arguments, or flirt with members of the opposite (or, indeed, the same) sex. And as language is a form of social action (and interaction), linguistic conventions become altered in the course of using language in social contexts.

For example, speakers may wish to get noticed, to be recognised as not being a member of a particular group, or, conversely, as belonging to the group. Exaggerating linguistic features, or accommodating towards the linguistic features of others, affords speakers ways of doing this. In one famous study, the sociolinguist William Labov observed change in the speech of those who lived on the island of Martha's Vineyard, off Cape Cod in Massachusetts. The speech of those who lived there all year round and identified strongly with the island and its traditional way of life – primarily fishing – was changing. Indeed, the speech of this group was seemingly reverting to features of spoken language closer to the island's traditional dialect. These included features of accent as well as grammar and vocabulary.

This was all happening at a time when Martha's Vineyard was beginning to become a desirable holiday getaway. Mainlanders were increasingly buying holiday homes on the island which were being occupied just for part of the year. Labov observed that salient features of speech that signalled the island's traditional accent were becoming more exaggerated. And this seemed to be an 'in-group' response to the influx of outsiders now inhabiting the island for just some of the year. Interestingly, many younger islanders, especially those who aspired to leave the island for the mainland, resisted this change, and continued to speak much more like the mainlanders.

Issues pertaining to social identity provide a powerful motivation for altered replication. After all, the way we speak is, in essence, an act of identity.[39] One function of the language we use is to identify ourselves with a particular social group. This means that, sometimes, salient features of speech, such as the pronunciation of a particular sound, or a particular word, are selected, diverging from a particular norm. And this can be the result of the desire to identify with others, whose language use is at odds with the norm.

While social dynamics can lead to speakers consciously altering the way they speak, another way in which linguemes can come to be altered is this: there is a general tendency amongst speakers to conserve effort, especially when using well-known words and expressions. William Croft provides an example from the community of Californian wine connoisseurs. While in the general English-speaking community, wine varieties are known by terms like *Cabernet Sauvignon, Zinfandel* and *Chardonnay*, in this speech community, where wine is a frequent topic of conversation, these terms have been shortened to *Cab, Zin* and *Chard*. As Croft observes: "The energy expended in an utterance becomes superfluous, the more frequently it is used, hence the shorter the expression for it is likely to be(come)."[40]

So far, I have been focusing on language change due to deliberate attempts by speakers to change their language. But language change can also be unintentional, due to pressures from within the language system itself. These processes are nevertheless grounded in language use. Take, for instance, the sound system in a given spoken language. Because human speech relies on a highly complex motor system in producing sounds, altered replication can occur through 'errors' in articulation. The articulatory system can overshoot or undershoot the sound it's attempting to produce, giving rise to a near (slightly altered) replication. Surprising as it may seem, speech errors can, and indeed do, give rise to a change that then spreads throughout an entire linguistic community.[41] In fact, once a particular 'error' has taken hold, this can even lead to a re-calibration of the sound system of a language: the new sound may occupy the same phonological space as an existing sound. And this can give rise to what linguists call sound chain shifts: resulting in wholesale changes to the accent of a language over time.

A chain shift involves a series of related sound changes. This often starts with a shift of one sound, giving rise to an elaborate chain reaction of changes. I like to think of chain shifts in terms of a game of musical chairs; when one sound moves to occupy the place of an adjacent sound, then the original sound has to move to occupy the place of the sound next to it. And the newly displaced sound has to move, and so on. The net effect is that a series of sounds move, forming a chain of shifts, and affecting many of the words in a language. But in sound shifts, it's not that sounds are in fact 'moving'. They are being produced in the same place in the mouth as they always were. It's actually that the sounds in words are moving.

A celebrated example is the Great Vowel Shift – first studied by Jens Otto Jespersen (1860–1943), a Danish linguist who coined the term.[42] This took effect in the early decades of the fifteenth century and, by the time of Shakespeare (1564–1616), had transformed the sound pattern of English. The Great Vowel Shift affected the seven long vowels of Middle English: the English spoken from roughly the time of the Norman conquest of England (1066) until about half a century after the death of Geoffrey Chaucer (around 1400). Words containing the seven 'long' vowels of English began to be produced with the tongue slightly higher in the mouth.[43] To give you a sense of the impact on the language, here are some examples. Before the vowel shift, the vowel in the word *date* was pronounced like 'dart', *feet* was pronounced like 'fate', *wipe* was pronounced akin to 'weep', *boot* was pronounced like 'boat', and the vowel in *house* was pronounced like 'whose'.

My point, in discussing chain shifts, is that these phenomena appear to be unintentional. Speakers may not always be deliberately altering the way they speak. The tendency in chain shifts, for long vowels in words to come to be produced with the tongue higher in the mouth, might be due to articulatory pressure for maintaining length. And conversely, a similar change applies to short vowels, but in the opposite direction: there is a tendency for the tongue to become lowered. But these changes, or at least their causes, are non-intentional. They don't arise due to speaker goals, but from purely mechanical system-internal factors. That said, the way this change – the altered replication – spreads *is* due to socio-cultural factors. After all, altered replications can only take hold if they are selected for during normal language use, and propagated through a linguistic community.

Altered replication is not restricted to sound change, but can also affect the form–meaning units of language. Recall, from Chapter 1, that form–function units are the stuff of language: they consist of anything bigger than individual sounds. These include affixes like the *-er* agentive marker, as in *teacher*; words like *red*, and *devil*; as well as larger units of grammar – our grammatical constructions, such as the passive voice construction. Altered replication of this kind involves a change in the relationship between form and meaning. For instance, the sentence *I'm going to the library* exemplifies the so-called 'be going to' construction. But in this sentence, what is being described is a physical path of motion. However, in a sentence such as the following, *I'm going to be an astronaut (when I grow up)*, *be going to* relates to future time, not motion on a path. How, then, has the *be going to* construction developed this more abstract future time meaning? And, in posing this question, I hasten to add that the future meaning has indeed evolved from the motion meaning, rather than vice versa.

An obvious implication of going somewhere is that the destination is located in the future. This means that an expression such as *be going to* has an implied future meaning. And this implied meaning crops up again, and again, during language use. It turns out that language users are exceptionally good at abstracting implied meanings from the contexts in which they hear linguistic expressions. Moreover, these implied meanings come to be reanalysed, in the minds of language users, as independent semantic units, detached from the contexts of use in which they were only implied. Over time, this process, of detaching the implied meaning from the original context, allows us to begin to apply what was once only an implied meaning to new contexts. And in these new contexts, it is only the implied meaning that is relevant. But the process is gradual.

For instance, in the early stages of change, *be going to* was applied to contexts which, strictly speaking, didn't involve motion, but were motion-like. For instance, the sentence *I'm going to eat* is future-like; it describes something set in the future. However, it also involves motion; to eat, one must first go to a venue where food can be purchased, found or prepared. Later on in the process of reanalysis, *be going to* develops meanings which are purely future in nature, demonstrating that *be going to* has shaken off the shackles of the usage context from which it first emerged. The result is a purely future meaning, which co-exists with the original spatial sense.[44]

This process of form–meaning reanalysis is not an intentional process. Rather, the reanalysis is non-intentional – speakers are not somehow attempting to signal identity by abstracting, over time, a future meaning from an original spatial meaning. Nevertheless, the way in which form–function reanalysis occurs involves usage pressures within the linguistic system; these pressures arise naturally, a consequence of the way language is used in real situations and contexts, and the ability of the human mind to draw inferences from patterns of use.

In the final analysis, language change results from breaking with convention, and selecting some of the new variants created as a result of this departure. The propagation of new forms is often due to intentional mechanisms relating to the expressive functions associated with language, driven by sociolinguistic processes such as accommodation, identity and prestige. But the cause of altered replication is just as likely to involve non-intentional mechanisms – including articulatory pressures and form–function reanalysis – as it is intentional change.

The myth of Proto-world

In my discussion of the usage-based factors that give rise to diversity, one evolutionary notion I have, thus far, neglected is that of lineage. In evolutionary terms, a lineage is a species. In linguistic terms, one type of lineage is an etymology: the history of a word, and its emergence and evolution over time. Another type is the relationship between languages: as older languages evolve, and fall by the wayside, mother tongues gradually morph into daughter languages.

The branch of linguistics devoted to studying lineages is historical linguistics. One issue that has exercised historical linguists is the challenge of identifying relationships between languages, and specifically the task of grouping languages into language families. The underlying assumption of such work is that all languages, ultimately, must be derived from a single language: what has, perhaps facetiously, been nick-named 'Proto-world'. After all, it is reasonable to assume that anatomically modern humans must have been capable of spoken language for all of their existence. And on this basis, it is often assumed that Proto-world came with *Homo sapiens* in the first dispersal out of Africa, some 100,000 or so years ago.

From the perspective of historical linguistics, a language family is a group of languages related through descent from a common ancestor.[45] The common ancestor is termed a proto-language. Linguists think there are around 350 language families, comprising all of the world's living languages.[46] Languages are considered to be related based on the degree to which they share linguistic features such as sounds, vocabulary and aspects of grammar. For instance, English is a Germanic language, closely related to modern German, Swedish, Dutch, Danish, Norwegian and Icelandic. The Germanic languages form a branch of the Indo-European language family.

The Indo-European languages are a family of several hundred related languages including most of the languages of Europe, the Iranian plateau, and South Asia. Indo-European languages are spoken by close to 3 billion people, representing almost half of the world's population. Indo-European itself has about 150 languages including Hindi and Urdu (400 million speakers), Bengali (200 million), Spanish (300 million), Portuguese (200 million), French (100 million), German (100 million), Russian (300 million), and English (400 million), in Europe and the Americas. With English, one can reach approximately 1 billion people in the world – if we include second-language users.

One theory suggests that the Indo-European family originated in the Steppes of south-east Russia, north of the Caspian Sea, around 5-7,000 years ago. These early Indo-Europeans, so the conventional story goes, then slowly dispersed, spreading west to Europe, south to the Mediterranean, north to Scandinavia, and east to India. While there is no direct evidence for the Indo-Europeans, the consensus amongst linguists – given what is known about rates of language change – is that Indo-European could not have existed prior to around 7,000 years ago at the earliest.[47]

In contrast, the celebrated archaeologist Professor Colin Renfrew has suggested, based on climatic and technological developments, that Indo-European might have existed before then, perhaps as early as 9,000 years ago, and may have originated not in the Russian steppes, but in Anatolia, which is today that part of Turkey located in Asia.[48] And recent evidence seems to favour Professor Renfrew's take on things.[49]

One logical consequence of the view that, ultimately, all languages are related is the thesis that all the languages that have ever existed are descended from a single ancestor: Proto-world. This is the thesis of monogenesis. And this thesis bears a chilling resemblance to the claims made by the language-as-instinct thesis. If all languages, and all language families, including Indo-European, are descended from a single mother tongue, then this potentially gives credence to the view that language emerged all at once, a genetic mutation (according to Chomsky), which bestowed, upon one lucky individual, the gift of language.

But Proto-world, like Universal Grammar, is a myth. For instance, historical linguistics has long recognised languages that can't be classified as belonging to any of the known language families. Such languages are known as isolates: they bear no correspondence to any of the languages around them. In effect, an isolate is a language family consisting of one member. Such an example is Basque, spoken in the so-called 'Basque country', a region that borders France and Spain, with around 665,000 native speakers. Little is known of its origins; but it is likely that an early form of the Basque language was present in Western Europe before the arrival of the Indo-European languages in the area. And while some language isolates have become so by virtue of the extinction of other languages, Basque has been an isolate for all of its documented existence. Of the 350 or so language families in the world, remarkably, 129 of these are isolates. In other words, isolates – for which it is not possible to establish a genetic relationship with any other language family – make up 37 per cent of all language families. As the historical linguist Lyle Campbell observes, "Seen from this perspective, isolates are not at all weird; they have as their 'cohorts' over one-third of the 'language families' of the world."[50]

But wait. An objection to my argument might be this: "Isolates don't undermine monogenesis. They just show that language changes fast. And over time, as related languages go extinct, remaining languages, vestiges of change, remain." But here it is: languages *do* emerge out of the blue, *and* without a lineage. Sign languages are a case in point. As congenitally deaf people have never experienced spoken language, self-evidently, sign languages cannot, then, be modifications of spoken languages to which they are 'genetically' related. In point of fact, sign languages have very little in common with spoken languages at all.

The use of signing is relatively slow compared to the speed of spoken words. Spoken words can be spoken at roughly double the rate at which signs can be produced. Yet the messages conveyed by sign languages are produced in roughly the same amount of time as those produced via spoken language, as attested by simultaneous translation of spoken and signed language. This is made possible as sign languages require fewer signs, compared to the numbers of spoken words required to convey a similar message. Things can happen simultaneously in the visual medium; relevant information can be compressed economically into signs. This allows the message to be transmittable, via signed communication, at a rate commensurable with that of spoken language. Consider the following illustration from a popular handbook of BSL signs:

Consider an instruction in spoken English such as 'turn right at the traffic lights'. In BSL, traffic lights (one sign) would be signed first, followed by turn right sign (one sign). This not only reflects the real order of events, a crucial and distinguishing feature of visual language, but uses classifying handshapes to indicate lights and vehicle, which are located in space with appropriate directional movement to suit the context. In this way, information is condensed into just two signs, enabling the expression of an instruction that would require six spoken words.[51]

Sign languages emerge wherever there are communities of deaf individuals. Over time, these stabilise into rich communicative systems. Moreover, sign languages emerge in markedly different contexts and ways.[52] For instance, sign languages have emerged in a home-setting, where signers developed their own sign language within a single family in Nicaragua.[53] In another case, the emergence of a sign language was found in a Bedouin group of deaf individuals living in Israel, as discussed in the previous chapter.[54] In another study, a sign language was found to emerge amongst a group of deaf and hearing individuals in Bali, all of whom signed.[55] In each case, there was no precursor for the language. The sign language gradually emerged, driven by the sorts of usage-based mechanisms I described earlier. The point, then, is this: an explanation for language change and diversity cannot rest on a lineage, traced back to some original mother of all languages, spoken by some outrageously lucky individual – Prometheus – who happened to inherit, in one fell swoop, a language gene. Languages emerge and develop wherever and whenever humans come together, but they take time to develop into fully fledged communicative systems – in Chapter 8, I will consider what it is about our species that makes language possible.

But there's one final objection the language-as-instinct crowd might make: "Universal Grammar doesn't mean all languages have to be descended from the mother of all languages, the language spoken by Prometheus. As we have an instinct for language – Universal Grammar – language can emerge all at once, in any human, and in any human community, home-sign languages being a case in point."

But, again, a number of studies have invalidated this sort of objection. For a fully fledged language to develop takes about three generations.[56] They never emerge fully formed from scratch. The best-documented example is the Al-Sayyid sign language: after seventy years, it is only amongst the younger members of the 150-or-so deaf members of the community that a fully fledged grammar is emerging.[57]

Adieu, Universal Grammar

Chomsky famously proposed a Universal Grammar, which he dubs "a general principle of linguistic structure on the basis of observation of a single language": English.[58] But if all languages are the same underneath, we would expect similar trajectories of change, even when languages differ. Take word order, for instance. I've shown that languages can differ widely. But if languages are guided by a Universal Grammar, we would expect to see commensurable patterns of change across language families.

Recent research by Michael Dunn and colleagues has investigated this: they examined the way in which word order patterns evolve over time. To do this, Dunn and his team used a specialised software system which looked at the development of different word order patterns across different language families – they examined changes, over time, within the Indo-European, Austronesian, Bantu and Uto-Aztecan family groups. These language families account, between them, for over a third of the world's languages. For instance, the Austronesian language family includes around 1,268 languages, with the oldest around 5,000 years old; Indo-European, including English, has about 449 languages, going back nearly 9,000 years on Renfrew's account; Bantu – an African language family – includes around 668 languages, with a lineage going back roughly 4,000 years; and Uto-Aztecan – from the Americas – has around 61 languages going back about 5,000 years. Dunn's finding was that word order develops in lineage-specific ways. In other words, and contrary to the language-as-instinct thesis, word order patterns follow the trajectory established within a particular language family, and continue to fan out beyond that; word order patterns are influenced by patterns established in the language family, and evolve in lineage-specific ways. Word order, as one aspect of grammatical structure, is not constrained by language universals, but is, apparently, likely to be a consequence of the evolutionary natural drift at play in the language lineage within which a given language participates. The startling conclusion is that languages appear to be drifting apart, diverging based on cultural and usage pressures, rather than being constrained by some over-arching universal principle or principles binding them together.[59]

In this chapter I have, I hope, convinced you that the notion of a Universal Grammar is at the very least on shaky ground. There are a great many languages that diverge, markedly, from English. In the face of such diversity, the claim for a Universal Grammar simply cannot be maintained. And so, we bid adieu to the myth.

But Chomsky's claim is made on the assumption that there is a hard-wired language faculty; language is presumed to be innate. This is the issue to which I now turn.

4   Is language innate?

Myth: *Knowledge of language is present at birth. It is encoded in the microcircuitry of the human brain. This allows children to learn language without parents (or anybody else) trying to teach them, or correcting their mistakes (e.g.,* I sitted down, *versus* I sat down). *Language is therefore an instinct, emerging naturally, rather than being learned by imitation, for instance; a minimum of exposure to the sounds and words of a specific language is sufficient for a language to grow in a speaker's mind.*

Children come into the world biologically prepared for language – from speech-production apparatus, to information-processing capacity, human infants are neurobiologically equipped to acquire spoken language in a way no other species is. And, although there are precursors of language evident in the communication systems of other animals, human language is qualitatively different from other non-human systems of communication in a number of ways, as I pointed out in Chapter 2.

On the face of it, it is nevertheless baffling that children manage to learn language at all. Let's consider the problem, beginning with an adult. Imagine *you* are suddenly transported to a foreign land. All around you are people jabbering away in a tongue you don't understand. You try and make out the words – but spoken language is not like the written form. There are no commas and full stops, and no white spaces between words to guide you, as you try to figure out what the individual words are. All you hear is this endless stream of gobbledygook. Now, children are in an even *worse* situation than this. As one leading expert has observed: "Not only do they not know what adults are trying to say, they do not even know *that* adults are trying to say something."[1]

In the light of this, the language-as-instinct thesis says that language, or at least the Universal Grammar that underpins language, is not learned: the challenge is simply – and clearly – too great. After all, so the language-as-instinct crowd believe, "A normal child acquires this knowledge on relatively slight exposure and without specific training."[2] Thus, grammatical knowledge of some kind *must* be present at birth. Consequently, linguistic knowledge *is* hard-wired into the microcircuitry of the human brain. Accordingly, the issue I address in this chapter is: are we born with knowledge of grammar, so that, in a profound sense, we don't in fact need to learn it?

The view that our mental grammar is innate, in a number of respects, is highly attractive – in fact it's brilliant: at a stroke it solves the problem of trying to account for how children learn language without being corrected by their parents and caregivers – scientists have established, following careful observations, that, for the most part, parents and caregivers don't systematically correct errors children make; rather they encourage the child in his/her communicative efforts by engaging with the message, rather than worrying about the form (for a long time my daughter said "I goed" versus "I went"; and my son repeatedly said "I doned a pooh" versus "I did a pooh"; and I was fascinated to see that their mother never once corrected either one, but simply laughed at how cute the things they said were – probably the typical parents' response).[3]

And even when parents do helpfully attempt to correct their off-spring, things typically back-fire. In the following real-life excerpt, recorded by psychologist David McNeill, one imagines the long-suffering mother pulling her hair out by the end:

> Child: Nobody don't like me.
> Mother: No, say "nobody likes me".
> Child: Nobody don't like me.
> (Eight repetitions of this exchange)
> Mother: No, now listen carefully; say "NOBODY LIKES ME".
> Child: Oh! Nobody don't likes me.[4]

Not only do children take their own sweet time to master grammar, their mastery of how to use language appropriately takes even longer. The following anecdote makes this point crystal clear: one morning when a mother was about to take a shower, she asked her son, then aged three, to be mindful of his sleeping baby sister, who was just then aged one. He replied: "Ok mum! So I must not shout at her, and I must not kill her with my sword!" At which point, the by-now nervous mother decided not to take that shower – I wonder why. Moreover, children have learned spoken language before they begin formal schooling. Children are not *taught* language, they just acquire it, seemingly automatically.

Chomsky's approach represented a type of speculative, or 'arm-chair', linguistics. His argument for innateness was purely logical, based on several assumptions about the nature of language, and the mind. Research that has investigated how children *actually* learn language, research not available to Chomsky in the 1950s and 1960s, makes the proposition of innateness in the Chomskyan sense highly unlikely. Indeed, the field of developmental psycholinguistics which studies how children acquire language was not yet established when Chomsky was formulating his ideas. And yet Chomsky has steadfastly continued to insist that language is innate. Writing in 2002, Chomsky says:

> It is hard to avoid the conclusion that a part of the human biological endowment is a specialized "language organ," the faculty of language (FL). Its initial state is an expression of the genes, comparable to the initial state of the visual system, and it appears to be a common human possession ... Accordingly, a typical child will acquire any language under appropriate conditions ... we can think of the initial state of FL as a device that maps experience into state L attained: a "language acquisition device" (LAD).[5]

What Chomsky is claiming is that language really *is* an "organ": it grows in the same way that a kidney or heart does. And there is a mechanism – a language acquisition device – that provides the blueprint for the grammar of any language: the so-called 'Universal Grammar' I discussed in the previous chapter. This language acquisition device, so the claim goes, allows us to make sense of the language we hear spoken around us: children come pre-equipped with knowledge that allows them to make sense of the apparent gobbledygook spoken by their parents and carers. They are born with a Universal Grammar that provides the genetically programmed scaffolding that allows language to grow in the child's mind, automatically and relatively effortlessly. Children pick up their mother tongue because language is an instinct: once exposed to it, the child fills in the superficial, surface properties – words, sounds and the grammatical idiosyncracies – of the local variety: English, Swahili, or whatever, all underwritten by the genetically determined Universal Grammar.

Nevertheless, despite its convenience, this sub-thesis of the language-as-instinct thesis – that grammatical knowledge is innate – is not tenable, in the light of recent, quite overwhelming, evidence from language learning, and recent findings from neurobiology.

An instinct for language?

In the previous chapter, I addressed, and rejected as a myth, one aspect of the language-as-instinct thesis: the argument for Universal Grammar. But the claim that knowledge of grammar is innate – the subject of this chapter – is not the same, quite, as the proposal that grammatical knowledge is universal. After all, grammar could, in principle, be universal in the sense conceived by Chomsky and Pinker, but not innate; for instance, all languages could develop along the same lines, giving rise to absolute universals of the Chomskyan type. And while such universals need not be present at birth, they could, at least in principle, emerge through natural cognitive development, perhaps due to a broadly similar trajectory of neurological development in all human brains during infancy and beyond. Alternatively, such universals could develop due to broadly common aspects of our physical environment.

However, the further claim made by the language-as-instinct thesis is that language – which is to say, Universal Grammar – is an instinct: it *is* something we are born with. For Chomsky, we should conceive of "the growth of language as analogous to the development of a bodily organ."[6] Chomsky has received staunch support from the psychologist Randy Gallistel. Gallistel claims that the language organ is an example of a wider class of "learning organs" that are in a very real sense part of the biology of a large number of species.[7] But conceiving of language as a "learning organ" paradoxically leaves relatively little room for the role of learning in shaping a language. The biological learning devices of Gallistel, of which the proposed "language organ" is a paradigm example, don't really allow for *learning* – at least, not in the ordinary sense of the term. Instead, they specify hard-wired knowledge that allows information to be interpreted, ironically, in the absence of learning. Chomsky himself is rather sceptical about the role of actual learning in the design structure of language. He suggests that: "a general learning theory ... seems to be dubious, unargued and without any empirical support".[8] In short, language is just too complex to be learned. And we appear to pick it up effortlessly at our mother's breast. Therefore, it must be innate.

Steven Pinker has eloquently articulated the claim that language is an instinct:

> Language is a complex, specialized skill, which develops in the
> child spontaneously, without conscious effort or formal
> instruction, is deployed without awareness of its underlying logic,
> is qualitatively the same in every individual, and is distinct from
> more general abilities to process information or behave
> intelligently. For these reasons some cognitive scientists have
> described language as a psychological faculty, a mental organ, a
> neural system, and a computational module. But I prefer the
> admittedly quaint term "instinct." It conveys the idea that people
> know how to talk in more or less the sense that spiders know how
> to spin webs. Web-spinning was not invented by some unsung
> spider genius and does not depend on having had the right
> education or on having an aptitude for architecture or the
> construction trades. Rather, spiders spin spider webs because they
> have spider brains, which give them the urge to spin and the
> competence to succeed.[9]

But the problem with comparing language with spider web-spinning is that language just isn't an instinct: not in the sense of the term as used by the layperson, nor as used by the scientist. Spider web-spinning, like other instinctive behaviours, emerges developmentally, without instruction, input or interference from any other member of a given species. Spiders spin webs whether they are exposed to artisan spiders performing web-spinning or not. Human language just doesn't emerge in this way. Exposure to language is required. And not any old input will do: there has to be lots of it, over several years, for language to develop. Moreover, language exposure must take place in a normal human socio-cultural context, resulting in distinct varieties; children grow up speaking the language of their mothers, carers and the community in which they live: a child exposed to the West African language Wolof will grow up speaking Wolof, whilst a child living in Lombardy, in Northern Italy, will grow up speaking Lombard.

Evidence of the critical importance of both human contact and language input comes from the heart-wrenchingly sad cases of feral children; whether by accident, by misfortune, or in some cases deliberately, such infants are isolated from normal human interaction. And these cases vividly demonstrate that, without exposure, language simply doesn't emerge.

A second way in which language isn't an instinct is that instinctive behaviour, such as web-spinning, is a stereotyped activity: it conforms to a relatively invariant routine and practice. Language is self-evidently not stereotyped in this sense. The world's languages differ in the most startling ways, a flavour of which I provided in the previous chapter. Languages can deploy sound systems; some, like sign languages do not. Of spoken languages, there is enormous divergence in the range and types of sounds deployed; vocabularies vary markedly, as do grammatical systems. French is incomprehensible to a monolingual speaker of English, while Mandarin is different again. In contrast, spiders' webs are broadly similar across all spiders of the same species: there aren't different 'dialects' or 'varieties' of spider webs. However you cut it, language is quite clearly not an instinct in the way that spider web-spinning most definitely is.

Arguments for the language instinct

There are two main arguments for language being innate, in the sense proposed by the language-as-instinct thesis. The first relates to the fact that children don't receive overt correction from their caregivers when they get things wrong. Chomsky wondered how it is that children acquire the grammatically well-formed sentences of their mother tongue, and just those sentences, rather than a larger set. For example, children of English-speakers acquire a Subject Verb Object (SVO) word order pattern, such as: *The supermodel kissed the window cleaner*. But logically they could produce sentence patterns that don't accord with English. A much smaller, but nevertheless significant subset of languages, uses a VSO word order, e.g.: *Kissed the supermodel the window cleaner*. Finally, there is the OSV pattern: *The window cleaner the supermodel kissed*. (See the table on page 75 in the previous chapter.) While this is in fact a vanishingly rare pattern in the world's languages, English-speaking infants don't appear mistakenly to produce grammatical patterns of this kind. The question is: why?

Chomsky argues that we should in fact expect errors of this sort – there is nothing in the language children hear around them that prohibits this rare grammatical pattern: for one thing, children don't get much language exposure; for another, children are not usually corrected by their carers even when they *do* make errors. This amounts to Chomsky's famous argument which he refers to as the poverty of the stimulus. The input children receive is impoverished, in the sense that the language exposure is partial, to say the least; and there is no negative evidence to warn them off incorrect grammatical patterns.

On first blush, this might seem like a somewhat counter-intuitive argument. After all, why would children start using a grammatical pattern – in fact a vanishingly rare pattern – that doesn't show up in the everyday language they are exposed to? To appreciate fully the poverty of the stimulus argument it is necessary to understand Chomsky's second argument. Chomsky was developing his language-as-instinct thesis in the 1950s and 1960s, at a time when it was not well understood what children in fact bring with them to the learning process. It was assumed that children had little to guide them in the learning process: children's minds, Chomsky thought, placed only very limited constraints on the hypotheses about what the grammar being acquired should look like – in other words, with limited learning capabilities, almost anything goes.

So, if children don't have much in the way of a robust set of learning principles to guide them, and coupled with the observation that their language input is impoverished, and, moreover, carers aren't very helpful when children do get it wrong, we should expect lots and lots of errors; the input (a.k.a. the stimulus) is pretty impoverished. In short, children acquiring English should be just as likely to produce sentences with an OSV pattern – *The supermodel the window cleaner ogled* – as the correct SVO pattern: *The window cleaner ogled the supermodel.* Yet children don't make these sorts of logical errors.

Chomsky's conclusion was that a blueprint for grammar must be innate. Our Universal Grammar provides human children with a language acquisition device: it allows children to pick language up without needing to *learn* it. Children come to the task with an inbuilt understanding of the various constraints that guide the nature of language, without going down blind alleys – producing nigh-on-impossible grammatical patterns in the language they are acquiring.[10]

Some studies have, somewhat triumphantly, claimed to have empirically 'confirmed' Chomsky's arguments for language innateness. In one study, this was investigated by examining the way children form questions in English. In English, a question is often made by 'moving' the verb to the front. In a sentence such as: *The window cleaner is bald*, the verb *is* is moved to the front:

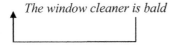

This yields the question: *Is the window cleaner bald?*

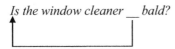

But if children merely have the sort of simple inductive learning capabilities assumed by Chomsky, they should reason that moving the verb to the front of the sentence is *always* the way in which questions are formed in English. For instance, in a sentence such as: *The man who is cleaning is bald*, the derived question could be: *Is the man who cleaning is bald?*

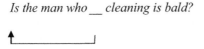

Not only is such a question ungrammatical, it has been duly 'confirmed' that children acquiring English do not make logical errors of this sort.[11] Hence, this finding was deemed to support Chomsky's argument: children don't make logical errors which we might otherwise expect. And as they don't have much in the way of learning principles to help them – children aren't that smart – and they receive little overt correction, they must have an innate language acquisition device helping them.

But here's the rub. This is not a finding about innateness, nor indeed about anything else. Just because children don't produce outlandish grammatical constructions when learning to form questions, this doesn't mean that Chomsky is right: that there is a Universal Grammar guiding them on the path to perfection in forming interrogatives. All this shows is that children don't produce the interrogatives that don't exist in their language!

Before moving on, let's clarify one aspect of the language-as-instinct thesis. As children learn language, they do produce lots and lots of errors; for instance, children say things like: *Look at those sheeps Daddy*; *Don't giggle me*; *I founded it out*; *Mummy crossed me* (= 'Mummy was cross with me / told me off'), and so on. But these are not the sorts of 'logical' errors Chomsky had in mind. Errors such as adding the plural marker *-s* to *sheep* is a consequence of the child having learned that the plural in English is formed by adding an *-s* marker. But this rule is then overgeneralised to *sheep*, which is an irregular plural. The 'logical' errors relate not to perfectly normal overgeneralisations such as these. Instead, they concern grammatical patterns alien to the language being learned.

From one perspective, Chomsky's argument is brilliant: children avoid making mistakes they might otherwise be expected to make because they come with a handy on-board computer, in the shape of a Universal Grammar. And this serves as a learning guide which takes the pain out of learning: children 'learn' without actually having to *learn*. Children pick up language because they already know what to look out for: the blueprint of language is written into their DNA.

From another perspective, the language-as-instinct thesis is utterly absurd. Why assume that children would ever produce, at least in principle, sentence patterns that they've never heard? After all, it could be that the absence of particular types of grammatical constructions in what a child hears, such as the non-existent OSV word order pattern in English, provides a line of evidence that guides the child to avoid precisely those sorts of grammatical patterns that no English speaker uses.

In fact, the philosopher of cognitive science Jesse Prinz makes exactly this point. He suggests that children "make predictions about what sentences or words they will hear while listening to adults. A failed prediction could be used as evidence that the rule underlying the prediction was wrong."[12] The consequence is that infants could actually have a rich source of negative evidence – learning what not to say from what they don't hear – without ever being corrected by their parents and carers. Just because children don't receive overt correction from carers does not mean they lack evidence as to what the grammar of their native language looks like. And so, it is plausible that children don't produce grammatical oddities that fly in the face of the native tongue they are learning, precisely because they have never heard such constructions.

While Chomsky assumes that absence of evidence provides no evidence, it may in fact be the case that children take absence of evidence for evidence of absence: children learn what not to say (and consequently what they should say), from what they don't hear. And as we shall see later in the chapter, researchers have now established that children do exactly this: they pre-emptively avoid particular grammatical constructions when they have heard other constructions used in similar contexts of use.[13] The poverty of the stimulus argument falls because a lack of overt correction does not mean children have no guidance as to what their grammar should look like.

A second problem for the language-as-instinct thesis is this. We now know that children bring with them far more than the simple-minded learning strategies assumed by Chomsky to the process of language acquisition. In the 1960s a mathematical proof was developed; this provided a principled basis to support the theoretical claims made by Chomsky. This was known as Gold's Theorem, after its author.[14] What this proof demonstrated, incontrovertibly, is that a grammar cannot be learned without negative evidence – without overt correction. This leads to the conclusion that languages are, accordingly, unlearnable. And as such, language must be innate.

But contemporary researchers have pointed out that "Gold's Theorem only applies if we make assumptions about ... learning ... that are wildly unlike any known nervous system".[15] As we shall see below, human infants are far smarter than Chomsky thought: they come to the task of language learning

equipped with a broad and sophisticated range of skills and
learning abilities not foreseen by Chomsky. Equipped with these,
children are more than able to acquire the grammar of their
mother tongue, without anyone having to assume they have
innate knowledge stuffed into their DNA at birth. In short,
Gold's Theorem, and the language-as-instinct thesis, radically
underestimate exactly what children are capable of.[16]

Lessons from neurobiology

If the language-as-instinct thesis is right, then linguistic knowledge, our Universal Grammar, must be represented in the microcircuitry of the human brain. If general learning abilities are
inadequate to account for language development, and there is
insufficient help provided in the input by way of negative evidence, then knowledge of language must, of necessity, be available
as part of neural organisation. It is only this level which provides
the coding power that would underlie our inborn knowledge of
language. But more than two decades of research in the field of
neurobiology – the scientific study of the nervous system, which
includes the brain, the spinal cord and the peripheral ganglia –
now shows this to be an extremely unlikely prospect.

The building blocks of the nervous system are neurons.
Neurons are cells that process and transmit information. This is
achieved by both chemical and electrical signals. The signalling is
achieved via synapses, which are the specialised connections with
other neurons. The human brain contains somewhere in the
region of 80 to 120 billion neurons, depending on gender and
age.[17] The majority of these are located in the cerebral cortex, the
outer layer of the brain associated with self-control, planning,
reasoning and abstract thought. In addition, each neuron is linked
to others by up to a staggering 10,000 synaptic connections.
Hence, the adult human brain is estimated to contain around
100–500 trillion (10^{14}) synaptic connections.[18] Moreover, for
every cubic millimetre, the cerebral cortex has about a billion

synaptic connections.[19] Finally, each synaptic connection can take up to ten different values.[20] The net result is that the "synaptic coding power of the human brain contains more potential states of connectivity than there are particles in the Universe!"[21]

For grammar to be innate, neurons would have to be encoded by genes – our genetic endowment. A gene is a molecular unit, consisting of stretches of genetic materials – DNA and RNA – that are passed on via sexual (and asexual) reproduction. A gene contains the information necessary to build and maintain the cells of a given organism. To specify our Universal Grammar, there would need to be a detailed mapping of information from genes to the neurons of the human cortex, providing the innate information to be encoded in the language processing areas of the brain. However, while there are 10^{14} synaptic connections, there are far fewer genes, something in the order of 10^6. Moreover, up to 30 per cent of human genes are taken up with the construction of the nervous system.[22] This leaves around 70 per cent of the already far smaller number of genes to control a massive potential cortical state space. If genes worked like letters in the alphabet, for instance, yielding an infinite combination of 'words', this might be possible. But this is not how genes work:[23] they don't have anything like the necessary coding power to ensure that Universal Grammar is etched into the microcircuitry of the human brain.

The response from the language-as-instinct crowd might be: "Hey wait. This all depends on what you think is 'in' Universal Grammar. There might be a 'light touch' Universal Grammar that only includes specific operations key to grammar: let's name them as 'recursion', or 'merge', or whatever." Yet, despite around forty years of trying to figure out what Universal Grammar looks like, there are no two language-as-instinct researchers who agree on what might be in there. And that is telling.

Moreover, if Universal Grammar really did amount to nothing more than a single core operation, such as recursion, something that our genetic coding could actually deal with, this still wouldn't be very helpful. If all our genetic blueprint told us was that recursion happens, learning would have to play a much greater role than Chomsky and co. are willing to concede.

Another possibility might be that innate knowledge occupies just a fraction of the potential connectivity of the brain. A much smaller region of this potential state space might be within the controllable range of our genetic encoding. However, it turns out that genes do not determine the job that individual neurons become specialised for.[24] Rather, the information that neurons process arises from the sorts of stimuli they happen to be exposed to. In other words, neurons are extremely flexible in terms of the type of information they can process.

For example, neurons located in the auditory region of the brain can take on a vision function if visual signals are transferred to them.[25] In experiments, cortical 'plugs' – sections of brain tissue – transplanted from one area of the brain to another take on the function associated with the input – for instance, visual processing – found in the new region.[26] Moreover, human children who suffer damage to the language processing areas of the brain can develop linguistic abilities in other brain regions not normally associated with language: if linguistic input is diverted due to damage, other areas can develop the ability to deal with it. More generally, synaptic sprouting occurs across the lifespan in response to new tasks – our brain tissue really does grow as we learn, and as we experience.[27] Experience shapes the way in which neurons develop, and even whether they live or die. Neurons are produced in massive quantities early in life. But those that are not used die out.[28]

Perhaps most startling of all, clear evidence of the flexibility of neurons comes from their successful transplantation across species. Transplants of cortical plugs from fetal pigs have been found to grow successfully in the brain of the adult rat.[29] As the eminent neurobiologist Pasco Rakic has put it, "heredity provides the clay of life and experience does the sculpting."[30]

This does not mean, of course, that there is no innate pre-specification, in terms of brain design. On the contrary, there is. But genetic pre-specification works at the larger-scale architectural level, rather than at the level of cortical detail – at the level of individual neurons.[31] Genetic information gives rise to general biases in terms of our overall brain plan. For instance, language processing develops in the left hemisphere of the cerebral cortex for about 95 per cent of normally developing humans.

The left hemisphere would appear, initially at least, to be biased towards processing perceptual detail, language being a paradigm example of an information type rich in perceptual detail – think of the fine auditory discriminations that humans must make in perceiving spoken language, distinguishing between a [p] as in *pig*, from a [b] as in *big*.[32] But such general biases don't provide the requisite coding power to encode something like a Universal Grammar.

In terms of the brain's microcircuitry, this all demonstrates that the determining factor appears to be experience, rather than innately prescribed information. The weight of evidence from neurobiology appears to quash the possibility that genetic information can provide anything like the detail that amounts to grammatical knowledge.[33]

Lessons from language learning

From the perspective of language acquisition – the study of how children learn their mother tongue – the problem for the language-as-instinct thesis is this. It assumes that children pick up adult-like language on the basis of an unchanging, fully formed Universal Grammar that children are born with. But if language is based on an innate Universal Grammar, then it should emerge all at once, with a minimum of exposure. Yet children's early language is anything but fully formed.

So here's the problem: why do children take several years to begin producing complex utterances, and several further years to develop adult-like competence? Why is there such a discrepancy between child and adult-like speech?

The language-as-instinct camp argues that the discrepancy is accounted for by continuous development in the child's linguistic competence. There are, they say, regular stages in the acquisition of particular grammatical structures; when one structure emerges in development, then this will be applied productively across the board to all other relevant grammatical structures. For instance, once a child comprehends "an utterance such as 'close the door!' he will be able to infer from the fact that the verb 'close' in English precedes its complement 'the door' that all verbs in English precede their complements".[34] The idea is that exposure to evidence that English word order is verb before object, a VO pattern, is sufficient for the child to understand that *all* verbs *always* precede objects.

In the most recent version of Universal Grammar, Chomsky proposed that it is made up of what he refers to as principles and parameters.[35] A principle relates to a high-level organisational function – word order, for instance – while each principle has a finite series of parameters, which work kind of like switches in the mind – as briefly introduced in the previous chapter. Children are therefore expecting to find word order patterns in the language they are exposed to because they are born with the principle 'word order'; and this forewarns them to be on the lookout for it. Moreover, they have switches that would correspond to the possible word order patterns exhibited by the world's languages. Once a child in an English-speaking environment has sufficient evidence that the word order pattern is subject-verb-object (SVO), *(S) The window cleaner (V) ogled (O) the supermodel*, the SVO parameter gets switched on. And, thereafter, the child's mind is altered: all canonical English sentences will be interpreted as SVO. In this way, Universal Grammar is supposed to provide a means of allowing the child to acquire any language, by flicking one switch or another. But upon exposure, there is no going back: the switch is flicked, and, at a stroke, the child's understanding is changed for all similar instances.

The consequence of this proposal is that language should be learned in jumps: once the switch gets flicked, the child 'gets' the way word order patterns in their mother tongue. But it turns out that this proposal, that children acquire language in discontinuous jumps, is wrong. A battery of studies on the stages that children go through during acquisition demonstrates, on the contrary, that there is little evidence to support wholesale jumps in acquisition, which would correspond to mental switches being flicked. Children are not able to generalise from specific examples of word order, and apply them across the board. Children acquire language in a far more gradual and piecemeal way; it develops in fits and starts. Moreover, their patterns of acquisition are heavily dependent on the specific types of language they are exposed to. And language is, initially, exclusively reliant upon concrete linguistic material. Children only very gradually begin to generalise over the expressions they master. They do this slowly, unevenly, forming linguistic categories that, ultimately, will give rise to a fully fledged grammatical system.

For instance, whenever my daughter did something commendable, she often heard the expression *good girl!* She initially seemed to learn this expression as an unanalysed chunk. When her baby brother did something warranting praise, she would commend him by saying *good girl.* Only later, after repeatedly hearing the expression *good boy!* aimed at her brother, did she start differentiating the terms in a gender-appropriate way.

What this anecdote reveals, and the theme that I develop in the rest of the chapter, is that learning a language is a bottom-up process. Children don't begin with pre-given rules that they are born with: language learning is not guided, magically, top-down, by innate knowledge. Children actually have to do the hard graft of working things out slowly, from the bottom up. They learn expressions as single chunks, and slowly, over time, with exposure and practice, they slowly build generalisations that allow them to start to form the grammar of the language they are acquiring. So, let's review the evidence.

Language learning proceeds in a piecemeal way

My first exhibit is the trajectory of language acquisition: this demonstrates that until the age of around three, child grammar develops in a piecemeal way. Kids first begin to produce identifiable 'words' from around 12 months of age. These first utterances are not, strictly speaking, words, however. A child's first words, intriguingly, are equivalent to whole phrases and sentences of an adult's speech, in terms of communicative intention. Moreover, these holistic phrases can serve quite distinct, albeit related, communicative functions. In one study, an infant first used the phrase *phone* in response to hearing the telephone ring. For her second use, she used the phrase to describe the activity of 'talking' on the phone. On the third occasion of use, she used *phone* to name the phone. And on her fourth use, she used the phrase as a request to be picked up in order to talk on the phone. What this reveals is that a child's initial forays into linguistic communication centre around a single item, whose communicative function is rounded out and extended through successive trials.

Examples of first words and their communicative functions[36]

Phrase	Communicative function
Rockin	*First use*: while rocking in a rocking chair
	Second use: as a request to rock in a rocking chair
	Third use: to name the rocking chair
Phone	*First use*: in response to hearing the telephone ring
	Second use: to describe activity of 'talking' on the phone
	Third use: to name the phone
	Fourth use: as a request to be picked up in order to talk on the phone
Towel	*First use*: using a towel to clean a spill
	Second use: to name the towel
Make	*First use*: as a request that a structure be built when playing with blocks
Mess	*First use*: to describe the state resulting from knocking down the blocks
	Second use: to indicate the desire to knock down the blocks

From around 18 months, infants begin combining words to produce multiword expressions. Some are straightforward combinations of earlier single-word phrases, such as *ball table*, to indicate "there's a ball on the table".[37] However, the multiword expressions often appear to be built around a specific word: a constant element that determines the communicative function of the utterance. This constant provides a 'pivot' from which other words can be hung.[38] Sometimes this pivot is an event word, such as *more*, for instance, *more milk*, or *more grapes*. Sometimes it can be a pronoun, or a more general type of expression, *I* __, or *It's* __ or *Where's* __.

Examples of pivot schemas[39]

More car	No bed	Other bib	Boot off	See baby	All broke	All done
More cereal	No down	Other bread	Light off	See pretty	All buttoned	milk
More cookie	No fix	Other milk	Pants off		All clean	All done
More fish					All done	now

These multiword combinations, which provide the earliest stage of syntax, have been dubbed 'pivot schemas': a rudimentary unit of grammar. They provide a schematic template that allows other words to be attached in order to convey a particular communicative function. But, interestingly, pivot schemas don't exhibit conventionalised word order.[40] For instance, children produced expressions such as *juice gone* and *gone juice* with the same communicative intention. This reveals that children's early multiword expressions are not due to some rule that's guiding the way they are formed: the prediction of the language-as-instinct thesis. Rather, the pivots are acquired and develop in an 'item-based' way. Their development is specific to the pivot schema itself: at this stage, children don't extend their pivot schema to contexts of use in which they haven't heard the pivot word used by their carers, as we'll see in more detail in a bit. In short, there is no evidence of an underlying rule-based system guiding the process of language acquisition.

From about 24 months of age, children begin to go beyond pivot schemas. This occurs as children start to acquire more complex syntax. From around this age, children begin to become aware that word order conveys meaning – in languages which exhibit a dominant word order. In studies involving sentences like *Make the bunny push the horse*, children from around two understand the following. They know that they should try and make the bunny push the horse, rather than the horse pushing the bunny. They understand that the sequence of the entities in the sentence conveys a doer of the action – usually the first noun phrase in the sentence (i.e., *the bunny*) – and an undergoer of the action – usually the second noun phrase in the sentence. (i.e., *the horse*).[41]

Nevertheless, children at this age are still not able to generalise pivot words beyond the contexts in which they have heard them. In particular, we now know that while children are adept at a wide range of different types of syntactic configurations – as below for the verb *to draw* – they remain extremely conservative in the way that they use pivot words until around the age of three. So, now consider the verb pivot *to draw*. It might be deployed in the following ways:

Draw ___.	(e.g., *Draw a flower*)
Draw ___ on ___.	(e.g., Draw a flower on the paper)
Draw ___ for ___.	(e.g., *Draw a flower for mummy*)
___draw on ___.	(e.g., *Lila draw on the paper*)

However, not all verbs are used in such a full range of syntactic contexts. While a child may use *to draw* in the range of distinct contexts just described, another verb, such as *to cut*, might be used in a much more restricted range (e.g., *cut* ___). Up until around 3 years of age, verbs behave as pivot 'islands': children seem to use verbs as if they were individual, isolated units of knowledge, specific to the pivot schemas they've been learned in.[42] Rather than being able to generalise across distinct verbs, and recognise that syntactic contexts might apply across the board, the pivot schemas adopt syntax in an item-based way: each pivot verb is associated with a verb-specific range of syntactic contexts in which it can be used.

Compelling evidence for this phenomenon comes from an experiment in which two- to three-year-old children were exposed to a nonsense verb *tamming*. Children were taught, through actions and images, that the meaning of *tamming* is 'rolling or spinning'. This was done using sentences which lacked a direct object, such as: *The sock is tamming*.[43] Children were then prompted to use *tamming* in a syntactic context with an object.

For instance, a child was shown a picture in which a dog was causing an object to 'tam'. The child was then asked: *What is the doggie doing?* A question such as this invites a response such as: *He's tamming the car* (= "the dog is causing the car to roll"). This sentence features a direct object, *the car*. Surprisingly, the experimenters found that children were unable to respond using sentences with a direct object.

There are two conclusions that arise from this finding. First, infants up to the age of about three are poor at the creative use of novel verbs such as *tamming*; second, they appear unable to generalise from one type of syntactic context (a sentence without an object), to another (involving a direct object). While children do have both syntactic templates stored in memory, they appear only able to apply words to the sentence types in which they've heard the specific words used. In short, a child's grammar up to the age of around three is learned in fits and starts, centring around specific pivot 'islands', rather than taking place in discontinuous jumps – which would have been expected if the language-as-instinct thesis were correct.

My final example concerns the use of the definite and indefinite articles: *the* and *a*. English-speaking children begin to use these between the ages of two and three. However, children at this age use the articles with completely different sets of nouns: while they may have heard *the doggie*, and be able to use *the* with *doggie*, they may not use *a* with *doggie*, even though they might use *a* with other nouns. Only later, after the age of around three, do children appear to be able to form more abstract syntactic patterns that facilitate the use of either article with any noun.

My point, in this part of the discussion, has been to show that grammar just doesn't develop in discontinuous jumps. If the language-as-instinct thesis were correct, we would expect that once children have evidence for a particular usage – for example, an indefinite article with a noun – then, hey presto, they should start using the indefinite article with nouns across the board. But children just don't do this. They learn to use the indefinite and definite articles in a piecemeal way, one noun at a time. Only later, from the age of around three onwards, do they begin to form generalisations across words and expressions.

Language learning is dependent on what children hear

This leads to exhibit two: what children say is directly grounded in what they hear. As has been implicit in the evidence I've been reviewing so far, language learning emerges from language use. Language learning studies show that over 90 per cent of children's earliest multiword expressions derive from the specific patterns of language they are exposed to.[44]

In one study, researchers found that verbs used by carers and parents directly correlate with the order in which children acquire the verbs.[45] For instance, the order in which verbs like *go*, *run* and *sip* are acquired, by children, is determined by how often the children were exposed to these words in the speech of their carers. In fact, there are two types of frequency effects that contribute to how quickly children pick up particular words. One is, straightforwardly, how often the child hears the word. If a child hears *run* more frequently than *go*, then they will start to produce *run* before *go*.

But another frequency effect also turns out to be important. The number of syntactic contexts in which a child hears the word also contributes to how quickly it is learned. As illustrated with the verb *to draw* above, if a verb is heard in a wide range of different syntactic contexts, then it will be learned more quickly. A more recent study, which looked at the acquisition of English by nine children, confirmed the importance of frequency of exposure in determining how quickly words are acquired.[46] It was found that, of the two factors, it is straightforward frequency which is most important; the more often a child hears a word, the more quickly he or she will begin producing it. And finally, another study has confirmed the importance of frequency of exposure in learning more complex aspects of grammar. Researchers have discovered that children learn to use complex sentences – sentences with two or more clauses – more quickly the more they hear sentences of this sort in their mothers' own language use.[47]

But according to the language-as-instinct thesis, how often a child hears a particular grammatical configuration should make not one iota of difference, in terms of mastering the construction. After all, one instance of exposure – or at most a few – should be enough to allow the child to flick the relevant parameter one way or another, and so completely master that aspect of his/her grammar. But, on the contrary, more and more studies, studies that examine what children *actually* hear, and what they *actually* say, are demonstrating this: language is learned from what children hear.

While this probably shouldn't be news at all, it actually contradicts the language-as-instinct thesis. As infants, our grammar is built from the ground up. We construct our mental grammars in piecemeal fashion, from what we hear, rather than relying on switches in our brains that allow us to bypass the hard work of figuring it all out – if only! In short, "the linguistic environment provides the raw materials out of which young children construct their linguistic inventories".[48]

Children don't hear what we think they hear

My final exhibit concerns the nature of the language children are exposed to. The standard assumption made by language-as-instinct theorists is that, while the linguistic input is impoverished, children nevertheless get what they need to flick their mental switches one way or another. But this assumes that the language children hear actually provides clear evidence for what their target mental grammar should look like. It assumes that parents and carers are exemplary models of pristine, grammatical speech. But a brief tour of what children actually hear shatters any illusions.

One leading study revealed the following.[49] Children hear between 5,000 and 7,000 utterances each day. Of these, nearly a third are questions and nearly half of the utterances used by mothers begin with just seventeen words: *what, that, it, you, are/aren't, do/does/did/don't, I, is, shall, A, can/can't, where, there, who, come, look* and *let's*. In addition, fixed syntactic contexts of the following sort are very common: *Are you . . .?, I'll . . ., It's . . ., Can you . . .?, Here's . . ., Let's . . ., Look at . . ., What did . . .?*

Furthermore, more than a fifth constitute a fragment or phrase – rather than a well-formed grammatical sentence. Moreover, only about 15 per cent of the total utterances feature what is presumed to be the typical subject-verb-object (SVO) word order of English. And around 30 per cent of the everyday utterances children are exposed to have no grammatical subject!

In addition, about 15 per cent of child-directed utterances include subjects that are not in the first position in the sentence. For instance, in the example *There are your toys*, the subject (*your toys*) appears after the verb.

And finally, the overwhelming majority of subjects that children do hear are pronouns – e.g. *I*, *me*, *my* – which encode different cases: subject, object, possessive and so on. This further complicates the daunting task facing the child. For instance, my daughter said *My do it* for a long time, rather than *I do it*, illustrating the challenge in figuring out the correct case roles associated with pronouns.

In short, contrary to what is assumed by language-as-instinct researchers, child-directed speech by adults doesn't readily provide the unequivocal exposure that is required to allow parameters to be set. One lesson to draw from this is: what we assume children hear is not actually the case. Rather than consisting of well-formed sentences, the linguistic exposure children are faced with is very much a hotch-potch. And it is these very utterances that children begin to acquire and produce.

So how *do* children learn language?

Given the weight of evidence – early grammatical development is item- rather than rule-based – how, then, do children acquire a functional and sophisticated grammatical system by around their fourth birthday? If language is not innate, what can human infants do that other species can't? What do human infants bring to the table, so to speak?

It turns out that children bring two broad types of skills to the language learning process. And these allow them to acquire language without requiring an innate Universal Grammar.

The first of these is a pattern-finding ability. This is a general cognitive skill that enables human infants to recognise patterns, and perform 'statistical' analyses over sequences of sounds and words. Infants who haven't yet begun to produce language – children under a year old – appear to employ this ability to figure out how individual sounds pattern into units such as words, phrases and utterances.

In one experiment, 8-month-old infants were able to recognise patterns in sounds they were exposed to.[50] This experiment relied on a preferential looking technique. This procedure is based on the fact that infants prefer to look towards the direction of familiar sounds rather than unfamiliar ones. In the experiment, infants were presented with two minutes of synthesised speech consisting of the four nonsense words *bidaku*, *padoti*, *golabu* and *tupiro*, each consisting of three syllables. These nonsense words were sequenced in different ways so that infants would hear a stream of repeated 'words' such as: *bidakupadotigolabubidakutupiropadoti. . .*, and so on. The infants were then exposed to new streams of synthesised speech, presented at the same time. The competing speech streams were played from separate speakers – one located to the infants' left and one to the right. While one recording contained 'words' from the original, the second recording contained the same syllables, but in different orders, so that none of the 'words' *bidaku*, *padoti*, *golabu* or *tupiro* featured. The researchers found that the babies consistently preferred to look towards the sound stream that contained some of the same 'words' as the original. This vividly illustrates that even children who have not yet begun to produce language are nevertheless able to recognise patterns of syllables forming 'words' in an auditory stream; and this provides compelling evidence for the pattern-finding ability.

Other research demonstrates that child pattern-finding skills are not limited to language.[51] Psychologists have also discovered that infants demonstrate the same skills when the experiment is repeated with non-linguistic tone sequences, and with visual, as opposed to auditory sequences. While we use our pattern-finding ability to help identify linguistic units from the gobbledygook that we hear as infants, this appears to be a general-purpose cognitive ability that is not specific to language. Moreover, this pattern-finding ability isn't restricted to humans: it is also apparent in our primate cousins. For instance, Tamarin monkeys demonstrate the same pattern-recognition abilities when exposed to the same sorts of auditory and visual sequencing experiments as I described, above, for human tots.[52]

Summary of human pattern-finding abilities[53]

Human pattern-finding abilities
The ability to relate similar objects and events, resulting in the formation of perceptual and conceptual categories for objects and events. Category formation aids recognition of events and objects.
The ability to form sensorimotor schemas based on recurrent perception of action. This is associated with the acquisition of basic sensorimotor skills, and the recognition of actions or events, such as crawling, walking, picking up an object, and so on.
The ability to perform distributional analysis on perceptual and behavioural sequences. This allows infants to identify and recognise recurrent combinations of elements in a sequence and thus identify and recognise sequences.
The ability to create analogies (recognition of similarity) between two or more wholes (including utterances), based on the functional similarity of some of the elements in the wholes.

So, if humans share pattern-finding abilities with other primates, then this alone cannot be the means by which we learn language, given that other primates do not have anything that is qualitatively similar to human language. What then leads human infants to acquire language? According to the eminent developmental psycholinguist Michael Tomasello, the answer is human cultural intelligence.

As I shall argue in Chapter 8, cultural intelligence predisposes us to being pro-social, which facilitates cooperative behaviours, of which language is the paradigmatic example. Human infants are social creatures from an early stage in the lifespan, and certainly way before the emergence of language. Pre-linguistic infants rec-ognise, and, moreover, prefer to look at, schematic drawings of human faces rather than drawings of other types of patterns.[54] They recognise other humans as animate beings distinct from other entities and objects.[55] And babies, from an early age, engage in proto-conversations with caregivers and parents, seemingly responding to a parent's chatter using babble in place of spoken language.[56] Strikingly, babies seem aware of the turn-taking conventions that guide human interaction. They don't babble at the same time as an adult is speaking: they wait their 'turn'.

While the pattern-finding skills described above are necessary to enable human infants to learn language, they are not, on their own, sufficient. Human cultural intelligence provides, in addition, a set of intention-reading abilities. These emerge most clearly from between 9 and 12 months. And these abilities allow human infants to begin the painstaking task of working out what the linguistic units mean, once extracted from the gobbledygook they hear. Intention-reading, then, allows the infants to begin to connect specific patterns in the auditory stream with meanings. But to make this leap, infants must also begin to understand that other humans are intentional agents: the gobbledygook is not random chatter, but something intentional and therefore mean-ingful; other humans are attempting to do something special: they are using the gobbledygook in an attempt to signal meaning.

Intention-reading relies on three elements. First, there must be a common ground allowing the infant to understand the adult's communicative attention. For example, when an infant and an adult are both looking at and playing with a toy, it is this three-way relationship between child, adult and toy that is the joint focus of attention: the common ground. This is the case even though other elements of the scene are still perceived – such as the child's clothes, or other objects in the vicinity. The second element requires that the child recognise that the use of language repre-sents a special kind of intention on the part of another: the intention to communicate. For instance, when the adult says *teddy bear*, the adult is identifying the toy that is the joint focus of attention. And they are using the sequence of sounds that make up this phrase to express the intention that the child follow their attention towards the object. In the diagram below, of a joint attentional frame, I have drawn this, where the unbroken arrow represents the communicative intention expressed by the adult. The dotted arrows represent shared attention.

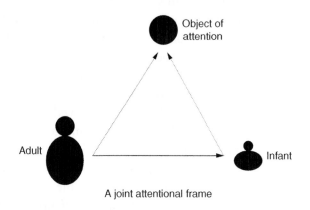

A joint attentional frame. Adapted from Tomasello (2003: 29).

Finally, language learning involves a special type of imitation: infants must not only be able to recognise an adult's intention to communicate; they must also be able to imitate this role in order to achieve a similar communicative attention. For example, the child must imitate the use of the linguistic expression *teddy bear* by an adult in directing attention to the object. And, crucially, the infant has acquired the expression only when he or she can use it in order to signal a communicative intention: that the adult recognise that the infant intends them to pay attention to the teddy bear.

There is very good evidence that children understand adult communicative intentions, and can learn such intentions, through imitation in this way. In one study, two groups of 18-month-old infants were shown two different actions.[57] In one, an adult successfully pulled the two pieces of an object apart. In a second, an adult tried but failed to pull the two pieces apart. However, both sets of infants, when invited to perform the action they had witnessed, successfully pulled the two pieces apart. This suggests that even the infants who had not witnessed pieces successfully pulled apart had understood the adult's intention.

In another experiment, 16-month-old infants were exposed to both intentional and 'accidental' actions.[58] The intentional action was marked vocally by the expression *there!* while the 'accidental' action was marked by *whoops!* The infants were then invited to perform the actions. Children who had witnessed the 'accidental' action were less likely to perform the action than those who had witnessed the intentional action. This reveals that children less than a year and a half old are able to distinguish intentional from non-intentional actions.

Summary of human intention-reading abilities

Human intention-reading abilities
The ability to co-ordinate or share attention, as when an infant and adult both attend to the same object.
The ability to follow attention and gesturing, as when an infant follows an adult's gesture or gaze in order to attend to an object.
The ability to actively direct attention of others, such as drawing attention to a particular object or event, for example by pointing.
The ability to engage in cultural (imitative) learning, such as imitating verbal cues in order to perform intentional actions.

Towards a theory of language learning

While language acquisition involves both a unique adaptation for things cultural and symbolic (intention reading), and a primate-wide set of skills for categorisation (pattern finding), this still doesn't explain, quite, how children construct a grammatical system.

The linguist Ronald Langacker, an influential proponent of the language-as-use thesis, has developed just such an account. Langacker proposes that the form–meaning units that make up an individual's mental grammar, such as words, idioms and other sorts of grammatical constructions, are derived from language use. These units are formed by the infant generalising across patterns of language use. For example, a speaker acquiring English will, as the result of frequent exposure, discover recurring words, phrases and sentences in the utterances he or she hears, together with the range of meanings associated with those units. With a lot of exposure, the child begins to abstract across different instances of use in order to draw out the common elements of the utterance. This involves setting aside points of difference.

By way of example, consider three sentences involving the preposition *in*. *The puppy is in the box*; *The flower is in the vase*; *There is a crack in the vase*. In each sentence the 'in' relationship is slightly different: while a puppy is fully enclosed by the box, the flower is only partially enclosed – in fact, only part of the flower's stem is in fact 'in' the vase. And in the last example, the crack is not 'in' the vase, but 'on' the exterior of the vase, although enclosed by the vase's exterior. These distinct meanings arise from context. Yet, common to each is the rather abstract notion of enclosure. Langacker proposes that what the child is doing is associating what she hears, the word form *in*, with an abstract mental schema, namely enclosure. Moreover, the schema for *in* specifies very little about the nature of the entity that is enclosed, nor much about the entity that does the enclosing. After all, in the examples we've just looked at, the details as to whether the entity is actually fully enclosed come from the linguistic context, rather than what is conveyed by *in* per se.

As we saw in Chapter 1, there are various kinds of linguistic units, and these, according to Langacker, make up our mental grammar. They can be words like 'cat', consisting of the three sound segments [k], [æ] and [t] that are represented as a unit [kæt]; idioms like [*He/she kick*-TENSE *the bucket*]; morphemes like the plural marker *-s* that are 'bound' to another word, or the agentive suffix *-er* in *teacher*; and larger, sentence-level constructions, such as the active voice construction (*The window cleaner ogled the supermodel*), and the passive voice construction (*The supermodel was ogled by the window cleaner*).

A consequence of Langacker's usage-based account is that the frequency with which a particular expression is heard has consequences for the resulting mental grammar that the child constructs. And this fits with the findings I've been reviewing in this chapter. How frequently a child hears a particular expression in fact determines how well established the expression comes to be in the child's developing mental grammar.

The linguist Joan Bybee[59] has conducted a significant amount of research on the nature of frequency and repetition in language use.[60] For instance, the semantically related nouns *falsehood* and *lie* crop up with different frequencies in the language we use on a daily basis. The noun *a lie*, as you might have guessed, is much more common than *a falsehood*. Bybee predicts that *lie* is therefore more firmly ingrained in our mental grammar than *falsehood*; after all, we saw earlier that greater frequency of an expression has been found to lead to earlier and more robust acquisition. I illustrate this distinction with the diagram below. In the diagram, the frequency of the two expressions results in *lie* being more ingrained in long-term memory, which I represent by bolding the box for the schema *lie*, but not *falsehood*.

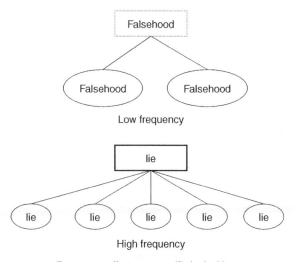

Frequency effects on specific lexical items

Frequency effects on specific lexical items.

I'll return to some of these issues when I describe the language-as-use view of our mental grammar in Chapter 8.

Learning what to say … from what isn't said

But the language-as-use account of how we learn language would not be complete without addressing how children learn what not to say, given that they receive no overt correction from caregivers. Recall that one of Chomsky's arguments for grammar being innate was exactly that: children do not make the sorts of logical errors they might otherwise make, and they receive little in the way of formal correction.

The linguist Adele Goldberg has recently provided evidence that children learn what to say – and what not to say – from what isn't said.[61] Despite Chomsky's claim that language exposure is insufficient for children to work out the rules of their language without an innate Universal Grammar, it turns out that children do in fact use lack of evidence of use as evidence for lack of use.

Consider the following two sentences:

> *The supermodel explained him the news.*
>
> *She saw the afraid window cleaner.*

These sentences will, most likely, feel a little weird; of course, they can be understood without too much trouble. But now compare them with the following sentences:

> *The supermodel gave him the news.*
>
> *She saw the scared window cleaner.*

I'm betting that the verb *gave*, and the adjective *scared* feel much more natural in these sentences. But why should the verb *explain* and adjective *afraid* be any less acceptable? There is no rule that prohibits them: after all, the sentences featuring *explain* and *afraid* are perfectly understandable, albeit somewhat weird-sounding.

Once researchers had examined large amounts of collected examples of people's spoken language – referred to as a corpus – it turns out that, in general terms, English speakers just don't use *explain* and *afraid* in sentences of this kind. So now consider the following usages of *explain* and *afraid*:

> *The supermodel explained the news to him.*
>
> *She saw the window cleaner who was afraid.*

Now, suddenly, *explain* and *afraid* seem perfectly fine: in these examples, they feel just right. But why, what's changed? In fact, little has changed. It turns out, when you examine lots and lots of sentences, drawn from what people actually say, English speakers appear nearly always to use *explain* immediately followed by the direct object *the news* – *explained the news* – rather than an indirect object *him*. And it also turns out that people appear not to use *afraid* before a noun; rather, they seem to use it as part of a relative clause, following *who* – for instance, *who was afraid*. There's no reason, on the face of it, why *afraid* couldn't be used before a noun – *the afraid window cleaner* – but English speakers *just don't* do this – it's a habit that has emerged over time, that's not visible until a linguist examines a corpus. As languages develop – any language, it doesn't have to be English – patterns of discourse develop. *Afraid* has developed slightly differently from *scared*, in the sense of what other bits of language it generally co-occurs with. And it turns out that humans are very sensitive to these usage-based patterns. Again, the patterns are not due to any specific rule of grammar: they are simply patterns of use.

And here's the really neat part: as children are learning language, they use these usage-based patterns to learn what *not* to say. For example, they learn that *scared* is used in contexts before the noun, as in *the scared window cleaner*. And they also learn that *scared* is semantically close to *afraid*. But they have a type of negative evidence – observed patterns of use – which demonstrates the different contexts in which *afraid* and *scared* normally occur. Children never, or almost never, hear *afraid* before the noun, as in *the afraid window cleaner*. In contrast, they frequently hear *scared* in just these sorts of contexts. And it turns out that children use this kind of negative evidence – evidence of not having heard a particular word or phrase in a specific context – to help them figure out how to use words and phrases. Part of what children do, when they learn their grammar, is to learn the usage patterns associated with words and other larger linguistic units.

And, in the final analysis, it turns out that children do indeed make use of usage patterns to infer how their grammar should look. They build their grammar from use, from what they actually hear, and, from what they don't hear.

But couldn't language emerge all at once?

While the evidence I've been reviewing suggests that language emerges gradually, in a piecemeal way, if language were an instinct, it should be able to emerge at once, quite abruptly. The linguist Derek Bickerton has claimed to have found such evidence in the guise of a creole. A creole is a language that emerges from a more rudimentary means of communication: a pidgin. Pidgins arise in situations where two or more people come together who don't share a common language. Such contact situations often arise along trade routes, and in more sinister scenarios such as the enforced slavery of peoples, as in enslavement of West Africans during the era of colonisation of the Americas by the great European powers. A pidgin provides a limited means of communication which takes bits of the languages from the native speakers involved, or alternatively from the linguistic context in which the individuals find themselves. But in cases where parents don't share a common language, and use a pidgin to communicate, their children learn the pidgin as their mother tongue. And in those cases, the children start to give the pidgin its own structure and organisation. This leads to the pidgin developing the same complexity and sophistication as any other natural language. Pidgins of this kind, full-blown languages, are known as creoles.

Bickerton claimed to have discovered that the Hawaiian Creole emerged all at once. His claim was based on documentary evidence of the spoken language. Using this evidence, Bickerton 'identified' features of the grammar which seemed to have emerged out of the blue. The children of pidgin-speaking parents appeared to have bestowed the pidgin with a grammatical system. But the children had no grammar to go on; after all, the pidgin didn't have one. The question that arises is this: how did the children turn the impoverished pidgin into a creole, and in so doing create a new language? This could only have happened, so Bickerton argued, if there were an innate pre-specification for language that allowed the children to furnish the lowly pidgin with a grammar, turning it into a language fit for purpose.[62]

However, Bickerton's claims are highly controversial. He based his argument for an innate linguistic architecture on documentary evidence from 70–100 years ago, rather than his own observations. Without actually knowing *exactly* what input the children were exposed to, we can't be sure that the children hadn't been exposed to languages other than the pidgin. And a number of commentators have made exactly this point: it is entirely possible that the children acquiring the creole may have been exposed to dominant languages in which the creole developed – some of the linguistic features that appear in the creole could only have come from these languages.[63] And, given that other 'new' languages, such as sign languages, take at least three generations to develop, as things stand, Bickerton's claims don't offer credible evidence for the view that language is innate.

Perhaps far better evidence, on the face of it, comes from findings reported by Susan Goldin-Meadow. Goldin-Meadow and her colleague Carolyn Mylander have studied the cases of congenitally deaf children, born to hearing parents. However, these children were not exposed to a sign language, because their parents either didn't know how to sign, or decided not to expose the children to sign language. Nevertheless, the children developed a communication system, referred to as 'home-sign'.[64]

Whenever we speak, we automatically use gestures that accompany our spoken language. Moreover, we cannot readily suppress these gestures: watch someone having a phone conversation. They will still be gesturing away even though the person on the other end of the line cannot see them. And even congenitally blind people still use gestures.[65] Research on the gestures people make demonstrates that they are minutely-co-timed to coincide, and in many cases precede, actual spoken language.[66] Look at someone talking and carefully watch their hands, and you'll see what I mean. And, as noted in Chapter 2, there are reasons to believe that gestures, a form of communication evident in our closest primate cousins, may have provided the basis for the development of spoken language over evolutionary time.[67] Moreover, we use gestures to help convey meaning: together, "speech and gesture form a composite communicative signal".[68]

The remarkable deaf children studied by Goldin-Meadow and Mylander used the normal gestures of their parents as their 'linguistic' input. And they developed a 'home-sign' language based on the gestures their mothers used – when speaking – in communicating with them. For instance, the children all produced pointing gestures that singled out and identified objects, people, places and so on. They used gestures to represent events or actions, such as two hands flapping to signal the action of a pet bird, or the pet bird itself. They combined these gestures into sequences, with a simple syntax, to convey meaning. They produced gestures that were used as modulators, such as headshakes to negate something. And they used hand shapes to provide the events or actions they were representing with a simple morphology – for instance, to show that the event was continuing, or had finished.

On the face of it, the discovery of a home-sign communication system suggests that language can indeed emerge all at once. And such a finding, if true, would be consistent with the language-as-instinct thesis. However, the home-sign system of Goldin-Meadow's children is very simple, compared to a fully fledged sign language such as ASL. Moreover, it is based on the gestures available in the input the children received. Indeed, the fact that home-sign systems emerge is in fact consistent with the language-as-use thesis. Children come pre-disposed to understand other humans as intentional agents who behave cooperatively: as I will propose in Chapter 8, children are born with a species-specific interactional intelligence. It is this that predisposes our species to develop communicative systems that are qualitatively different from those of other animals. Although speech is unavailable to those children developing home-sign, the language-as-use thesis predicts that children, very soon after entering the world, interpret the gestures that adults use as signalling communicative intentions. So, the existence of home-sign is not in itself evidence for language being innate.

It's all about language use!

The language-as-instinct thesis takes the view that a child is born with a pre-specified Universal Grammar. This provides the underlying rules that allow a language to emerge on the basis of minimal linguistic input. This view assumes that the rapid acquisition of an infinitely creative system of language can only be plausibly accounted for by a small and efficient set of innate principles and parameters.

But, on the contrary, language acquisition involves "a prodigious amount of actual learning".[69] Language emerges in an item-based way: individual expressions are learned from the input children are exposed to. And usage-based processes such as frequency and repetition allow children to learn language in chunks.[70] And, painstakingly, abstraction takes place allowing the child to begin to form schemas. At first the schemas themselves are restricted. And only later do they evolve into fully fledged generalisations across instances of language use. This is what the evidence shows us. A grammar emerges from use, rather than being innate. Indeed, language acquisition is all about language use. And, far from the child coming to the business of language-learning virtually empty-handed, there is a battery of general learning mechanisms that are deployed. The child is adept at pattern-finding, and comes equipped with a species-specific ability to recognise communicative intentions, and, moreover, a pro-social desire to communicate.

And finally, usage-based factors guide the construction of a grammar in the mind of the child. These include the ability to abstract across instances of use in order to construct schemas, and to be guided by frequency in entrenching these and associating the schemas – the 'meanings' – with units of linguistic form such as words. The view of mental organisation that emerges couldn't be further from the old view.[71]

In many ways, the new view, the language-as-use thesis, is liberating, removing the shackles of the past. The old Hegelian argument, that language is innate, a consequence of a language learning organ, explains away language acquisition using smoke and mirrors: let there be language! This approach has been deliciously described as amounting to "Irrational nativist exuberance" by Barbara Scholz and Geoff Pullum.[72]

Rather than getting unduly carried away à la nativists, what should impress us is how much children bring to the table in constructing their mother tongue. But, in the final analysis, language arises from language use, rather than some mysterious, innate, Universal Grammar. We learn our language from our mother, our father, our siblings and those around us. And, in the end, that should not surprise us.[73]

5 Is language a distinct module in the mind?

Myth: *Language forms a distinct faculty or module of mind. The language module occupies a dedicated neural architecture in the brain: it is specialised for processing grammar and is inaccessible to other mental modules. It emerges on a pre-specified developmental trajectory and cannot be guided or influenced by other types of information from elsewhere in the mind.*

In western thought there has been a venerable tradition in which the mind has been conceived of in terms of distinct faculties. Scholastic thought in the Middle Ages, associated most notably with the theologian Thomas Aquinas, proposed that mental functions were attributes of specific parts of the mind. With the advent of cognitive science in the 1950s, the digital computer became the analogy of choice for the human mind. Computers, like human brains, appeared to constitute a mechanism capable of complex reasoning. Cognitive science took the computational processes deployed by computers as an analogy for how the brain computes the mind. In the mind-as-computer metaphor, the information processing performed by computers is much like human cognition.

From the mind-as-computer perspective, the notion of associating function with location/parts makes intuitive sense. In everyday life the objects and entities we encounter are modular, with the digital computer being the paradigmatic example. The physical components of a computer – the hardware – form a system that is subdivided into component parts – modules – that can be independently created, and which are associated, almost exclusively, with very specific functions. For instance, a hard drive, a printer, a CPU – made of modular microchips and a motherboard – a disk reader and a monitor are all distinct modular parts. They perform specific roles and can be connected, disconnected, reconnected and replaced without qualitatively impacting on the performance of the whole.

While the idea that the mind is a computer has been a central and highly influential heuristic in cognitive science, the radical proposal that the mind, like the computer, is also modular, was made by philosopher of mind Jerry Fodor. In a now classic book, *Modularity of Mind*, published back in 1983, Fodor proposed that language is the paradigmatic example of a mental module.[1] And this view, from the language-as-instinct perspective, makes perfect sense.

According to Fodor, a mental module is realised in dedicated neural architecture. It is designed to deal with a specific and restricted type of information, and is encapsulated – it is impervious to the workings of other modules. As a consequence, a module can be impaired, resulting in the breakdown of just those aspects of behaviour associated with the module, while other aspects of mind continue functioning normally. And as a module deals with a specific type of information, the module will emerge at the particular point during the life cycle when the information it processes begins to emerge. Hence, a module is activated, in developmental terms, following a schedule that is specific to the module.

One consequence of all this is that mental modules must be innate. After all, if a module processes a specific type of information, and 'switches on' when the organism begins to receive the information that it is specialised for, the module must already be programmed as part of the human genome.

As we saw in the previous chapter, the language-as-instinct thesis contends that the principles of grammar that form the core of language are too complex to be learnable without negative feedback. They are universal, and hence must be innate. As highly specialised and innate knowledge of this sort takes the form of a module, on Fodor's account, then the language instinct must, in fact, be a module. The fact that the modular view of mind meshes precisely with the language-as-instinct thesis is no coincidence. Both Chomsky and Fodor were early advocates of the computational view of mind. And Fodor's 1983 publication on modularity owes much to a joint seminar they taught together at the Massachusetts Institute of Technology.

On the face of it, the idea that the mind is modular might make intuitive sense. In our everyday lives, we associate component parts of physical artefacts with specific functions. Modularity of design is both a practical and sensible approach to the manufacture not just of computer hardware, but of many, many aspects of everyday commodities, from cars to children's toys. Indeed, the desk I am working at, whilst I write this book, is in fact a modular office 'suite'. It comprises a desk, a shelving unit, a printer stand and a set of drawers on wheels. Each of these component 'modules' can be interchanged, and combined in different ways, and with different items from the ones I have.

However, the evidence, as will become clear below, provides very little grounds for thinking that language is a module of mind, or indeed that the mind is modular in the way supposed by the language-as-instinct thesis. In fact, the broad array of evidence now available makes clear that the relationship between language and cognition is extremely complex. This leads to the conclusion that the modular view of mind provides an overly simplistic view of the nature of human cognition. And it calls into question the nature of the relationship between language and other aspects of cognition. It requires a revised view of the nature and organisation of grammar. These are all issues I touch upon in this chapter.

On grammar genes and chatterboxes

According to Steven Pinker, for language to be an instinct, and therefore to count as a module, "it should have an identifiable seat in the brain, and perhaps even a special set of genes that help wire it into place. Disrupt these genes or neurons, and language should suffer while the other parts of intelligence carry on; spare them in an otherwise damaged brain, and you should have a retarded individual with intact language, a linguistic idiot savant."[2] He then makes the following claim: "There are several kinds of neurological and genetic impairments that compromise language while sparing cognition and vice versa."[3] Hence, language must be a distinct module in the mind.

For language to be a distinct module, we require a demonstration of three things. First, there must be an identifiable location or system in the brain that is associated solely with grammar. Second, there must be a dissociation between grammar and other types of cognitive behaviour, including other types of linguistic knowledge which are not innate, such as the development of vocabulary. The reason for this is as follows: if one type of knowledge, for example grammar, and just that, can be knocked out, while other aspects of mental function continue to work just fine, this would provide evidence that distinct intelligences are insulated from one another, working as encapsulated units, kind of like separate reactors in a nuclear power station which are housed in separate bunkers – if there is damage to one, the others remain unaffected – pretty important in a nuclear power station. And third, there must be a clear trajectory of development showing that grammar emerges relative to its own specific time-scale, and independent of maturational trajectories of other types of information. Let's examine, then, the claims that have been advanced to support each of these.

The brain is divided into two halves: a left and a right hemisphere. This is referred to as lateralisation, and is true of any organism more complex than a worm. In humans – and unlike in other primates, including Great Apes such as chimpanzees – the lateralisation is asymmetric. In 1877, Paul Broca, the French neurologist, wrote: "Man is, of all the animals, the one whose brain in the normal state is the most asymmetrical. He is also the one who possesses most acquired faculties. Among these the faculty of articulate language holds pride of place. It is this that distinguishes us the most clearly from the animals."[4]

In human beings, the language areas – such as Broca's area, so called after Paul Broca – is typically found in the left hemisphere. This is the case for nearly all right-handed people, who account for 90 per cent of the population.[5] Indeed, handedness is another human-specific consequence of brain lateralisation – the hemispheres typically control the opposite part of the body. Intriguingly, while around 20 per cent of left-handers have their language areas in the right hemisphere, 68 per cent of them have at least some language abilities in both hemispheres.

Lateralisation was uncovered by the pioneering work of Paul Broca, working in France, and later Carl Wernicke, based in what was then Germany. Both Broca and Wernicke conducted post-mortems on patients who had suffered severe language deficits. Broca's patients could understand speech with little difficulty, but were severely impaired in what they could utter. Broca's most celebrated patient could produce just one word: *tan*. In contrast, Wernicke's patients could produce language, but had severe difficulties in understanding it.

Difficulty in producing or understanding language is known as aphasia. And Broca's aphasia is an 'expressive' aphasia: it turns out that it results from a wholesale failure to be able to construct sentences and produce language – an inability to express oneself. In less severe cases, patients with Broca's aphasia are capable of slow, laborious and often slurred sequences of words. Their grammar is problematic, seldom making use of regular grammatical endings such as *-ed* for the past tense.[6] And Broca's patients have a tendency to leave out the small grammatical words such as *of*, *to* and *for*, rendering their speech disjointed. In contrast, damage to Wernicke's area causes a 'receptive' aphasia, as comprehension, rather than production, is impaired.

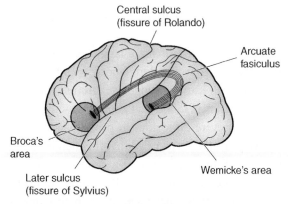

Approximate locations of Broca's and Wernicke's areas on the frontal and posterior portions of the cerebral cortex respectively.

Broca's area seems to involve more than simply the motor coordination essential for producing well-formed utterances: it involves the ability to process grammar itself. For example, when Broca's aphasics hear sentences in a passive form, they often misunderstand – if I were to say *The supermodel slapped the window cleaner*, they may understand that I am instead conveying that the window cleaner slapped the supermodel.

Because of its role in producing grammar, might Broca's area be the seat of the language module? While Pinker admits that "No one has yet found a language organ or a grammar gene",[7] Broca's area is nevertheless a likely candidate. A patient who suffers a stroke or bullet wound to Broca's area suffers an instant and catastrophic language impairment. But intriguingly, other aspects of intellect appear to remain intact. This suggests the sort of dissociation between language and other aspects of cognition that is required to provide evidence for a language module.

In the case of one Broca's aphasic, the cognitive scientist Howard Gardner reports that, while language was severely compromised, other mental faculties appeared to remain intact. Gardner wrote: "[The patient] was alert, attentive and fully aware of where he was. Intellectual functions not closely tied to language, such as knowledge of right and left, ability to draw with the left (unpracticed) hand, to calculate, read maps, set clocks, make constructions, or carry out commands, were all preserved. His Intelligence Quotient (IQ) in nonverbal areas was in the high average range."[8]

But what of a genetic basis for a language module? One study examined a family from London whose members all appeared to have difficulties in learning language.[9] Across three generations of the family, researchers found that about half – thirty members of the family – had severe difficulties in pronunciation, morphology and syntax. Moreover, tests revealed that the members of the family who were affected appeared to have a genetic mutation affecting one particular gene, known as FOXP2. Some supporters of the language-as-instinct thesis have seized upon this finding as evidence that language really is a genetically determined module.

But for language to be a distinct module, there must also be a dissociation between grammar and other cognitive abilities – as appears to be the case with Broca's aphasia. But to clinch the case, we need a second dissociation: whereby intelligence is compromised, but language is unaffected. And the result of the two dissociations is a so-called 'double dissociation'.

Exhibit A, in Pinker's case, is those unfortunates who suffer from what he dubs the chatterbox syndrome: these individuals would appear, on the face of it, to exhibit just such a dissociation. Chatterbox syndrome sufferers have a genetic disorder that results from a defective gene on chromosome 11. This results in severe mental retardation, but appears to leave language otherwise unaffected – hence Pinker's label: linguistic idiot savants.

The chatterbox syndrome is most often associated with patients who have what is more commonly referred to as Williams Syndrome. Sufferers have a distinct elfin appearance, sharp chins, and broad foreheads. While their grammatical abilities are often at or above average, they suffer from severe intellectual impairments: IQ is typically no more than 50 – compare this to the average IQ range which is 84–114 in the normal population. Consequently, linguistic idiot savants struggle with everyday tasks ranging from tying shoe laces to being able to distinguish their left from their right.

In contrast to linguistic savants, other individuals suffer from what is often referred to as specific language impairment (SLI). Patients with SLI have normal intelligence, but as suggested by the term, have deficits with their language. Unlike individuals with Broca's aphasia, involving an acquired loss of language, SLI results from a genetic abnormality. The members of the London family I discussed earlier, with the defect on the FOXP2 gene, all suffer from SLI. Unlike the severe impact on language of Broca's aphasia, the affected Londoners give the impression of "a tourist struggling in a foreign city".[10] They report that they find speaking strenuous, and palpably do make frequent grammatical errors. For instance, they use pronouns – words like *she* or *it* – incorrectly. And like Broca's aphasics, they make errors in inflectional morphology, such as the failure to correctly use the plural -s marker, or the -ed past-tense marker.

Together, the chatterbox syndrome and SLI appear to point to a double dissociation between language and other aspects of intelligence: language can be impaired in the case of SLI, while normal intellect is preserved. But in the case of the linguistic savants, language is preserved, while intelligence suffers.

The third and final line of evidence relates to the developmental trajectory of the language module. According to the language-as-instinct thesis, what is innate about language concerns our grammar, and specifically the elements shared by all humans regardless of the language they ultimately end up speaking. This component, as we have seen in earlier chapters, has been referred to by Chomsky as Universal Grammar (or UG for short). Chomsky describes the situation as follows: "For language or any other internal module, its growth and development in the individual involves . . . a genetic endowment that converts data to experience and guides the general course of development . . . For language we can analyse the genetic into a component specific to human language (UG)."[11]

While Chomsky is sometimes difficult to understand, even for many professional linguists, I like to quote him for the following reason. Many cognitive scientists who work outside linguistics are often shocked to discover that a major tranche of Anglo-American linguistics still adheres to the quite extreme view that grammar is a distinct module of mind. Many neuroscientists, in particular, think that modularity is way too simplistic a view to take, and that, while different areas of the brain exhibit degrees of specialisation, there is always significant cross-talk, which makes strict modularity untenable up-front. In case anyone thought that Chomsky, or his swathes of fervent followers, had recanted, think again: the quote, above, is from 2011. And the language-as-instinct thesis, which today remains the single largest 'school' in Anglo-American linguistics, has little empirical basis, sustaining itself in an institutional hegemony which, in the view of some, seeks to maintain the status quo regardless of the actual facts: reputations have been built upon the idea of the language-as-instinct thesis; for these researchers, the prospect of the Universal Grammar thesis being wrong doesn't bear thinking about. For Chomsky, language is self-evidently a module. And the 'data' that Chomsky speaks of are found in the language infants are exposed to, namely the words that children hear amongst the "blooming, buzzing confusion" (= the gobbledygook), appropriating the words of the eminent psychologist William James.

According to the language-as-instinct thesis, evidence for a distinct maturational trajectory for the language module, for Universal Grammar, comes from the seemingly discontinuous jump from speaking in one or two words to the rapid onset of a fully fledged grammar: joining up strings of words. One day, vocabulary, and the next, grammar: grammar emerges seemingly out of nowhere, overnight.

Researchers subscribing to the language-as-instinct thesis describe the trajectory for language acquisition in the following terms. The sound system of a language, our phonology, makes its first appearance in babbling, which involves repeating syllables such as *ba-ba-ba*, from 6 to 8 months of age. Meaningful speech begins to emerge between 10 and 12 months with first words. Vocabulary growth is initially slow, at least for the first 50–100 words. But then, between 16 and 20 months of age, most children display a burst in vocabulary acquisition; 2-word combinations appear between 18 and 20 months. But then, between 24 and 30 months, children show an acceleration in terms of complexity of word combinations, with the seemingly abrupt emergence of grammar. And, by 3 to 3.5 years of age, most children have mastered the basic word combinations and grammatical patterns of their language.

The assumption is that a language acquisition device gets 'turned on', allowing grammar to begin to emerge. The neurolinguist John Locke has proposed that just such a 'grammatical analysis mechanism' begins operating shortly before the child's second birthday, allowing the rapid emergence of grammar to take place between 2 and 3 years of age. Locke claims that it is developmentally programmed not to turn on before as it needs a basic amount of vocabulary to have been learned. Words must be learned painstakingly, from the blooming, buzzing confusion of the talk of caregivers, parents and siblings; but once the language module kicks in, the emergence of grammar is rapid, and relatively effortless: as "language is a module ... learning ... [is] ... irrelevant to its development".[12] Hence, principles of Universal Grammar facilitate the swift development of grammar.

The chatterbox fallacy

But does the chatterbox syndrome really exist? Are there really language savants whose language is an island of perfection in an otherwise degraded intellect? Is there a grammar gene? And does a developmentally pre-programmed language acquisition device kick in from around 20 months of age leading to the rapid flowering of an innately pre-specified Universal Grammar? More recent and more careful studies appear to undermine all of these proposals.

Let's begin with the issue of localisation: whether the brain has areas specialised for grammar, and nothing else. While it has been known for well over 100 years that Broca's area is correlated with grammar production, it doesn't follow that this brain area is dedicated to language to the exclusion of all else. We now know that every component of Broca's area exhibits significant levels of activation in the planning of various nonverbal motor tasks,[13] and even our ability to recognise discordant chord sequences in music.[14] Further complicating the situation is the discovery that impairment of Broca's area does not inevitably mean that language is irrevocably damaged.[15] For instance, in one recent case, a computer engineer had a slow-growing tumour removed from his brain, resulting in damage to Broca's area. Yet this resulted in minimal linguistic impairment, and the patient was able to return to work and communicate normally within 3 months of the brain resection. In other cases, damage to Broca's area resulting in more serious linguistic impairment corrects itself over time, especially in children. This suggests that language can 'move' to neighbouring brain regions, calling into question the specialised role of Broca's area.[16]

In a further twist, the preserved brains of two of Broca's patients were re-examined using modern high-resolution magnetic resonance imaging. The first patient, Leborgne, was the one I mentioned earlier who was only able to utter the word *tan*. The second, Lelong, could only produce five words: *yes, no, three, always* and a mispronunciation of his own name: *lelo*. It was found that damage to other areas of the brain may also have contributed to the severe disruption to language production exhibited by both Leborgne and Lelong.[17]

Recent experiments further illustrate that Broca's area, far from being uniquely dedicated to language production, is associated with a range of non-linguistic tasks involving the recognition of actions. For instance, Broca's area allows us to perceive and even interpret the action of others; it is also the location of mirror neurons which fire in response to specific actions of others, especially gestures, and hand shadows.[18] As language may have evolved from gesture, the relation between Broca's area and language production may be a consequence of its role in processing and recognising manual actions.[19] And, more damaging still to the language-as-instinct thesis, there remains considerable disagreement about the precise location of Broca's area in the brain, across laboratories and studies that have investigated it.[20] Indeed, the neurolinguist Friedmann Pulvermüller has reported that the production of language appears to be highly distributed, being located in every lobe of the human brain.[21]

Let's now briefly reconsider the role of FOXP2 as the putative grammar gene. There are reasons to be extremely sceptical of this claim.[22] First of all, the gene is not specific to language. It appears to impact on the ability to sequence muscles of the face and mouth that are not involved in language. It is also implicated in general intelligence. Members of the London family affected by the genetic mutation have, sadly, a consistently lower IQ measure than other family members, by around 18 points on average. And IQ is a measure of general intelligence, rather than language.[23] In addition, FOXP2 is also found in other mammals – so it's not specific to humans. The human version of the gene is very similar to that found in gorillas, orang-utans and rhesus macaque monkeys.[24] And finally, FOXP2 appears to be important for the development of the heart, gut and lungs. As a prominent expert explains: "While something about the normal version of human FOXP2 seems to help an individual to develop language, the gene itself does not contain a blue-print for grammar."[25]

The second line of evidence – the dissociation between language and other aspects of intelligence – is equally suspect: the double dissociations turn out to be not what they seem. While those with Williams Syndrome do indeed exhibit perhaps surprisingly good linguistic abilities, at least relative to their diminished visual–spatial and reasoning capabilities,[26] it doesn't follow they are linguistic savants.[27] The linguistic abilities of Williams Syndrome sufferers, more often than not, fall below the ability of normal children and young adults of the same age. This is scarcely surprising given that they have IQs of around 50.

While a handful of Williams Syndrome subjects have been found to have comparable phonological memory, and memory for novel words at or above mental-age as compared to normal subjects, their performance is invariably below in terms of vocabulary, sentence understanding and their ability to form sentences.[28] Moreover, and in spite of their ultimate relative success with language acquisition, Williams Syndrome patients are late talkers: they are severely delayed compared to normally developing children, in both their word production and comprehension.[29] Williams Syndrome patients can often acquire quite erudite vocabularies, and master complex grammatical structures.[30] This is unusual for people with such low IQ scores. However, the strategies they use are quite different from those of normal children. The psychologist Anette Karmiloff-Smith has found that, while normal children expect new words to refer to a whole object, this is not the assumption made by Williams Syndrome sufferers.

They "take a new word to refer just as readily to a part of an object, say, its handle ... they show an atypical tendency to focus on parts". [31] Moreover, they find it difficult to judge whether sentences are ungrammatical or not, and have difficulty producing sentences with relatively complex grammar – for instance, sentences involving a relative clause (a clause introduced by *who, which* or *that*), such as: *The window cleaner who was bald loved the supermodel.*

What this reveals is that the so-called chatterbox syndrome' relates to a deficit in linguistic performance; it also relates to an abnormal trajectory of linguistic development compared to typical populations of language learners. In short, it is not accurate to conclude that Williams Syndrome subjects are linguistic savants.

The claim made by Pinker is that patients with Williams Syndrome diverge from patients suffering from SLI. SLI is typically diagnosed between 3 and 4 years of age, following the expected burst in the development of grammar witnessed in normal children. However, following more than 40 years of research, it now appears that SLI is better characterised not as a substandard deviance in terms of linguistic development, but rather as a delay. [32] SLI sufferers exhibit qualitatively similar linguistic abilities to normally developing younger children.

In addition, recent studies reveal that SLI may be more than simply a problem with language. SLI children perform significantly below children of the same age on non-linguistic tasks, such as the ability to imagine objects, and the ability to rotate them mentally, [33] the ability to engage in symbolic play – pretending that an object such as a block represents something else, such as a phone [34] – and the ability to shift attention from one object or task to another. [35] This suggests that SLI may not, in fact, be an impairment specific to language after all. SLI appears to have a more general cause.

In terms of the delay to language experienced by SLI sufferers, the ability to build words from smaller units – morphology – appears to be the consistently most affected type of linguistic knowledge. Moreover, it has long been known that morphology is difficult to perceive – after all, the affixes that are added to words, such as the plural *-s* marker, or the *-ed* past-tense marker, are little sound units that are often difficult to hear, especially in rapid speech. And hence it may be that SLI is in fact not a consequence of language per se, but due to a difficulty in hearing, or processing certain kinds of auditory cues,[36] or perhaps in establishing mental rules for sound combination due to issues with phonological development.[37] Either way, the difficulty seems *not* to be a problem with grammatical development. Instead, it has to do with the perception and formation of representations for acoustically weak elements of grammatical marking. All in all, linguistic savants turn out not to be as linguistically sophisticated as originally claimed; and SLI appears not to relate exclusively to linguistic deficits, or, ultimately to be caused by a difficulty with developing grammatical competence per se.

Finally, let's re-consider the claim for a discontinuous jump from vocabulary to the sudden emergence of grammar from around the age of two – recall that, according to the language-as-instinct thesis, vocabulary acquisition is not guided by our innate Universal Grammar: vocabulary has to be learned. Up until the 1970s, before detailed longitudinal studies had been conducted – studies that followed the development of children over time – it seemed reasonable to think that children acquired words quite slowly at first, but picking up speed shortly before the age of a year and a half. But then, from around 20 months onwards, grammar emerges, seemingly abruptly.

However, with the advent of a raft of detailed studies following the trajectory of child language acquisition, across both individuals and populations, in English- and non-English-speaking contexts, it is now clear that this picture of a discontinuous jump is not in fact accurate. We now know that acquisition of grammar is contingent on the acquisition of vocabulary.[38] The development of grammar is continuous with that of vocabulary growth, and is closely tied to vocabulary acquisition. The single best estimate of how developed a child's grammar is at 28 months – right in the heart of the grammar 'burst' – is total vocabulary size at 20 months – right in the middle of the vocabulary burst. The utterances of 20-month-old and 28-month-old children are statistically identical in terms of how many words they know compared to how complex their grammar is.[39]

Performance on grammar appears to correlate closely with vocabulary size right across the 16- to 30-month age range. The language-as-instinct thesis predicts that we should find that once a specific threshold of words has been acquired, the two decouple. But this turns out not to be the case. Moreover, the correlation is not due to a child's age. Age is a surprisingly poor predictor of both vocabulary and grammar in the 16- to 30-month age range. When vocabulary size is kept constant at different age ranges, and experimenters examine the difference in grammatical complexity, age accounts for a surprisingly low 0.8 per cent of the variance on grammar. In contrast, when age is kept constant, and different vocabulary sizes are examined, vocabulary size accounts for 32.3 per cent of children's grammatical complexity.[40] And this finding is not unique to children learning English – it is the pattern across other languages too.[41]

What these findings reveal is that, far from being a unique type of encapsulated knowledge, grammar appears to be closely related to and predicted by vocabulary acquisition. It does not, it seems, emerge on its own independent developmental trajectory, as would be expected if grammar were indeed a distinct module of mind, an instinct.

One objection to my conclusion might be that grammatical 'function' words, such as *to*, *of* and so on are being included in the count of vocabulary. As these might be considered to be part of grammar, they may be artificially inflating the size of the acquired vocabulary; as such, they could be blurring the picture of discontinuity between vocabulary acquisition and grammar onset that might otherwise be the case. Yet, once these 'little' grammatical words are removed from the vocabulary count, the pattern remains. Indeed, if anything, the pattern of a correlation between the growth of vocabulary and the accompanying emergence of grammar is even more starkly represented than when including the original function words.[42]

A second possible objection might be that we really need to examine the development of individual children, by examining individual trajectories of development, rather than taking averages at different periods from populations of children. To counter this, twenty-eight children were followed from 12 to 30 months of age. Researchers observed the children on a monthly basis, in free play, carefully observing, recording and videotaping their language use. Some more formal tests of word and grammar comprehension were also employed. And the same correlation was found: each of these individual children, remarkably, exhibited a correlation between vocabulary size and growth of grammar.[43]

What about in atypical populations: children who develop grammar at a normal rate despite vocabulary scores that are abnormally high or low for their age? Late talkers are those in the bottom 10th percentile for vocabulary in the absence of retardation, neurological impairment, autism, deafness or any other obvious biomedical cause for delay. In contrast, early talkers are in the top 10th percentile for expressive vocabulary. One of the major findings of the late Elizabeth Bates, a leading psycholinguist, is that there is no evidence for a dissociation between vocabulary and grammar in atypical populations of children either.[44]

In summary, the relationship between grammar and vocabulary acquisition is not discontinuous: it is incontrovertibly continuous. Grammar appears *not* to develop according to a unique time course, relative to vocabulary, as would be the case if it were indeed a distinct module of mind. Grammar is dependent upon vocabulary acquisition: the relationship between the two does not dissociate at any point in life.

Alas, poor Darwin

The modular view of mind has a long history, arising from a materialist tradition in which mental functions are localised in specific regions of the brain. In 1784, a German physician named Franz Joseph Gall claimed that character, thoughts and emotions are generated by specific brain regions. He developed an approach, known as phrenology, which mapped various personality traits onto specific brain regions.

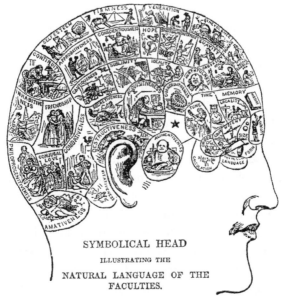

A phrenologist's representation of the brain. (Symbolical head showing the natural language of the faculties (litho), English School (nineteenth century) / Private Collection / The Stapleton Collection / The Bridgeman Art Library.)

Although phrenology became extremely popular in the nineteenth century, it was soon being disparaged. In 1843, François Magendie called it "a pseudo-science of the present day". Despite its bad press, arising from its stereotyping of intelligence along ethnic lines based on measurements of skull size, and its concomitant racist overtones, phrenology was nevertheless an important step. Arguably for the first time, phrenology represented an attempt to understand human behaviour in neurological rather than purely philosophical terms.

The modular view of mind, while not directly related to phrenology, nevertheless takes a narrow one-to-one view of mind function and brain localisation. Indeed, researchers who have taken a modular view of language have extrapolated away from this, claiming that other types of intelligence might be modular too. Pinker speaks for all arch-modularists when he wonders whether "maybe the rest of cognition is a bunch of instincts too – complex circuits, each dedicated to solving a particular family of computational problems posed by the ways of life we adopted millions of years ago".[45] Pinker proposes that abilities as diverse as the following are all distinct modules of mind: intuitive mechanics, intuitive biology, number, mental maps for large territories, habitat selection, recognition of danger, detection of food contamination, and on the list goes.[46]

This radical view – that the mind consists entirely of different kinds of modules – has, in fact, been worked out in some detail by the self-dubbed evolutionary psychologists Leda Cosmides and John Tooby. And so-called 'evolutionary psychology' achieves an apotheosis of sorts in their 1992 volume *The Adapted Mind*. Pinker himself also advocates massive modularity; he claims that this explains how the mind works.[47] The idea, in essence, is that: "Like a swiss army knife, the mind is an assembly of specialised tools, each of which has been designed for some particular purpose."[48] Modules evolved for dedicated functions, ranging from "choosing a mate, choosing one's diet, seeing, spatial orientation, face recognition", to our ability to engage in mind-reading – attributing particular mental states to other people – and, of course, our ability to process grammar.[49] And as these modules evolved to provide an evolutionary advantage, they are sometimes referred to as *Darwinian modules*.

So far, so good. But here's the difficulty. Language has been proposed, by the massive modularity crowd – Cosmides, Tooby and Pinker – as the best example of a module. And, as we've seen, in the case of language, modularity fails. Evidence for other putative modules is necessarily far harder to come by. Evidence for large-scale neurological systems that are domain-specific – that are specialised for processing just one genre of information, whether it be language, visual input or whatever – is scarce indeed. In neuroimaging studies, for instance, the proposal for a mind-reading module has been investigated. When subjects process beliefs about others, the following brain areas light up: language processing areas in the left frontal cortex, visuospatial areas in right temporal parietal regions, and the amygdala, associated with emotions. In short, mind-reading appears to exploit a network of brain structures – not a single dedicated area. And these same structures are implicated by a range of other, often quite disparate, competencies.[50]

The massive modularity crowd have countered this, and might put their response this way: "Hang on a sec; our modules, Darwinian modules, don't have to be localised. Nor do they have to be informationally encapsulated: the brain is functionally, *not* physically modular – neurological systems, which might overlap with others, *just have* evolved to perform specific functions." On this account, modules are now only semi-autonomous.[51] One of the most famous modules proposed is the cheater detection module.[52] This module, it's been claimed, evolved to detect cheaters – individuals who defy contractual and other social norms – and is supposed to feed into an intricate reasoning system. And indeed, damage to certain parts of the brain – the orbito-frontal cortex and amygdala – results in an inability to reason about social norms, providing some support for a putative cheater detection module.[53]

However, a significant difficulty for massive modularity is a logical one. And this has been raised by Jerry Fodor, of all people, the contemporary architect-in-chief of the modular view of mind. Imagine that there is a mental module for perceiving human faces, a module for perceiving animal faces, and a module for everything else. Now, if we perceive an animal's face, it should be processed by the animal recognition module; if it is a human face, by the human recognition module, and so on. But, if a piece of information enters the brain, how do we know which module it is to be processed by? The question then becomes, how does the mind know which type of information it is, and hence to which module it can be assigned? This requires a meta-module, one that already knows the difference between human faces and animal faces and everything else. The problem for the massive modular view is that, as modules only process a specific type of information – they are domain-specific – then having the entire mind comprised of modules means there is no central intelligence that can join things up, and decide which module should look after which item of information.[54]

But the massive modularists get around this by claiming that not all intelligences are modular – there must be some general processor available for general learning. Piloting an airbus, programming a computer or reading, for instance, can't have evolved dedicated modules, they argue: these competences all emerged relatively recently.[55]

In Fodor's version of modularity, which preceded massive modularity, he took the view that modules could only ever work for low-level perceptual phenomena, rather than higher-level thought processes.[56] There had to be a *central intelligence*, a non-modular Big Brother looking out for the mind more generally. But Fodor's modularity comes unstuck due to the claim that modules should be informationally encapsulated: they deal with a specific genre of information, and do not permit cross-talk with other modules. There are numerous examples in which modules do appear to speak to each other.

One very famous example is the so-called 'McGurk effect', named after the Scottish psychologist Harry McGurk who discovered it.[57] In the McGurk effect, a video in which a person is seen to be saying a particular sound, for instance [b], is played to subjects; but what they in fact hear is a different sound, for instance [g]. And the result is that the audience perceives a blend of the two sounds: the sound seen and heard. This demonstrates that visual and auditory experiences interfere with each other – which should not be possible if the mind really were modular.

Another example relates to so-called 'touch illusions'. When subjects are tapped on a limb, their assessment of how many taps they experience can be influenced by what they hear. For instance, hearing multiple sounds while experiencing a single tap can give rise to the illusion that there were multiple taps.[58] Again, modularity predicts that this should be impossible as different modules are prohibited from interfering with information emanating from each other.

The massive modularity worldview is built upon a radical nativist stance. In part, this seems to arise from a phobia of the role of learning and experience. For instance, stereoscopic vision – our ability to see objects with height, width and depth – turns out to emerge gradually, and in some cases fails to develop; experience and learning may play a role in the development of this fundamental aspect of vision. Yet in his book *The Blank Slate*, which advocates a massively modular approach to the mind, Pinker claims that there must surely be an innate mechanism that programmes the development of stereoscopic vision. But any such mechanism would require genes to speculate about input they are unable to predict, as conceded by Pinker himself. Yet Pinker nevertheless prefers the prospect that stereoscopic vision is underwritten by genetics, no matter how suspect such an account might be, as it avoids, Pinker complains, "the tiresome lesson that stereoscopic vision, like everything else, is a mixture of nature and nurture".[59]

Massive modularity seeks to clothe its rationalist stance in the cloak of evolutionary respectability. But ultimately it gets Darwin wrong. The modern neo-Darwinian synthesis had, by the mid-1980s, been largely accepted as the broadly correct account of evolution. And as evidence accrued, it came to be viewed as fact, rather than just a theory, as the evolutionary biologist Richard Dawkins has been at pains to point out.[60] But if you are a committed rationalist, how do you account for the evolution of a cognitively modern mind?

The notion of mental modules fits the nativist bill. On this reverse-engineering account, modules can be traced back to Holocene-era contexts that gave rise to them, way before the advent of farming and fixed human settlements, around 12,000 years ago. And as such, new modules have arisen, in response to specific contexts, affording an adaptive advantage. But, as many commentators have noted, it is often difficult to construct genetically and ecologically plausible scenarios that would have given rise to the putative mental modules posited by massive modularity.[61] For instance, in what context would the cheater detection module have been triggered, such that we have a specialised module for detecting those likely to break contracts?

But if Darwinian modules are not encapsulated, and they don't have to be localised in specific regions of the brain, isn't this more or less the same as saying that humans are smart, and we have general intelligence that allows us to do lots of clever things? Not quite. The proposal for Darwinian modules assumes that a module evolved for a specific purpose. And, hence, the prediction is that the neurological systems that underlie specific modules should have evolved at different rates, and in different ways from other modules. Much like a patch-work quilt, the brain is a mosaic of different modules that evolved independently and for different functions.

However, recent research appears to undermine this prediction. Neuroscientist, and Professor of Philosophy, Steven Quartz has used recent findings on the evolution of the mammalian brain to draw the conclusion that massive modularity gets Darwin wrong.[62] Research mapping the evolutionary development of the mammalian brain, including *Homo sapiens*, shows that the brain has evolved in a coordinated, rather than a mosaic fashion.[63] Studying eleven adult human brain parts, such as the cerebellum, the striatum and, critically, the neocortex, researchers have discovered that the brain has evolved as an ensemble, rather than tacking on specialised modules – the prediction made by massive modularity. This research concerns the development of brain volume, by examining the ratio of brain parts with respect to one another, over evolutionary time. If brain development involved a mosaic pattern of evolution, as assumed by massive modularity, then the ratio of size of brain parts, relative to each other, would change, so Quartz contends.

But this is not what has happened. In fact, the component parts of the mammalian brain have remained consistently coordinated, in terms of their relative size, over evolutionary time. Quartz claims that this reveals the brain to have evolved in a coordinated trajectory, rather than a mosaic pattern, with different parts evolving at different rates. In short, massive modularity fails to make the grade as "a comprehensive theory of the . . . interaction of brain, body, and world" in everyday mental life.[64] And even the philosopher Edouard Machery, who has argued against Quartz's assertion, concedes that there "are very few examples [if any] of uncontroversial Darwinian modules".[65]

A final problem for massive modularity is that it fails what I dubbed, in Chapter 3, the good science test. It is nigh on impossible to falsify the thesis of massive modularity: given the context-based nature of human action and interaction, it is, for all practical purposes, virtually impossible to dissociate elements of human behaviour and attribute them to distinct modules.[66] For instance, when we detect potential cheaters, this arises in complex contexts involving social interaction and behaviour, and, in contemporary life, within legally constrained processes. But due to the complexity of these contexts, it is virtually impossible to identify distinct stereotyped behaviour types that form the 'input' of a hypothesised dedicated cheater detection module.

Ultimately, the notion of modules, whether the encapsulated type of Fodor, or the – as it turns out – ironically named *Darwinian* modules of massive modularity, goes against the lessons and findings arising from the neo-Darwinian synthesis. Mental capacities, it would seem, are just not domain-specific in the way required by the modular perspective; on the contrary, they require – and indeed entail – co-evolution of brain parts, in coordinated fashion. The analogy with a Swiss-army knife, or a computer, whereby components can be added on without materially affecting and being affected by the rest of the apparatus is demonstrably not the way evolution works. Evolution simply doesn't work in discontinuous jumps, in fits and starts, evolving modules in mosaic fashion that are specialised for performing just one function.

So, what's the alternative to modularity?

Evolution works in an incremental way, working not to the design of a pre-conceived blue-print, nor even driven by external pressures alone. Rather, it works opportunistically, and in response to and in conjunction with changes elsewhere, giving rise, quite often, to a process of co-evolution between parts. Before considering the human brain and language, first let's consider a relatively simple example: the giraffe's neck.

A giraffe's long neck has entailed quantitative variations to the basic neck plan of the giraffe. And, as a result, this has allowed contemporary giraffes to reach tastier leaves that refresh the parts other animals cannot reach. But the evolution of a longer neck has required and co-occurred with a range of other changes. These include cardiovascular changes enabling blood to be pumped the considerably greater distance to the giraffe's brain. Also required was a co-evolution of the giraffe's body parts: a shortening of the hind legs relative to the front legs to prevent the long-necked giraffe from falling over. Moreover, in the giraffe the route of the laryngeal nerve is such that it travels from the brain to the larynx by looping around the aortic arch. This results in about 20 feet of extra nerve! Unlike the shortening of the giraffe's hind legs, this is simply a co-evolved redundancy, what is sometimes dubbed 'poor' design. But the larger point is that evolution is not a mechanistic process whereby hard-wired units can be selectively inserted into – or indeed, removed from – the human brain – or indeed any other organism.

In the case of language, the quantitative variations resulting from co-evolution would have led to deep and extensive changes to the nature of the human brain. In addition to the anatomical changes required to produce spoken language, and the system for controlling the relevant musculo-skeletal system, changes from the primate memory system would have been required to facilitate our ability to produce well-formed sentences; as we saw in Chapter 2, chimps have poor short-term memories which makes complex syntax problematic. Also required is a system for encoding concepts, and aligning those with auditory symbols, and for recognising intentions, which involves aligning mind-reading abilities with language. Indeed, there is considerable evidence that human mind-reading skills arise through social experience and language training.[67] Moreover, language centres have evolved from areas dealing with other, evolutionarily earlier functions, from which language may have developed. The role of Broca's area in grammar production might, on this account, be co-located with the brain's centre for recognising hand gestures precisely because language may have evolved from an earlier form of gestured Proto-language.

The evolutionary anthropologist Terrence Deacon has argued persuasively that co-evolution has driven the interdependence of language and the brain – wherein changes in one part of the brain entail changes in another part. And co-evolution is an established pattern in evolutionary development.[68] For instance, nectar-eating insects such as bees have co-evolved with flowers to the mutual advantage of each, as we saw in Chapter 1.[69] The change to both bees and flowers, involving ultra-violet reflectance of nectar by flowers, and the ability to perceive in the UV range in bees, has apparently been one of co-evolution.

A recent development has been the rise of Complexity Theory, which now allows scientists to model how co-evolution of language and the brain may have come about. Complexity Theory proposes that any system can be understood as self-organising, adapting to changes elsewhere in the system. Aspects of the system can serve as attractors, causing a reorganisation elsewhere as a response. For instance, traffic flow on motorways and highways is a good example of a self-organising system. Attractors such as traffic lights, intersections, roundabouts and so on affect and thus organise the traffic. But other attractors also play a role, such as the tendency of drivers to rubber-neck when passing a broken-down or crashed car on the hard shoulder of a motorway, resulting in long tail-backs as drivers slow to gawp at the spectacle: this is a form of self-organising behaviour, the result of attractors – here, a broken-down car – operating in the system.

The psychologists Ray Gibbs and Guy Van Orden have proposed that the co-evolved, and evolving, relationship between language and the brain can be thought of as a self-organising system: a complex adaptive system.[70]

That said, I am not, I hasten to add, denying a role for other types of evolutionary adaptations. For instance, recent evidence suggests that human infants may have innate mechanisms to discriminate between distinct types of syllables – e.g., *ba* versus *ga* – and to distinguish between male versus female voices up to 3 months prior to birth.[71] But the ability to discriminate between acoustic signals is the result of evolutionary natural drift,[72] a consequence of a further specialisation of a pre-existing set of parsing abilities, our pattern-recognition abilities, an adaption found in other primates. And even such adaptations self-organise in response to other attributes of the neurological system that language, and the competences that underpin it, are part of.

But if there aren't innately pre-specified modules, we still need to account for the fact that the human brain, nevertheless, exhibits significant levels of specialisation within neurological circuits, albeit with varying degrees of cross-talk. How do we account for the fact that Broca's area, for instance, is more or less specialised for the production of language, and is closely implicated in language deficits such as expressive aphasia, albeit with the various caveats I highlighted earlier in the chapter?

The psychologist Annette Kamiloff-Smith suggests that, while the brain is not modular at birth – the proposal of Fodor, Chomsky and other language-as-instinct researchers – neurological circuits in the brain nevertheless become specialised for distinct functions.[73] This takes place, she maintains, as we develop from infants into adulthood. This process of modularisation arises from normal development, giving rise to specialisation of brain function, without having to assume the untenable view of innate modularity.

The idea is this. At birth, children's brains respond to information they receive via the senses in a fairly distributed way: activation is fairly widespread across the brain, albeit as constrained by the gross-architectural biases that are genetically determined – perceptual details, including language, tend to be biased for processing by the left hemisphere, for instance. But, with time, specific circuits come to be selectively activated in response to specific genres of information. This process of modularisation, or specialisation, can be viewed as a self-organising response as the child's brain develops and marshals resources in an efficient way. But, crucially, this process is affected by experience: by environmental input. Human brains are not modular, but specific circuits become increasingly specialised as the brain becomes more efficient in response to the range of information it must grapple with.

What's all the fuss anyway?

In the final analysis, why does it matter whether the mind is modular or not? Who cares? I maintain that we should all care: anyone who relies on language to get by –pretty much all of us – has a vested interest in the nature of language and how it hooks up to the mind. The notion of modularity, and, in particular, modularity of the classic type associated with Fodor, is central to the worldview of the language-as-instinct thesis, even today. The world's best-selling linguistics textbook, by Professor Victoria Fromkin and colleagues, presents the thesis of language modularity as established fact. In its most recent (tenth) edition, the book proclaims that: "selectivity in both acquisition and impairment points to a strongly modularized [innate] language faculty, language is separate from other cognitive systems".[74] And this latest edition now also includes an entire sub-section of a chapter devoted to the "evidence" to support linguistic modularity.

My point in citing the Fromkin textbook is to demonstrate, again, that the myth of language modularity – of a language faculty – has become institutionalised via retellings which are now immune to counterevidence. And while classic modularity *à la* Fodor is, at very best, a controversial perspective, it is widely peddled as established doctrine by core readings in the language sciences, readings used to train tomorrow's research scientists, and language educators and professionals. As a graduate student in the United States, the introductory classes I took in linguistics used the Fromkin textbook. And even today at my own university in the United Kingdom, the most recent edition of the Fromkin textbook – which, more than ever, embraces classic Fodorian modularity as *de rigeur* – is used as the primary text to educate *all* first-year undergraduate linguistics *and* English language students.

But as we've seen in this chapter, modularity makes all sorts of inaccurate predictions: why would the mind be modular in the sense of the language-as-instinct thesis? It doesn't make sense, given what we now know about evolution and the mind. But sometimes some scientists *seem* to go out of their way not to make sense. Language is clearly qualitatively different from the communication systems of other species. And human brains/minds are capable of singularities not evident elsewhere in nature. But does that mean we have to invoke sleight of hand to explain away hard problems? Human language and the human mind are qualitatively different from anything else in nature, but does this mean we need to invent just-so stories that pander to this seeming divergence? If so, then we must indeed invoke hopeful monster explanations: sudden and discontinuous macro-evolutionary changes. If we claim that language emerged from one sudden mutation, it is then but a short leap onto the slippery slope of claiming that everything is specialised. And this leads from Fodorian modularity to the unfalsifiable and, ultimately, implausible worldview of massive modularity.

6   Is there a universal Mentalese?

Myth: *Meaning in natural languages, like English or Japanese,
derives, ultimately, from a universal language of thought:
Mentalese. Mentalese is the mind's internal or private language,
and makes thought possible. It is universal in the sense that all
humans are born with it. It is language-like, consisting of symbols,
which can be combined by rules of mental syntax. Without
Mentalese we could not learn the meanings of words in any
naturally occurring language – spoken or signed.*

The attentive reader will have noticed that, up until this point, we
haven't focused on meaning. The purpose of language, ultimately,
is to convey ideas – meanings; hence this is an issue with which
we must grapple, and to which we now turn – in this, and the
next chapter. In the language-as-instinct thesis, in addition to a
Universal Grammar, the human mind also comes pre-equipped
with a universal 'language of thought': Mentalese. According to
Jerry Fodor, who first advocated a language of thought back in
the 1970s, it is precisely due to the existence of Mentalese that
the meanings of any natural language – spoken or signed – can be
learned at all.[1]

Everyone agrees that meaning is not the same as thought.
If it were, language would determine thought, and you and
I would not be able to think without language. But lots of evidence
clearly demonstrates that language doesn't single-handedly make
thought possible. Babies – who lack language – nevertheless have
sophisticated thought processes, and form often quite complex
concepts. And so do many other species. Moreover, pre-linguistic
human infants, squirrel monkeys, scrub jays and many other
species all do this in the absence of language.[2]

The question then is: how do we develop mental representations –
concepts – that allow us to learn the meaning of the words in

our language? The language-as-instinct thesis proposes that we are born with a mental operating system – Mentalese – that allows us to represent ideas and mental states. As we proceed though our life journey, from birth onwards, experience is filtered, allowing us to build up ideas based on experience. But the architecture and 'grammatical' principles that allow us to manipulate mental representations – to produce complex thought – are present at birth: we enter the world pre-equipped with Mentalese.

But Mentalese brings of a lot of baggage with it; to believe in Mentalese as an account of the human mind you also have to make some specific, and as it turns out erroneous, assumptions about the mind. It commits you to the stance that the mind is essentially a computer, functioning and behaving like a large-scale information processor. For instance, Mentalese consists of symbols – the equivalent of words. But the symbols that make up our universal language of thought don't directly correspond to things in the world, and in our experience. While they are meant to represent entities such as chairs and tables, and more ephemeral experiences such as love and fear, they do so utilising a logical language that is wholly unlike the vivid, phenomenological experiences and mental states that we are often viscerally aware of.

The crux of the matter turns on the nature of human concepts. Everyone agrees that concepts are the "central timber of our mental lives".[3] But the language-as-instinct thesis maintains that concepts bear no relation to the ideas they represent: whether that be stuff in the world, such as doorknobs, supermodels and tax evasion, or concepts arising from our subjective experience, such as lust or unrequited love. For the language-as-instinct thesis, concepts are abstract logical relations. All concepts, whatever their stripe, are couched in an operating system distinct from the experience types that the concepts relate to. This operating system is Mentalese.

In contrast, the language-as-use thesis that I'm advocating claims that concepts are directly grounded in the experiences they derive from and relate to. For instance, a concept for a doorknob is very much like our perceptual experience of a doorknob.

And this is because concepts are 'stored' in the very brain regions that process the perceptual experiences in the first place: concepts are directly embodied in experience, and the brain states that perceive and so represent experiences.

Mentalese and the computational mind

So where does meaning come from? For example, how do we come by the knowledge that the word *cat* conveys the idea of a four-legged furry creature, which sports whiskers, a tail and says "meow"? We might reply that it is because we learned it from our caregiver, who pointed to a particular coherent set of perceptual stimuli – a bundle of fur, whiskers, legs, pointy ears and so on – while uttering the sounds that make up the word *cat*. But this begs the very question: how did our caregiver come by that meaning, and associate it with the word *cat*? From their caregiver? But what about the very first person, before there was a caregiver? How do we get out of this infinite regress?

According to the language-as-instinct thesis, we acquire the meanings associated with words because we have a pre-existing language of thought – Mentalese – that allows us to acquire the meanings to begin with. On this account, the reason that children, any normally developing children, can grow up learning to use the words of their mother tongue – Icelandic, Tongan, English or whatever – is because we are all born with a universal language of thought: Mentalese. Language learning is thus underwritten by our language of thought, which provides a kind of backstop that makes learning possible. As Jerry Fodor has put it: "One cannot learn a language unless one has a language."[4] And, as Pinker summarises, "Knowing a language, then, is knowing how to translate Mentalese into strings of words."[5] And without Mentalese, learning a natural language such as English would be impossible.

Mentalese, it is claimed, is our internal, private language that makes thought possible.[6] It is made up of concepts that can be combined. And their composition enables rational thought.[7] One reason for supposing that there is such a thing as Mentalese, in addition to, and indeed prior to, a natural language such as English, is this. We are able to think, and to draw inferences, even in the absence of spoken language. For instance, individuals who suffer brain trauma to Broca's area, and suffer a catastrophic loss of language, can nevertheless still think.

In one such case, as we saw in the previous chapter, an individual who had lost the ability to speak retained otherwise normal intelligence. He could read maps, and set clocks, he could do mathematical calculations, and was otherwise fully alert and attentive. Moreover, there is compelling evidence that human babies who have not yet acquired language nevertheless are capable of basic types of thought processes.

In one experiment, 5-month-old babies were found to be capable of mental arithmetic. This experiment cleverly made use of the so-called 'habituation effect': when a baby becomes bored with a particular scene it is attending to, it begins to lose interest, and looks away, searching for something more interesting. But when a particular scene is unusual in some way, this piques the baby's interest and it looks at the scene with renewed attention. The developmental psychologist Karen Wynn took advantage of this effect.[8]

In the experiment, babies were shown two Mickey Mouse dolls on a stage. As they started to lose interest, a screen came up to block the stage, and a hand visibly removed one of the dolls. When the screen was lowered, if one Mickey Mouse character was visible, the babies looked briefly and then quickly lost interest. However, if two or more dolls were visible, something completely unexpected, they were captivated. Based on a series of similar experiments, Wynn concluded that babies must be able to keep track of the number of items on the stage, adding and subtracting as necessary. And to be able to do so, they must be able to process information, and to reason based on their adding and taking away: they must be capable of rational thought.

It is not only pre-linguistic humans that are capable of thought. Evidence points to other species being capable of thought processes. One example relates to the ability to draw inferences from a sequence of events or observations in order to reason about other aspects of the sequence. For instance, if I tell you that Pussy Galore is older than James Bond, and that Auric Goldfinger is older than Pussy Galore, you can infer that Goldfinger is older than James Bond. This type of reasoning is referred to as transitive inference by ethologists – the ability to draw an indirect inference. Ethologists study animal behaviour. And they have discovered that a range of species, especially those who live in large social groups, such as primates – for instance, squirrel monkeys[9] – and birds – for instance, pinyon jays[10] – are capable of making inferences of this kind.

So what would Mentalese, the language of thought, look like? The short answer is that, as it is an internal 'language', it would be very much language-like. Just like a spoken language, it would have the equivalent of words, its symbols. But clearly the symbols of Mentalese would have to be qualitatively different: as it is a language of thought, they wouldn't have sounds associated with them. And the symbols would be associated with meanings – the states, experiences and objects in the world that they represent. Moreover, the symbols could be combined using rules of mental syntax. And the syntactic rules could combine the symbols to form complex propositions. These propositions would be semantically interpretable, allowing us to have complex thoughts.

But Mentalese would have to be simpler, in certain ways, than spoken languages. Language-specific distinctions would not be present. For instance, while English makes use of prepositions, such as *in* and *on*, which appear in a position before the noun – *in the garage, on the table*, etc. – spatial relations of this kind are encoded after the noun, as postpositions, in many languages – for instance, Japanese. Mentalese wouldn't encode distinctions such as this. Nor would it need to bother with how words are pronounced. But in other ways it would need to be far more complex.

For instance, consider the use of *red* in the following two English sentences: *The teacher scrawled in red ink all over the pupil's exercise book*, versus *The red squirrel is in danger of becoming extinct in the British Isles.* In each sentence the word is the same. But the meaning is quite different. The first type of *red* is a vivid, true red. But the second is a dun or browny red. These distinct meanings are presumably not coming from language. After all, how could the same word form, *red*, 'carry' two quite distinct perceptual hues? The answer is that it doesn't. Mentalese would have to have rich representations that correspond to the range of concepts we have for 'red': 'red' comes in all manner of hues, ranging from Superman's cape to henna, from fire to the colour of a lover's lips, and everything in between. Language is restricted, constrained by the vocal–auditory time pressures that envelop it: sounds and words come one at a time, in a sequence, and must be processed serially as we hear them. In contrast, Mentalese doesn't face these sorts of constraints; it must be able to represent a rich and complex array of ideas. And being a language of thought, symbols don't have to line up in a one-to-one correspondence with linguistic forms.

Consider another example: *The president changes every five years.* This sentence is ambiguous, turning on the distinction between a role – president – and the individual who occupies the role. The presidency (role) might be occupied by a new incumbent every five years; or the individual who occupies the role might get noticeably older, fatter or balder, every five years. Either way, Mentalese needs to be able to capture 'logical' distinctions such as this, differentiating between role versus value; and it must do so in a way that avoids the kind of imprecision apparent in natural language.

But if thought relies on a representational medium – Mentalese – that is independent of spoken languages such as English, does it really have to be language-like? The answer to this question in fact depends on how you think the mind works. As we began to see in the previous chapter, the language-as-instinct thesis assumes that the mind functions in ways that are broadly similar to the way a computer works. And for reasons I'll come to, if the mind is broadly computer-like, then the operating system that runs it will be language-like: enter Mentalese.

The contemporary, interdisciplinary project of cognitive science emerged, in the 1950s, on the premise that the mind could be understood in terms of a computer. Like human minds, computers are able to produce feats of complex 'reasoning'. And, like human organisms, computers make use of language. But a computer has different sorts of languages for different functions.

First off, a computer has its own internal 'machine' language. A computer's machine language makes use of the symbols that the computer itself can interpret and run to produce outputs in response to commands from the outside world – from us, the computer users. This machine code is binary, involving sequences of 1s and 0s. The 1s and 0s are referred to as 'bits'. The sequences of bits are constrained by the rules of the specific machine language. A sequence of bits, usually eight, but sometimes more, is referred to as a byte. And the sequence of bytes comprises the computer's internal machine language. But for computer programmers who get the computer to perform the sorts of operations computer users – you and me – find useful, machine code is way too complex to interact with. Programmers talk to a computer using a higher-level language, such as Java or C+. And a compiler translates the computer's internal machine code into the programming language and vice versa.

On this analogy, the mind has its own internal language, Mentalese, which makes use of discrete symbols that can be combined, following mind-internal rules. The mind's hardware is the human brain, which 'computes' the series of mental states we refer to as the mind. Specific neurons constitute distinct symbols in the brain's machine code. And patterns of activation – sequences of neurons oscillating – give rise to physical states that correspond to patterns of thought. But these mental states are then translated into an input/output language: English, Icelandic, Swahili or whatever. The input/output language allows us to 'translate' our thoughts so that, in the absence of telepathy, we can communicate with others around us.

The idea that thought involves computation of physical symbols can, in fact, be traced back to the seventeenth century English philosopher Thomas Hobbes. In *Leviathan*, Hobbes argued that reasoning involved computation: "When a man reasoneth, he does nothing else but conceive a sum total from addition of parcels; or conceive a remainder from subtraction of one sume [*sic*] from another . . . These operations are not incident to numbers only, but to all manner of things that can be added together, and taken one out of another."[11]

For Hobbes, thought involved addition and subtraction of ideas. In contemporary accounts of the computational mind, Mentalese consists of formal symbols or tokens; and these can be manipulated in rule-governed ways, similar to how words are combined to produce syntactically well-formed strings in a natural language such as English. In short, meaning arises from the manipulation of mental representations – formal symbols – following the syntactic rules dictated by Mentalese.

But what's the evidence that the mind really is a computer, processing and manipulating physical states and symbols in this way? According to Fodor, this follows because "The only psychological models of psychological processes that seem even remotely plausible represent such processes as computational."[12] As he has famously put it, the computational mind is "the only game in town". And, being the only game in town, it follows that thought is facilitated by a language of thought common to all human minds: a universal Mentalese.

Wherefore meaning?

One significant challenge for the Mentalese story is to explain where meaning comes from. The reason for thinking there is such a thing as Mentalese is that it provides language with its semantic grounding: it represents mental states as well as objects in the world that language can then encode. But what grounds Mentalese? Where does Mentalese get its meanings, its concepts, from? And this is the insoluble problem that faces Mentalese.

This grounding problem has three specific variants. The first relates to a problem of symbol grounding.[13] If Mentalese consists of symbols that relate to states of affairs – for instance, the state of affairs associated with being a cat, a doorknob or a supermodel – such that we thereby know what it means to be a cat, doorknob, supermodel or whatever, how do these symbols acquire their meanings? In Mentalese, the symbols are arbitrarily related to the thing that they represent. This means that the symbols bear no obvious similarity to what they stand for.

For instance, one way of annotating a symbol for 'cat' in Mentalese might be to use distinctive features. For instance, in Mentalese, a cat might be represented by [+tail, +whiskers, +four legs] and so on, where the + symbol indicates that a particular feature is present. At the neurological level, these distinctive features would correspond to a sequence of arbitrarily related neurons. But the point is, whether we use distinctive features or arbitrarily related neurons to capture the representation, there is no obvious relationship between the symbol and the thing it represents. The symbol isn't in fact meaningful per se. We might know that the symbol represents the state of cathood, but we *still* don't actually know what a cat is as a result. In short, unless you've actually experienced a cat, for instance by interacting with it in the real world, the Mentalese symbol, on its own, is insufficient to tell you what a cat is, what it looks like, what it feels like, and all the phenomenologically real experiences that you and I associate with cathood.

The problem has been famously illustrated by the philosopher John Searle in his Chinese Room thought experiment. Searle asks us to imagine an English-speaker alone in a room, the Chinese Room. The man doesn't know a word of Chinese. However, in the Chinese Room there are instructions, in English, for manipulating Chinese characters. This allows the English speaker to make sentences in Chinese, by following the rules, and so being able to combine the Chinese characters. Outside the room there's a Chinese man. And the man inside the Chinese Room can communicate with the Chinaman on the outside by passing notes through a small aperture. But the aperture is too small to be able to see who is on the other side. Using the same set of English instructions, the man in the Chinese Room can convert the Chinese characters from notes he receives into English, and construct new messages in response, by using his instruction manual to translate his English message into Chinese symbols. And in this way, not only can the two people continue a dialogue, the man on the outside has little inkling that the man in the Chinese Room doesn't in fact know Chinese. The messages in Chinese that the man in the room receives are hopelessly meaningless to him. He *can* communicate. But he can only do so by following a set of instructions which allows him to translate Chinese symbols into English and vice versa.

The point is that the instruction manual in the Chinese Room is analogous to Mentalese. It allows us to translate symbols. But the mere fact that we know how to use the instruction manual doesn't mean that we know what the symbols represent: for the man stuck in the Chinese Room, they are not grounded in the world beyond the instruction manual.

The second problem concerns how symbols in Mentalese are interpreted: the problem of interpretation grounding.[14] The problem goes like this: if thoughts are internal representations in our heads, how do they get interpreted as being representations of whatever they are representations of? This would require another you, a miniature version of you – a homunculus – inside your head to do the interpreting. But then who does the interpretation of the representation inside the homunculus' head that is a representation of your representation? And this requires an even littler you inside the first homunculus' head. In philosophy of cognitive science, homunculus arguments are circular and therefore always fail. And they fail because they are explaining a phenomenon in terms of the very phenomenon they are attempting to account for.

Pinker acknowledges this, saying "The computational theory of mind also rehabilitates once and for all the infamous homunculus." But, as he so often does when confronted with an all but insurmountable objection, he ridicules the objection. Hence, the objection to Mentalese on the grounds that it is guilty of being a homunculus argument is, in fact, merely an attempt by scientists "to show how tough-minded they are"[15] (one suspects that Pinker is implying such scientists are really prima donnas engaged in intellectual posturing – and we shouldn't therefore take their picky counter-arguments too seriously!).

He continues by belittling these – one assumes – overly prim theoreticians, who talk down to computer scientists. After all, Pinker contends, such theoreticians would have it that "if the engineer is correct his workstation must contain hordes of little elves".[16] Pinker then points out, almost indignantly, that "Talk of homunculi is indispensable in computer science. Data structures are read and interpreted and examined and recognized and revised all the time, and the subroutines that are unashamedly called 'agents', 'demons', 'supervisors', 'monitors', 'interpreters' and 'executives'. Why doesn't all this talk lead to an infinite regress?" Pinker asks, rhetorically.[17]

Pinker's serious point – and he does have one – is that if the mind were essentially an information processor, in broadly the same way as a computer, then, just like in a computer, each homunculus would not be looking at a representation of everything all at once: "The intelligence of the system emerges from the activities of the not-so-intelligent mechanical demons inside it."[18] This argument assumes that each homunculus is doing a bit less than the homunculus it is inside, and thus each homunculus is actually half as intelligent as its predecessor. Interpretation is grounded when a point is reached such that the final homunculus is so stupid that all he can do is say "yes" or "no". But this argument – like the suggestion that grumpy theoreticians are being self-righteous in pointing out circularity – is disingenuous. Even a "yes"/"no" response involves an interpretation of a representation. And a further homunculus would still be required to interpret that representation. Pinker's attempt to defend the computational view of mind from the homunculus argument fails.[19]

The third problem concerns the syntactocentric nature of Mentalese. In proposing Mentalese as the mind's private language, Fodor was taking his lead from Chomsky's work on natural language in which Fodor collaborated. Chomsky argued that the core attribute of language is syntax – our ability to string words together to form grammatically well-formed sentences. On this account, we know that *ogled window the cleaner window the through supermodel the* is an ungrammatical sentence (cf. *The window cleaner ogled the supermodel through the window*) because it doesn't conform to the syntax of English: English provides rules for how words can be combined into grammatically well-formed sentences, as we saw in Chapter 3. Similarly, Mentalese has rules which operate on the symbols to produce "grammatically" well-formed thoughts. But this perspective assumes that syntax can be separated from meaning: such an assumption underlies the modular approach to language and mind I discussed in the previous chapter.

Chomsky provided, as early as 1957, what he claimed was a demonstration of the separability of syntax from semantics: he claimed that sentences can be judged to be grammatically well formed even when they are not semantically interpretable. His famous example is this:

Colorless green ideas sleep furiously[20]

Clearly something cannot be both colourless and green; and ideas, being abstract notions, cannot possibly sleep. And as sleep is a state implying relaxation and calm, this is at odds with the idea captured by "furiously". Yet the sentence is otherwise grammatical, albeit that it makes little sense, on a first pass at least.

But Chomsky's sentence, and his argument, entail that any grammatical combination involving 'adjective – adjective –noun – verb – adverb', which is the grammatical structure of his "Colorless green ideas" sentence, should be grammatical, even when meaningless. But, as the commentator Brendan Wallace has demonstrated, this is not the case. Consider the following sentence, where 'paragraph' is a verb meaning 'to separate into paragraphs':

Arboreal mammary media paragraph well[21]

This sentence has exactly the same grammatical structure as Chomsky's sentence. Yet, it is grammatically horrible for most normal, native speakers of English. This shows that, when words are selected whose meanings are entirely discordant, the sentence ends up being ungrammatical too. Meaning and syntax, on this evidence, would seem to be far more closely linked than Chomsky, Pinker and Fodor allow.

It then remains to explain why Chomsky's "Colorless green ideas" sentence is grammatical, yet semantically nonsensical. The answer turns on the fact that meaning is made up of a number of different elements in a sentence. These include different words, and the overall grammatical construction of the sentence itself – an issue I shall address in more detail in Chapter 8. And any of those elements can have multiple meanings. For instance, the word *green* can relate to the colour green, or it can mean environmentally friendly. Equally, *colourless* can mean lacking colour, or lacking real substance – for instance, an 'idea' can lack 'substance'. *Sleep* can describe a particular activity engaged in by humans and other organisms involving closed eyes, heavy breathing, and so on. It can also refer to a state of not paying attention, and so forth.

Moreover, sentences are typically interpreted in a context: a real-life situation, rather than being decontextualised and placed on a page as Chomsky and other linguists often do, in much the same way as nineteenth-century butterfly collectors would pin their dead specimens to the pages of their albums – the lifeless butterflies, denied the freedom to move around and express themselves, quickly shed their once vivid colours. Ultimately, because words and sentences exhibit individually, and severally, a divergent semantic potential, and because their context of use further contributes to this, a sentence almost never has a single, fixed interpretation. The meaning of a sentence is not, therefore, an all-or-nothing matter. There are degrees to which words are semantically interpretable.[22]

By way of example, focus on the word *began* below:

> *John began the novel*
>
> *John began the magazine*
>
> *John began the dictionary*

People I've asked tell me that the sentences become semantically odder as you progress down the list. A novel is something that has a clear progression. Chapters are sequenced and thus there is a beginning, a middle and an end: hence it is perfectly reasonable to 'begin' a novel. A magazine, on the other hand, consists of a series of articles, and often adverts and images. While you might begin an article, the way in which we interact with magazines is less like our approach to novels; we don't inevitably start at the beginning and work our way through in sequence. And, as a beginning implies the first point in a sequence, *began* is less readily used in such a context. This is even more so with a dictionary, which is a work of reference. Dictionaries are not read in that way, and hence the last sentence feels quite weird indeed.

But the dictionary example can be interpreted as being semantically OK if certain conditions are met. And these come from the context of its use. For instance, the African-American civil rights figure Malcolm X famously read a dictionary in prison from cover to cover – a dictionary being the only book available to him. And, in this context, the semantic acceptability of the sentence moves higher up the scale of normality.

My point, then, is that, just as sentences can be more or less grammatical, so too sentences can be more or less semantically interpretable. Finding a sentence that requires some work to interpret – as in the "Colorless green ideas" sentence – doesn't render the sentence's syntax bad. "Colorless green ideas" might, in certain contexts, refer to proposals for an ineffective environmental policy, one that lacks in bite. It is a semantically interpretable sentence, at least in principle. And that is why it is judged to be grammatically well formed. But if you have a sentence in which the semantics don't work, whatever mental gymnastics you perform, and no matter how creative you are in coming up with a likely context of use that works, the sentence will never be grammatical. And this is the case with the "Arboreal mammary" sentence.

The essential problem is that representations, in the language-as-instinct thesis, are divorced from meaning. And this problem is inherited by the account of Mentalese proposed by Fodor and adopted by Pinker and others. Mentalese involves symbols that are not grounded, and are explicitly stripped of any semantic content. Computations on them are purely formal and causal, and produce strings of symbols. But being stripped of their semantic clothes, their less than scantily clad bare bones carry no meaning.

In point of fact, syntax and meaning are not separable. And by attempting to separate them, Mentalese fails to do the job it is supposed to do: to provide a scaffolding for meaning that supports complex thought, and the acquisition of language.

Fodor's retort

One way to circumvent the grounding problems I've been discussing is to claim that Mentalese is innate – does this sound familiar? At a stroke, the grounding problems, and the issue of homunculi, disappear. Mentalese is in everyone's heads because we are born with the set of symbols on which Mentalese runs. And this move neatly solves the conundrum of the relationship between the concepts that help Mentalese run, and the states of affairs – presumably in the real world – that they are representations of. The grounding problem is resolved, as the symbols that make up Mentalese are in our heads to begin with.

But could it really be the case that all concepts are innate – which is what such a view commits us to? Concepts such as *red*, *doorknob* and *supermodel* would presumably, on this view, be hard-wired into the microcircuitry of the human brain, in the same way as Universal Grammar. Fodor's position in his classic 1975 book *The Language of Thought* is more or less precisely this. And Fodor thought that concepts had to be innate because they couldn't be learned; to learn concepts would necessarily require hypothesis formation and subsequent confirmation: it would require a set of concepts to already be in situ for the learning process to occur in the first place; there already have to be at least some concepts in place that can be used to make sense of the ones being learned. And so, Fodor reasoned, there must be a core set of conceptual primitives – innate concepts – that humans come into the world pre-equipped with.

On the face of it, this argument is brilliant. If we are born with a core set of primitive concepts, we each have the conceptual resources, at least in principle, to represent all the concepts we might ever need. After all, primitives can be combined, using the conceptual syntax of Mentalese, to construct more complex concepts.

But on this account, how do we then obtain the rich and varied kaleidoscope of ideas and concepts we end up with, from underwater basket-weaving to mediaeval musicology? The symbols for complex concepts still have to get aligned somehow with the things in the real world that they are representations of. Fodor claimed that the range of concepts that populate our language of thought get triggered by our experiences when interacting in our socio-physical world of experience. For instance, when we perceive the experiences 'green' or 'triangular' in the world 'out there', this somehow triggers a concept, or, rather, a symbol, that then comes to represent these experiences in Mentalese.

But a problem with this account still exists. Take the concept 'doorknob'. How does this get triggered in the mind, by experience? Are we really to think that we are, in some sense, born with the semantic value of doorknobhood, or the potential to construct it from conceptual primitives? And by interacting with doorknobs, when we enter and leave rooms and buildings, this innate capacity for doorknobhood gets triggered? This seems somewhat far-fetched.

And in later work, Fodor does attempt to address the – frankly, preposterous – claim that concepts such as 'doorknob' might in fact be hard-wired into the human brain at birth.[23] He argues that it is not that we are born with a prior concept – or a conceptual potential, which then gets triggered by experience. Rather, a symbol becomes locked to the experience of stereotypical instances in the world. And this is achieved with the help of experience.[24] On this revised account, we aren't, in fact, born with the semantic value for 'doorknobhood', such that we know what doorknobs are before we interact with them. Instead, Fodor now contends, a mental symbol acts as a place-marker in Mentalese, which becomes 'locked' to our experiences, in the external world, upon interacting with doorknobs. Hence, our 'concept' for doorknobhood is merely a token; the meaning associated with it is to be found in the external world. Hence, symbols, in Mentalese, provide an index to an experience type – for instance, 'doorknobhood'.

But this revised account gives rise to a further problem. How do symbols get to lock to their experience types in the world 'out there'? How does symbol X know to lock to experience Y? Fodor concludes that this is not the proper concern of cognitive psychology. In other words, we don't know, and, staggering as it may seem, he suggests we shouldn't really worry too much about that. Writing in 2008, he says: "maybe there aren't any innate ideas after all".[25] What we have, then, are merely innate mechanisms, that lock symbols in the mind to experiences in the world.

In the final analysis, the attempt to solve grounding by making representations innate is flawed – whether the concepts themselves are innate, as in early Fodor, or whether a 'locking' mechanism is invoked that ties them to experiences, as in the later Fodor. If mental representations are innate then learning must be excluded. But this then leads to other problems. Ultimately, saving a nativist account of concepts – one that is bent on excluding learning – seems to be too tall an order.

Intelligent bodies, embodied minds

The virtually insurmountable grounding problem faced by Mentalese is a consequence of the view of mind it assumes: the mind is an information processor, a computer. In particular, the computational mind requires that representations are neutral with respect to action and behaviour. In Mentalese, the symbol that represents the state of affairs in the world – that it is locked to – is quite unlike the thing it represents.

Traditionally, psychology has distinguished between perception, cognition and action – the so-called 'sense-think-act' model. While the brain constructs perceptual representations of the world, by converting energy signals from the external environment into nerve signals that the brain can recognise, in response, perceptual images or percepts are constructed. A percept, such as an image of a cat, or the sensation of being touched gently down one's spine, for instance, involves the temporal integration of different sensory experiences from various parts of the cerebral cortex. Now, in Mentalese, these percepts would somehow have to facilitate locking between another symbol, an abstract concept in the language of thought, and the state of affairs in the real world. But the symbol in Mentalese is abstract: it bears no relation to the cat, nor to the sensuous experience of being stroked on the back.

The alternative view, the one advanced by the language-as-use thesis, is that the representations that arise in human minds are, in fact, closely related to and resemble what it is that they represent. As human bodies interact with and act on our environment, the mental representations that arise reflect the nature of our embodied experience.[26] The philosopher of cognitive science Andy Clark has argued that the concepts assumed in Mentalese are action-neutral. What he means is that Mentalese believes our concepts are detached from context, from the real-life situations in which they arise: such concepts assume a neutral, or objective 'God's eye' view of the world.[27] But, such a view of the world is impossible (unless you're God): concepts arise from *our* understanding of and *our* interaction with the world. Concepts are *always* situated; they can never be perspective- or action-neutral.

Clark's point is that intelligent behaviour is geared towards acting *in* the world. And having bodies that are adapted to the ecological niche we inhabit makes it easier for our brains to support and control them. For instance, learning to walk is relatively easy for humans because we are born with 'intelligent' legs: our legs 'know' how to walk. Human legs are unusually long compared to those of other primates: they have evolved exclusively for bipedalism. Our legs are 171 per cent of the length of the human trunk, on average. This compares to 111 per cent for orang-utans and 128 per cent for chimpanzees. Human calf and gluteal muscles are adapted for walking upright on two legs, while the knee caps constrain the degrees of motion possible.[28]

Other aspects of the human organism have evolved in response to bipedalism: the human centre of gravity has shifted, so that we don't topple over. And this has resulted from the reorganisation of our internal organs compared to our primate cousins. This reorganisation is a co-evolutionary adaptation to our gradual shift to bipedalism: it's no good having intelligent legs that allow you to walk if you keep falling over like someone perpetually drunk. Moreover, the human double S-shape vertical column serves as a shock-absorber.[29]

From this sort of perspective, concepts arise from intelligent bodies: our mental representations emulate the experiences they are representations of.[30] The representations are analogue, providing action-orientated representations.[31] They are analogue in the sense of being 'like' or 'similar' to the things they are representations of. And their purpose is to help the body perform its 'intelligent' behaviour; hence they should be geared towards action. A concept for a 'doorknob', for instance, doesn't just tell its human owner what a knoorknob looks and feels like. It also tells us what doorknobs are for, and *how* to use them to open doors: a concept for 'doorknobhood' arises from our embodied interaction with doorknobs.

So if, as I am claiming, representations directly reflect our intelligent bodies – our embodiment – then there should be reflexes of them in our minds. Our concepts should reflect our embodiment.

Metaphors we live by

In their now classic work, linguist George Lakoff and philosopher Mark Johnson have argued that abstract concepts – concepts like 'love', 'justice', 'inflation' and 'time' – are built from embodied experience.[32] The body of evidence they provide appears to be overwhelming, coming from language but providing insight into the nature and structure of thought. The sorts of experiences that we use to structure abstract ideas, according to Lakoff and Johnson, arise from our interaction in and with the world. This structuring comes from our experience of moving about in space, from picking up and putting down objects, and from bumping into things. It derives from giving objects to others, and from receiving things in return. It is these sorts of experiences that provide us with the inferential structure that makes up our understanding of relatively abstract states like 'love', 'death', 'time' and countless others. Lakoff and Johnson propose that complex sets of abstract concepts in our minds are structured in terms of more concrete sets of embodied experiences.

Take the example of the concept 'love'. One particularly common way in which we talk and think about a love relationship is in terms of journeys. Consider the following everyday expressions which we might use to describe aspects of a love relationship:

> Look *how far* we've *come*. We're at *a crossroads*. We'll just have to *go our separate ways*. We can't *turn back* now. I don't think this relationship is *going anywhere*. *Where* are we? We're *stuck*.

It's been *a long, bumpy road.* This relationship is *a dead-end street.*
We're just *spinning our wheels.* Our marriage is *on the rocks.*
This relationship *is foundering.*[33]

On the face of it, these expressions literally relate to travel: I have
italicised the relevant 'travel' terms to make it easier to pick them
out. Yet no one gets confused. If you, in attempting a heart-to-
heart about the state of your relationship, said to your lover
"We're at a crossroads", you would be bemused at the very least
if he or she started discussing which way to drive. We effortlessly
understand that an expression such as this has very little to do
with a literal journey.

Lakoff and Johnson contend that abstract concepts such
as 'love' are systematically structured in terms of more concrete
embodied experiences, in this case journeys. In poetry, and
rhetoric, using language from one domain to talk about
something else is typically referred to as metaphor. Lakoff
and Johnson point out that the structuring of more abstract
concepts, in terms of more concrete embodied experiences,
is metaphor-like. But, crucially, the difference is that, in
understanding love in terms of journeys, this amounts to more
than mere word-play. These 'conceptual' metaphors seem
to provide the mind with a foundational structuring principle;
they allow us to articulate complex and abstract ideas, by
drawing on some of the experiences we know and understand best of all: our embodied interactions with the socio-
physical world.

In fact, our understanding of 'love' constitutes a large-scale
body of knowledge: a domain. Moreover, the domain of LOVE
is made up of a range of distinct, albeit related, concepts.
These include concepts for 'lovers', the love 'relationship', 'events'
that take place in the love relationship, 'difficulties' that take place
in the relationship, 'progress' we make in resolving these difficulties, and in developing the relationship, and so on. We also have
concepts for the 'choices' about what to do in the relationship,
such as moving in together, whether to split up, the nature of

the 'intimate side' of the relationship, and, more generally, the shared and separate 'goals' we might have for the relationship.

Similarly, in our minds we represent a range of concepts relating to the domain of JOURNEY. These include concepts for the 'travellers', the 'vehicle' used for the journey – plane, train or automobile – the 'distance' covered, 'obstacles' encountered, such as traffic jams that lead to delays and hence impediments to the progress of the journey, our decisions about the 'direction' and the 'route' to be taken, and our knowledge about 'destinations'.

The conceptual metaphor LOVE IS A JOURNEY provides us with the conceptual resources for systematically drawing on notions from the domain of JOURNEY, and using them to add structure to, and so understand better, corresponding ideas in the more abstract domain of LOVE. For instance, the lovers in the domain of LOVE are structured in terms of travellers so that we understand lovers *in terms of* travellers. Similarly, the love relationship itself is structured in terms of the vehicle used on the journey. For this reason, we can talk about marriage *foundering, being on the rocks*, or *stuck in a rut* and understand expressions such as these as relating, not literally to a journey, but rather, to two people in a long-term love relationship that is troubled in some way.

Moreover, it must be the case that we have knowledge of the sort specified by the conceptual metaphor stored in our heads. If this were not so, we wouldn't be able to understand these English expressions. The linguistic expressions provide an important line of evidence for the existence of the conceptual metaphor. I have summarised the correspondences between the two domains that make up the conceptual metaphor LOVE IS A JOURNEY in the table below. In the table, the arrow signals that content is projected from a more concrete concept in the domain of JOURNEY onto a more abstract, corresponding concept in the domain of LOVE. For instance, the concept for travellers from the domain of JOURNEY maps onto the concept for lovers in the domain of LOVE. These corresponding concepts are thus established as paired concepts within the conceptual metaphor.

While language reveals how the knowledge in our minds is organised, language also shows there to be a directionality

Correspondences that populate the LOVE IS A JOURNEY conceptual metaphor

Source domain: Journey		Target domain: Love
TRAVELLERS	→	LOVERS
VEHICLE	→	LOVE RELATIONSHIP
JOURNEY	→	EVENTS IN THE RELATIONSHIP
DISTANCE COVERED	→	PROGRESS MADE
OBSTACLES ENCOUNTERED	→	DIFFICULTIES EXPERIENCED
DECISIONS ABOUT DIRECTION	→	CHOICES ABOUT WHAT TO DO
DESTINATION OF THE JOURNEY	→	GOALS OF THE RELATIONSHIP

associated with this patterning. While we speak of, and think about, love in terms of journeys, the reverse doesn't hold. After all, we don't make use of expressions relating to love relationships in order to discuss journeys. For example, the expression *They have just got married* cannot mean *They have just started their journey*, whereas *They have just started their journey* can mean *They have just got married*. This asymmetric patterning in language reveals a directionality in our minds. The correspondences themselves are asymmetric, as represented by the arrows in the table for LOVE IS A JOURNEY: they go in one direction.

The point, then, of this discussion is the following: language points to conceptual metaphors. But conceptual metaphors are knowledge structures in our minds, rather than in language per se, although they facilitate language use. And, crucially, what this demonstrates is the embodied nature of our minds. Abstract ideas, such as 'love', are systematically structured, and not in a perspective-neutral way. On the contrary, our concept of love is structured in terms of embodied experience: our experience of engaging in long-term, purposeful activities such as journeys.

Embodiment effects in the brain

Conceptual metaphors provide an important line of evidence for the embodied nature of our minds. Their presumed existence reveals that concepts are not simply logical relations that lock to states of affairs in the world. Concepts directly reflect our embodied action and interaction in and with the world. But, while suggestive, the evidence provided by Lakoff and Johnson is indirect. After all, they use evidence from language to *infer* the existence of conceptual metaphors. They claim that conceptual metaphors – knowledge structures that project content drawn from embodied experience onto abstract concepts – must exist, because this is what language appears to be telling us. We talk about love in terms of journeys, in order to understand better the nature of love. And from that, we can conclude, they suggest, that conceptual metaphors must underlie such language use. But is there more direct evidence? Can we find additional support from experimental psychology and cognitive neuroscience, which examine what the brain is actually doing when it's processing language, and the concepts upon which language draws?

Everyone agrees that language draws on concepts. In order to be able to use language to communicate, we encode and so externalise concepts. When we use language to 'get our ideas across', the 'ideas' are our concepts, which we're using language to convey. When I tell a work colleague why I'm so tired, over a morning coffee – I was kept awake by two cats yowling at one another outside in the small hours for what seemed an eternity – I'm drawing on my concepts, my mental representations of the world. And I'm assuming my colleague also has concepts for cats and the territorial displays they engage in, in order to understand my narrative.

Direct evidence for the nature of concepts comes from patterns of activation in the brain when we use language, and when we comprehend it. If concepts are embodied, as claimed by the language-as-use thesis, then we *would* expect to see the brain regions that process particular experiences lighting up when we use language to describe those same experiences. For instance, we know that when someone uses a hammer to knock in a nail, or even when they watch another person wield a hammer, a particular region of the brain's motor cortex becomes active. If our concept for 'hammer' is embodied, then we would expect to see the same region of the brain light up when we use or understand language to describe a hammering event. This is because – so the language-as-use thesis claims – concepts are directly grounded in the experiences they are representations of. In terms of brain activity, concepts arise directly from the perceptual experiences that give rise to concepts. Hence, automatic and instantaneous activation of the brain region that processes hammering, when we also talk about a hammering event, would constitute an embodiment effect: a directly observable trace of the embodied nature of concepts when we use language. And embodiment effects would provide a direct means of confirming Lakoff and Johnson's contention that concepts are embodied.

But Mentalese, which assumes that the mind is essentially a computer, takes the view that concepts are abstract symbols. And as we've seen, these symbols get locked to states of affairs in the world, rather than actually embodying the states of affairs. Consequently, concepts in Mentalese bear no relation to the experiences and states that they are locked to. In Mentalese, concepts are abstract logical relations, they are disembodied symbols – which is why Mentalese has such a hard time accounting for how concepts are grounded, and, thus, how they obtain their meaning. Consequently, Mentalese predicts that there should be no such thing as embodiment effects: when concepts are deployed in language use, this does not involve sensorimotor regions of the brain. When we draw on concepts to describe a hammer, it is irrelevant whether the motor cortex becomes active or not. In other words, we are perfectly capable of discussing hammering nails into planks of wood without our motor cortex ever becoming activated.

Recent research by experimental psychologists has studied human behaviour during language use. And work by neuroscientists now allows us direct glimpses into the working of the brain as we produce and comprehend language. Both types of information reveal that embodiment effects do indeed occur.

One type of embodiment effect relates to the specific brain regions that are activated when we use certain words, or types of words. For instance, specific parts of the outer layer of the brain, the cortex, process and store sensory information: visual, auditory and tactile experience. Other parts of the cortex process motor information: information relating to hand or body movements. And finally, other regions of the brain, below the cortex – such as the amygdala – process and store emotional experience. Recent findings have shown that each of these brain regions is automatically, and immediately, activated when corresponding body-based language is understood.[34]

For example, brain regions that are active during the processing of actions, such as using tools like hammers, screwdrivers and saws, are automatically activated when we hear or read sentences relating to using tools of these kinds.[35] Put another way, when you or I understand an expression such as *He hammered the nail*, there is automatic and immediate activation of that part of the brain that is normally engaged when we perceive or enact hammering. Understanding language seems to require activation of just those parts of the brain responsible for the actions to begin with. This, then, constitutes an embodiment effect. If the brain's perceptual system for processing hammering played no essential role in our concept for hammering, as predicted by Mentalese, then the use of language should not – or need not – lead to direct activation of just that part of the brain that processes our experience of hammering. What this shows is that concepts relating to 'hammering', encoded and externalised via language, are more directly grounded in embodied states than Mentalese assumes.

Here's another example: regions of the brain that process visual information are activated when we comprehend words and sentences relating to visual information, such as object shape and orientation.[36] For instance, visual processing areas of the brain responsible for recognising distinct animal shapes become activated when we hear or see certain animal words.[37] And finally, language involving emotional responses also results in automatic activation of the relevant brain regions. For instance, threat words such as *destroy* and *mutilate* automatically activate parts of the amygdala.[38] This is an evolutionarily older part of the subcortical brain. The amygdala has been established, by neurobiologists, as being involved in emotional processing.[39]

Thus far, I've been discussing one type of embodiment effect: the automatic and immediate activation of brain regions in order to understand corresponding linguistic expressions. Another type of embodiment effect is behaviour. Human subjects, when using or understanding language, behave, in a myriad subtle ways, as if they are engaged in the sensorimotor activity that corresponds to the sensorimotor language; it is as if language primes language users for particular actions. For instance, when reading about throwing a dart in a game of darts in a pub, we automatically activate muscle systems which ready the hand grip common to dart throwing; when we use or hear language, the eye and hand movements of subjects are consistent with the sensorimotor activity being described.[40] It is as if language facilitates the vicarious experience of the events being described in language. The psycholinguist Rolf Zwaan has described this in terms of language users being immersed experiencers. He contends that "language is a set of cues to the comprehender to construct an experiential (perception plus action) simulation of the described situation".[41] And this could only be so if language provides direct access to representations of body-based states: concepts are embodied.

Behavioural evidence for immersion in embodied states, when using language, comes from the psychology lab. In one experiment, subjects were asked to judge whether action sentences such as *He closed the drawer* were meaningful or not.[42] Subjects did this by pressing one of two buttons, which were located sequentially in front of the subject. The button signalling that a sentence was meaningful was closer to the subject and thus involved them moving their hand towards their body, the same direction of motor control required to open a drawer. It was found that responses – judging whether the sentences were correct or not – were faster when the direction of motion corresponded to that described in the sentence. This finding supports the idea that bodily motor states are automatically activated when reading a corresponding sentence. But when the action required to press the button was at odds with the action described by the sentence, the response was slower. What this shows is that motor actions that are contrary to the actions described in language seem to interfere with our understanding of the actions being described. And here's the money shot: this can only be the case if understanding language involves activation of just those sorts of embodied experiences described by the language – in this case the actual activation of muscle groups required to open or close drawers.

Strikingly, and consistent with the idea that more abstract concepts like 'love' and 'justice' are structured in terms of more concrete concepts, abstract concepts also appear to exhibit embodiment effects. Lakoff and Johnson have argued that we conceptualise communication as physical transfer, for instance.[43] Evidence for this comes from linguistic examples, as when we say things like *I couldn't get my ideas across*, *Put it into words*, and so on. The cognitive scientist Arthur Glenberg, who carried out the experiments involving opening and closing drawers that I've been describing, found the same pattern applied to abstract concepts.

Consider a sentence like *I gave him some words of wisdom*. Metaphorically, this involves transferring the *words of wisdom* – some advice – from the speaker to the listener, which is to say: a pattern of motion away from the body. The time taken to say whether the sentence was semantically acceptable was quicker when the button to be pressed involved an action away from, rather than towards, the subjects' bodies. So, physical action that accorded with the metaphorical 'action' facilitated faster under-standing of the linguistic expression. This reveals an embodiment effect for abstract language, a conclusion in keeping with the findings uncovered, on the basis of analysing language, by Lakoff and Johnson.

Further evidence for abstract concepts being structured, at least in part, by sensorimotor experience comes from the work of the psychologist Daniel Casasanto.[44] In one experiment, he and a colleague investigated abstract concepts such as 'pride' and 'shame': people were asked to recount experiences that had either made them proud, or ashamed. They did so whilst simultaneously moving marbles either from a lower tray to a higher tray, or vice versa. Lakoff and Johnson have observed that positive experiences are metaphorically conceptualised as being up, while negative experiences are metaphorically understood to be down, as when we say: *She's down in the dumps, I'm feeling low* or *He's a bit down today.* Casasanto found that the speed and efficiency of the autobiographical retelling was influenced by whether the direction of the marble movements was congruent with the autobiographical memory: upwards for pride, downwards for shame. This provides further compelling evidence that even abstract language appears to involve automatic activation of sensorimotor experiences in the brain: we understand what the words *pride* and *shame* mean, in part, by virtue of the upward and downward trajectories which metaphorically structure them. And this knowledge is automatically activated when we use language to describe experiences that made us proud or ashamed.

Overall, contemporary research in cognitive neuroscience and experimental psychology demonstrates that concepts appear to be embodied. Concepts are not disembodied and ungrounded symbols as conceived by proponents of Mentalese.

So, where does this leave us?

In *The Language Instinct*, Pinker claims that Mentalese, and the computational mind, are "as fundamental to cognitive science as the cell doctrine is to biology and plate tectonics is to geology." This is certainly true of what has been referred to as first-generation cognitive science.[45] But since the 1980s, and with the development of a variety of techniques for directly observing what the brain is doing when it processes information – techniques that range from neuroimaging to measuring the electrical pulses given off by the brain during activity – the view enshrined by Mentalese looks increasingly untenable.

One difficulty for Mentalese is that it wants concepts to be innate – Fodor assumed that concepts already had to be in place for language learning to take place. And so, in some form or another, we must be born with some sort of conceptual representation.[46] Another difficulty is that the view of the mind assumed by Mentalese, and the larger language-as-instinct ecosystem of beliefs, is that of a computer. Hence, Mentalese is a logical operating system, and representations are perspective-neutral. But the evidence suggests that the mind is embodied: concepts are not abstract symbols that capture perspective-neutral relations between concepts and the states of affairs that hold in the world. Concepts derive from the world itself, and specifically our egocentric, embodied view of the world. Abstract concepts are constructed from more concrete experiences. And even concrete concepts such as hammers and hammering – you can't get much more concrete than that – are directly tied to the experiences that the concepts are representations of. Concepts are not meaningless symbols that get locked to experiences. Rather, concepts derive from the experiences themselves. Moreover, the same brain structures that process our perception of experiences also appear to play a constitutive role in how those same experiences are represented when the experience itself has faded from view. Language activates the same brain regions, when we communicate, as are activated when we process and perceive those self-same experiences in the 'here and now'.

Mentalese is supposed to provide a "preexisting conceptual space, programmed into our biological nature", and words are then essentially labels for our pre-existing concepts.[47] Mentalese provides a biologically programmed operating system that allows us to acquire linguistic meaning in the first place. But, in this chapter, I have been arguing that Mentalese is wrong because its view of the mind, and the nature of mental representations – concepts – is wrong. It is also wrong because it's consequently forced to deny, or at the very least to restrict, any significant role for learning and experience.

The language-as-instinct thesis is an example of radical nativism.[48] But it actually amounts to a false choice, by largely denying experience a meaningful role in the formation of concepts. I have been claiming, in previous chapters, that humans do bring a lot of innate machinery to the table. For instance, we now know that humans are exceptionally adept at pattern-recognition and intention-reading. In part, these abilities are underscored by sophisticated abstraction facilities that allow us to build exquisitely complex relational knowledge, and detailed knowledge about experiences, including the sounds and grammatical patterns we decipher from the gobbledygook we start with as infants, and which, ultimately, becomes our mother tongue(s). These abilities amount to innately prescribed neurological constraints, and these guide learning in top-down fashion. But there is still learning, and learning draws upon experience. And in the case of language learning, the experience is the language input we are immersed in even before birth.

In the final analysis, the received choice between nature (nativism) and nurture (experience) unduly polarises the situation. I am not trying to persuade you that innate specifications play no role: they do, and they drive the learning process. But we do learn, and our repository of concepts emerges from experience and the learning process.

7   Is thought independent of language?

Myth: *Thought is independent of and cannot be dramatically influenced by language. The idea that systematic patterns in grammatical and semantic representations across languages give rise to corresponding differences in patterns of thought across communities (the principle of linguistic relativity) is utterly wrong.*

The Holy Roman Emperor, Charles V, who ruled from 1519 to 1556, is often claimed to have uttered the following: "I speak Spanish to God, Italian to Women, French to Men, and German to my Horse." The idea, of course, is that each language has a particular character associated with it, which lends itself to specific functions: Spanish is the *Linguica Domnichi*, literally 'Language of God'; Italian is the 'Language of Love'; French is the 'Language of Diplomacy'; and German, with – some say – harsh, guttural sounds, is ideal for giving orders. But a number of researchers have gone further than this. It has been proposed that the distinct character of a language gives rise to wholesale differences in the way its native speakers think, and the manner in which we perceive the world: different languages entail a distinctive worldview. The way a language encodes space, time, colour, or any other domain has profound consequences for how its speakers perceive those domains of experience in their everyday lives. This idea is often referred to as linguistic relativity: differences across languages give rise to corresponding differences in how speakers of a given language think, and how they perceive the world.

But the claim made by linguistic relativity amounts to more than simply the idea that we use language to influence the thoughts of others. After all, as observed by cognitive scientists Paul Bloom and Frank Keil, "nobody doubts that language can inform, convince, persuade, soothe, dismay, encourage and so on".[1] It is a truism, then, that language influences thought: we do so almost every time we use language. Even a banal expression such as *Shut the door on your way out, please* illustrates this: we deploy language countless times a day in order to try and shape the thoughts of others.

The principle of linguistic relativity is more than this: it amounts to the claim that habitual ways of thinking, and of perceiving the world, are fundamentally influenced by structural differences across languages. The most famous exponent of this idea was the American linguist Benjamin Lee Whorf. Whorf, writing in the 1940s, claimed the following:

> We dissect nature along lines laid down by our native language. The categories and types that we isolate from the world of phenomena we do not find there because they stare every observer in the face; on the contrary, the world is presented in a kaleidoscope flux of impressions which has to be organized by our minds – and this means largely by the linguistic systems of our minds. We cut nature up, organize it into concepts, and ascribe significances as we do, largely because ... [it] is codified in the patterns of our language.[2]

But in *The Language Instinct*, Steven Pinker is quite clear:

> it is wrong, all wrong. The idea that thought is the same thing as language is an example of what can be called a conventional absurdity: a statement that goes against all common sense but that everyone believes because they dimly recall having heard it somewhere and because it is so pregnant with implications.[3]

Pinker goes on:

> there is no scientific evidence that languages dramatically shape their speakers' ways of thinking ... The idea that language shapes thinking seemed plausible when scientists were in the dark about how thinking works or even how to study it. Now that cognitive scientists know how to think about thinking, there is less of a temptation to equate it with language just because words are more palpable than thoughts.[4]

Of course, Pinker, and other language-as-instinct rationalists *would* argue against the relativistic effects of languages on thought, wouldn't they? After all, the language-as-instinct thesis assumes there is a language of thought, Mentalese, independent and quite separate from language. And Mentalese, at least in part, must be innate. For without Mentalese, natural languages like English, Malay and Mandarin couldn't be acquired in the first place. If natural languages were then capable of influencing and modifying thought, and our language of thought, this would undermine the presumed existence of an innately prescribed Mentalese. The language-as-instinct thesis maintains that we all share the same set of innately specified psychological faculties. On this account, the mind is largely a biological construction, and variability due to cultural and linguistic differences is negligible.

But, as we shall see in this chapter, there is now a significant body of evidence which makes it clear that the distinctive nature of languages does influence the habitual nature of how speakers of different languages think, and perceive the world. For instance, Greek speakers who use different terms for light blue (*ghalazio*) and dark blue (*ble*) can more easily discriminate shades of blue; English speakers, who lack this linguistic distinction, are less able to do this. In terms of space, speakers of languages that primarily employ absolute spatial coordinates, such as the Aboriginal language Guugu Yimithirr, carry out non-linguistic spatial tasks differently from speakers of languages that primarily employ relational spatial coordinates, such as English and Dutch. In terms of gender, Spanish and German speakers show effects of grammatical gender on classification, when asked to assign either a male or female voice to an animate object in a picture; English speakers, who lack grammatical gender, don't show this effect. Findings like these paint a very different picture from the one portrayed by the 'language myth'. Language augments and influences habitual thought and perception;[5] the language we happen to speak influences how we perceive the world. And, ultimately, it is the language-as-instinct thesis that is "wrong, all wrong."

Who's afraid of the Big Bad Whorf?

Psychologist Daniel Casasanto has noted, in an article whose title gives this section its heading, that some researchers find Whorf's principle of linguistic relativity to be threatening.[6] But why is Whorf such a bogeyman for some? And what makes his notion of linguistic relativity such a dangerous idea?

The rationalists fear linguistic relativity – the very idea of it – and they hate it, with a passion: it directly contradicts everything they stand for – if relativism is anywhere near right, then the rationalist house burns down, or collapses, like a tower of cards without a foundation. And this fear and loathing in parts of the Academy can often, paradoxically, be highly irrational indeed. Relativity is often criticised without argumentative support, or ridiculed, just for the audacity of existing as an intellectual idea to begin with. Jerry Fodor, more candid than most about his irrational fear, just hates it. He says: "The thing is: I hate relativism. I hate relativism more than I hate anything else, excepting, maybe, fiberglass powerboats."[7] Fodor continues, illustrating further his irrational contempt: "surely, *surely*, no one but a relativist would drive a fiberglass powerboat".[8]

Fodor's objection is that relativism overlooks what he deems to be "the fixed structure of human nature".[9] Mentalese provides *the* fixed structure – as we saw in the previous chapter. If language could interfere with this innate set of concepts, then the fixed structure would no longer be fixed – anathema to a rationalist.

Others are more coy, but no less damning. Pinker's strategy is to set up straw men, which he then eloquently – but mercilessly – ridicules.[10] But don't be fooled, there is no serious argument presented – not on this occasion. Pinker takes an untenable and extreme version of what he claims Whorf said, and then pokes fun at it – a common modus operandi employed by those who are afraid. Pinker argues that Whorf was wrong because he equated language with thought: that Whorf assumes that language causes or determines thought in the first place. This is the "conventional absurdity" that Pinker refers to in the first of his quotations above. For Pinker, Whorf was either romantically naïve about the effects of language, or, worse, like the poorly read and ill-educated, credulous.

But this argument is a classic straw man: it is set up to fail, being made of straw. Whorf never claimed that language determined thought. As we shall see, the thesis of linguistic determinism, which nobody believes, and which Whorf explicitly rejected, was attributed to him long after his death. But Pinker has bought into the very myths peddled by the rationalist tradition for which he is cheerleader-in-chief, and which lives in fear of linguistic relativity. In the final analysis, the language-as-instinct crowd should be afraid, very afraid: linguistic relativity, once and for all, explodes the myth of the language-as-instinct thesis.

The rise of the Sapir–Whorf hypothesis

Benjamin Lee Whorf became interested in linguistics in 1924, and studied it, as a hobby, alongside his full-time job as an engineer. In 1931, Whorf began to attend university classes on a part-time basis, studying with one of the leading linguists of the time, Edward Sapir.[11] Amongst other things covered in his teaching, Sapir touched on what he referred to as "relativity of concepts . . . [and] the relativity of the form of thought which results from linguistic study".[12] The notion of the relativistic effect of different languages on thought captured Whorf's imagination; and so he became captivated by the idea that he was to develop and become famous for. Because Whorf's claims have often been disputed and misrepresented since his death, let's see exactly what his formulation of his principle of linguistic relativity was:

> Users of markedly different grammars are pointed by their
> grammars toward different types of observations and different
> evaluations of externally similar acts of observation, and hence
> are not equivalent as observers but must arrive at somewhat
> different views of the world.[13]

Indeed, as pointed out by the Whorf scholar, Penny Lee, post-war research rarely ever took Whorf's principle, or his statements, as their starting point.[14] Rather, his writings were, on the contrary, ignored, and his ideas largely distorted.[15]

For one thing, the so-called 'Sapir–Whorf hypothesis' was not due to either Sapir or Whorf. Sapir – whose research was not primarily concerned with relativity – and Whorf were lumped together: the term 'Sapir–Whorf hypothesis' was coined in the 1950s, over ten years after both men had been dead – Sapir died in 1939, and Whorf in 1941.[16] Moreover, Whorf's principle emanated from an anthropological research tradition; it was not, strictly speaking, a hypothesis. But, in the 1950s, psychologists Eric Lenneberg and Roger Brown sought to test empirically the notion of linguistic relativity. And to do so, they reformulated it in such a way that it could be tested, producing two testable formulations.[17] One, the so-called 'strong version' of relativity, holds that language causes a cognitive restructuring: language causes or determines thought. This is otherwise known as linguistic determinism, Pinker's "conventional absurdity". The second hypothesis, which came to be known as the 'weak version', claims instead that language influences a cognitive restructuring, rather than causing it. But neither formulation of the so-called 'Sapir–Whorf hypothesis' was due to Whorf, or Sapir. Indeed, on the issue of linguistic determinism, Whorf was explicit in arguing against it, saying the following:

> The tremendous importance of language cannot, in my opinion, be taken to mean necessarily that nothing is back of it of the nature of what has traditionally been called 'mind'. My own studies suggest, to me, that language, for all its kingly role, is in some sense a superficial embroidery upon deeper processes of consciousness, which are necessary before any communication, signalling, or symbolism whatsoever can occur.[18]

This demonstrates that, in point of fact, Whorf actually believed in something like the 'fixed structure' that Fodor claims is lacking in relativity. The delicious irony arising from it all is that

Pinker derides Whorf on the basis of the 'strong version' of the Sapir–Whorf hypothesis: linguistic determinism – language causes thought. But this strong version was a hypothesis not created by Whorf, but imagined by rationalist psychologists who were dead set against Whorf and linguistic relativity anyway. Moreover, Whorf explicitly disagreed with the thesis that was posthumously attributed to him. The issue of linguistic determinism became, incorrectly and disingenuously, associated with Whorf, growing in the rationalist sub-conscious like a cancer – Whorf was clearly wrong, they reasoned.

In more general terms, defenders of the language-as-instinct thesis have taken a leaf out of the casebook of Noam Chomsky. If you thought that academics play nicely, and fight fair, think again. Successful ideas are the currency, and they guarantee tenure, promotion, influence and fame; and they allow the successful academic to attract Ph.D. students who go out and evangelise, and so help to build intellectual empires. The best defence against ideas that threaten is ridicule. And, since the 1950s, until the intervention of John Lucy in the 1990s – whom I discuss below – relativity was largely dismissed; the study of linguistic relativity was, in effect, off-limits to several generations of researchers.

Born to colour the world?

The work which did more than any other to discredit Whorf's principle of linguistic relativity was the book *Basic Color Terms*, written by Brent Berlin and Paul Kay and published in 1969. As Stephen Levinson has put it: "No single work has done more to undermine the doctrine of linguistic relativity."[19]

Berlin and Kay argued that the colour domain exhibits cross-linguistic universals. And these are a consequence of an innate neurological pre-specification: colour perception is constrained by innate neurological mechanisms; humans are born with a colour sense. Based on an examination of twenty languages, and surveying the literature of a further close-to-eighty languages,

Berlin and Kay 'found' the following: languages are remarkably consistent in the number of colour terms they have, and in terms of the hues these pick out – Berlin and Kay used the idea of a 'focal hue' to capture the 'finding' that a colour term such as *red* consistently seems to pick out the vivid, truly red hue across languages that have a word for 'red', rather than say the dun or browny red hue associated with the colouring of a fox or a red squirrel. They concluded, from this, that colour terminology is universal, rather than being relativistic. And, this being the case, it was assumed that comparable universals would be found in most other domains.[20]

The publication of *Basic Color Terms* was widely praised as a landmark event, and it is still considered to be a classic by sociobiologists, evolutionary psychologists and ecological cognitive scientists alike.[21] Berlin and Kay argued that, despite the apparent diversity in the way different languages represent colour, this seeming diversity is, in fact, tightly constrained by universal building blocks for colour in the brain. They claimed that all humans share "species-specific bio-morphological structures" that govern the human colour sense.[22] And the fact that different languages exhibit a divergent set of colour terms is determined by evolutionary forces, shaped by human biology. In other words, colour terms emerge following a 'natural law' whereby more technologically advanced cultures develop more colour terms, but always as determined by our innately prescribed colour sense.

The colour terms apparent across the languages of the world emerge "in a continuous series, each later stage 'transcending' earlier stages in differentiation marking a metamorphosis along the path towards its *telos*", resulting in a full complement of colour terms.[23] This means that the inventory of colour terms each language possesses is not random or arbitrary: differences follow from an innately specified sequence of basic colour terms.

Before examining what the evolutionary sequence is, let's first consider the notion of a 'basic colour term'. According to Berlin and Kay, a basic colour term fulfils a number of quite specific criteria. First off, it must be a single word: so words like *reddy-brown* are excluded. Second, it cannot include affixes: hence terms such as *bluish*, that add the affix *-ish* to *blue*, also don't count. Third, the hues covered by a term cannot be included in the range covered by another more encompassing term. For instance, the word *crimson* covers a narrower range of hues subsumed by the more general term *red*. Hence, on this basis, *crimson* doesn't count as a basic colour term. In addition, a basic colour term must apply across the board; it may not be restricted to a specific type of entity. For instance, the colour term *blonde* only applies to hair, and hence doesn't count as a basic colour term. And finally, the colour described by the term must be psychologically salient for all speakers of the language. For instance, while the colours black and white are presumably psychologically salient in English, the colour of my mother's freezer isn't, at least not for speakers beyond my immediate family members.

Based on these criteria, Berlin and Kay claimed that the world's languages exhibit a possible maximum of eleven colour terms. And, by happy coincidence, English just happens to be such a language: a language that has completed the evolutionary trajectory and developed a complete set of basic colour terms. And these are black and white, red, green, yellow, blue, brown, purple, pink, orange and grey. Crucially, however, any given language need not exhibit the full set of eleven basic colour terms. And this brings us back to the idea of an evolutionary trajectory: Berlin and Kay thought that languages could be at different points in realising the full set of basic colour terms. A more technologically 'advanced' language, such as English, was already there, a consequence of cultural factors that help to progress the development of the full set of possible terms.

According to Berlin and Kay, the evolutionary sequence is as follows:

  (i)   all languages start with terms for black and white;
 (ii)   the third basic colour term a language develops will be red;
(iii)   the fourth basic colour term will be either green or yellow, although not both;

(iv) the fifth term will be either green or yellow, depending on what the fourth term developed was, such that the language now contains basic colour terms for both green *and* yellow;

(v) the sixth basic colour term developed will be a term for blue;

(vi) finally, a language will develop terms for brown, purple, pink, orange and/or grey, eventually leading to the full set: eleven basic colour terms.

In their cross-linguistic survey, Berlin and Kay found languages at each of the points on this trajectory; moreover, no language was found to contravene it. For instance, while a language such as Dani, spoken in the central highlands of western Papua New Guinea, contained two colour terms, for 'black' and 'white', languages such as English, Russian and others had reached the acme, in terms of the potential range of basic colour terms that is possible.

While the evolutionary sequence was based on a survey of different languages, Berlin and Kay argued that the order of the sequence is tightly determined by innate biological factors in terms of our colour sense. Writing in 1978, Kay and his colleague McDaniel claimed that: "basic color categories ... can be derived directly from the neural response patterns that underlie the perception of color".[24] In short, the brain has a hard-wired semantic code for colour. And this code consists of 'atoms', which manifest themselves as basic colour terms. The reason for there being just eleven basic colour terms is determined by our biology.

Moreover, even the order of the basic colour terms in the evolutionary trajectory was claimed to be determined by biological constraints. Kay and McDaniel argued that, of the eleven basic colour terms, six can be considered to be more fundamental. These are the colour 'atoms' that give rise to the English basic colour terms: *black*, *white*, plus the primary colours *red*, *yellow*, *green* and *blue*. And these appear earlier in the evolutionary sequence, as attested by languages that have just those terms and not later ones.

But this then presents a potential problem. Does this then mean that a language that is less far along the evolutionary trajectory – in terms of developing basic colour terms – cannot describe the full range of the colour spectrum? Apparently not. For instance, in Dani, which has, recall, just two basic colour terms, the term *mili* (black) can be used to express a wider range of colours than those associated with English *black*. It can be used to refer to cool and dark shades, including blue, green and black.[25] And *mola* (white) can be used for warm/light colours including red and yellow, as well as white.[26] Indeed, as cognitive psychologist Rosch Heider showed, the Dani are still able to categorise objects by colours for which they have no words.

In response to this finding, Kay and McDaniel proposed that, at the neurological level, colour atoms give rise to composite colour categories. And, in terms of language, those that have not evolved the full complement of basic colour terms are not disadvantaged: they can still refer to the totality of colour space. As in the case of Dani, the fewer basic colour terms a language has, the wider the spectrum of hues – and even colours – those terms can encompass.

In addition to identifying the set of eleven basic colour terms, Berlin and Kay, and their various collaborators, invited subjects to identify the hue that each basic colour term best designated. The idea here was to attempt to establish the ideal or focal hue for each term. In one procedure, a subject was shown a Munsell colour chart – a chart containing different colour 'chips', 330 of them in total, covering the colour spectrum. Each subject was then required to identify the chips that the basic colour term could apply to: for instance, the colour chip that best matched the designation of a basic colour term, for instance *red*. As Berlin and Kay reported: "it is rare that a category focus is displaced by more than two adjacent chips".[27] In short, no matter how broad the range of shades a basic colour term could be used to describe when referring to objects in the world, Berlin and Kay found that a basic colour term *always* had a closely delimited ideal or focal hue.

On the face of it, Berlin and Kay's proposed evolutionary trajectory for basic colour terms accords with findings from colour science. It was first proposed, as early as the 1800s, that the human visual system involves three paired colour systems, allowing humans to extract black and white, as well as the colours red and green, and blue and yellow, from visual experience. In the twentieth century, three types of cone photopigments were identified in the human retina.[28] And in the 1990s, pioneering vision scientists Russell and Karen de Valois proposed distinct brain circuits that facilitate the neurobiological basis for these paired colour systems.[29] Those findings and proposals seem to support the priority and evolutionary sequence of the basic colour terms identified by Berlin and Kay based on their cross-linguistic survey. Colour has a genetic basis, and appears to give rise to semantic universals that mirror this relative priority of colour perception in the human visual system and brain.

The body of work initiated by Berlin and Kay, culminating in the publication of the World Color Survey in 2009, had seemed to strike the death knell for linguistic relativity. Language, so it appeared, is tightly constrained by neurobiology. Cross-linguistic variation – at least in the domain of colour – is always determined by underlying semantic universals that are innately specified. And variation in colour across languages is a consequence of where a given language is at, in terms of lexicalising the eleven possible basic colour terms.

The research tradition initiated by Berlin and Kay has garnered further support from research on human babies prior to the acquisition of language. In one study, sixteen 4-month-old babies were exposed to lights of different colours. Pre-linguistic infants appeared to be better able to recognise focal colours associated with basic colour terms than the hues surrounding focal colours.[30] And so, the ability to recognise focal colours cannot be an artefact of language, as the 4-month-olds have yet to acquire it. This lent yet further support to the idea that basic colour terms – to which focal hues are supposed to be tied – are indeed a consequence of biological pre-specification, rather than being a consequence of language and/or culture.

The neo-Whorfian critique

In the 1990s, John Lucy published two volumes which helped re-establish linguistic relativity as a respectable arena of enquiry. Lucy, a Professor at the University of Chicago, and an expert in linguistic and psychological anthropology, mounted and led a sustained critique of the theory of basic colour terms.[31] Other researchers also pointed to a raft of theoretical and methodological problems with the approach adopted by Berlin and Kay.[32]

The neo-Whorfians have made four main criticisms of this research tradition as it relates to linguistic relativity.[33] First off, the theoretical construct of the 'basic colour term' is based on English. It is then assumed that basic colour terms – based on English – correspond to an innate biological specification. But the assumption that basic colour terms – based on English – correspond to universal semantic constraints, due to our common biology, biases the findings in advance. The 'finding' that other languages also have basic colour terms is a consequence of a self-fufilling prophecy: as English has been 'found' to exhibit basic colour terms, all other languages will too. But this is no way to investigate putative cross-linguistic universals; it assumes, much like Chomsky did, that colour in all of the world's languages will be, underlyingly, English-like. And as we shall see, other languages often do things in startlingly different ways.

Second, the linguistic analysis Berlin and Kay conducted was not very rigorous – to say the least. For most of the languages they 'examined', Berlin and Kay relied on second-hand sources, as they had no first-hand knowledge of the languages they were hoping to find basic colour terms in. To give you a sense of the problem, it is not even clear whether many of the putative basic colour terms Berlin and Kay 'uncovered', were from the same lexical class; for instance, in English, the basic colour terms – *white, black, red* and so on – are all adjectives. Yet, for many of the world's languages, colour expressions often come from different lexical classes. As we shall see shortly, one language, Yélî Dnye, draws its colour terms from several lexical classes, none of which is adjectives. And the Yélî language is far from exceptional in this regard. The difficulty here is that, without a more detailed linguistic analysis, there is relatively little basis for the assumption that what is being compared involves comparable words. And, that being the case, can we still claim that we are dealing with basic colour terms?

Third, many other languages do not conceptualise colour as an abstract domain independent of the objects that colour happens to be a property of. For instance, some languages do not even have a word corresponding to the English word *colour* – as we shall see later. This shows that colour is often not conceptualised as a stand-alone property in the way that it is in English. In many languages, colour is treated in combination with other surface properties. For English speakers this might sound a little odd. But think about the English 'colour' term *roan*: this encodes a surface pattern, rather than strictly colour – in this case, brown interspersed with white, as when we describe a horse as 'roan'. Some languages combine colour with other properties, such as dessication, as in the Old Germanic word *saur*, which meant yellow and dry. The problem, then, is that in languages with relatively simple colour technology – arguably the majority of the world's languages – lexical systems that combine colour with other aspects of an object's appearance are artificially excluded from being basic colour terms – as English is being used as the reference point. And this, then, distorts the true picture of how colour is represented in language, as the analysis only focuses on those linguistic features that correspond to the 'norm' derived from English.[34]

And finally, the 'basic colour term' project is flawed, in so far as it constitutes a riposte to linguistic relativity; as John Lucy has tellingly observed, linguistic relativity is the thesis that language influences non-linguistic aspects of thought: one cannot demonstrate that it is wrong by investigating the effect of our innate colour sense on language.[35] In fact, one has to demonstrate the reverse: that language doesn't influence psychophysics (in the domain of colour). Hence, the theory of basic colour terms cannot be said to refute the principle of linguistic relativity as ironically, it wasn't in fact investigating it.

The neo-Whorfian critique, led by John Lucy and others, argued that, at its core, the approach taken by Berlin and Kay adopted an unwarranted ethnocentric approach that biased findings in advance. And, in so doing, it failed to rule out the possibility that what other languages and cultures were doing was developing divergent semantic systems – rather than there being a single universal system – in the domain of colour, albeit an adaptation to a common human set of neurobiological constraints. By taking the English language in general, and in particular the culture of the English-speaking peoples – the British Isles, North America and the Antipodes – as its point of reference, it not only failed to establish what different linguistic systems – especially in non-western cultures – were doing, but led, inevitably, to the conclusion that all languages, even when strikingly diverse in terms of their colour systems, were essentially English-like.[36]

Lessons from Rossel Island

Since the original publication of Berlin and Kay's 1969 book, counter-examples have often been uncovered. For instance, Ainu hu – an ethnic language spoken on the northern Japanese island of Hokkaidō, and unrelated to Japanese – has a word that covers both 'red' and 'green', which, according to Berlin and Kay, are supposed to occupy distinct stages in the development of colour terms; this should therefore be impossible – as we have seen throughout this book, language, and the human mind, continue to surprise us.

In response to such examples, the evolutionary pattern first developed in 1969 underwent a series of revisions in later research, involving greater flexibility in terms of the sequence.[37] But what has remained is the claim that there is a single evolutionary sequence, it is universal, *and* it governs all languages.

Yet this principle would appear to be undermined in a devastating way by findings from one particular language: Yélî Dnye.

Yélî Dnye is spoken on Rossel Island, with a population of around 3,500 people. Rossel is a remote island, part of Papua New Guinea, in Oceania. As we saw in Chapter 3, it only takes one counter-example to invalidate a presumed universal pattern. And Yélî Dnye appears to be exactly that: it invalidates the claims for semantic universals made by Berlin and Kay – and, as we also saw in that chapter, the often quite striking diversity exhibited by human languages teaches us to be wary of positing absolute universals. Moreover, the general lesson is that, while rationalist explanations are appealing – they straightforwardly contrive to solve the problem of language learning and diversity – culture and usage are key in the development of a linguistic colour system – as we shall see below. While the Yélî language doesn't invalidate the findings from vision science – that humans have a biological specialisation for perceiving colour – the case of Rossel Island nevertheless illustrates the following: language develops in ways that, while constrained by biology, adopt often surprisingly divergent solutions. And these solutions arise due to language-specific usage-based pressures.

The colour system in Yélî Dnye has been studied extensively by linguistic anthropologist Stephen Levinson.[38] Levinson argues that the lesson from Rossel Island is that each of the following claims made by Berlin and Kay is demonstrably false:

Claim 1:   All languages have basic colour terms
Claim 2:   The colour spectrum is so salient a perceptual field
           that all cultures must systematically and
           exhaustively name the colour space
Claim 3:   For those basic colour terms that exist in any given
           language, there are corresponding focal colours –
           there is an ideal hue that is the prototypical shade
           for a given basic colour term
Claim 4:   The emergence of colour terms follows a universal
           evolutionary pattern

A noteworthy feature of Rossel Island culture is this: there is little interest in colour. For instance, there is no native artwork or handiwork in colour. The exception to this is hand-woven patterned baskets, which are usually uncoloured, or, if coloured, are black or blue. Moreover, the Rossel language doesn't have a word that corresponds to the English word *colour*: the domain of colour appears not to be a salient conceptual category independent of objects. For instance, in Yélî, it is not normally possible to ask what colour something is, as one can in English. Levinson reports that the equivalent question would be: *U pââ ló nté?* This translates as "Its body, what is it like?" Furthermore, colours are not usually associated with objects as a whole, but rather with surfaces. For instance, in Yélî it's not possible to say things such as *Europeans are white*, or *white man*. Rather, a Yélî speaker would convey this idea by saying the equivalent of: *The skin of Europeans is white*.

In terms of colour expressions, Yélî doesn't have a single lexical class from which colour reference is drawn. Yélî colour expressions are derived in two ways: from terms adapted from object names, or by using phrasal descriptions and similes, e.g., *like the parrot* (where "parrot" designates a particular species of parrot that happens to be red in colour). Moreover, when such expressions are derived from object terms, they are not strictly colour expressions, as they retain reference to the colour quality of the object from which they are derived. For instance, the Yélî word for a red parrot species on the island is *mtye*. This gives rise to the term *mtyemtye*, which is a doubling (or reduplication), of the word for 'parrot'. The derived word can be translated as "red like the red parrot".

In terms of the status of Yélî colour terms as basic colour expressions, all appear to fall foul of the criteria outlined by Berlin and Kay. None is a single, unreduplicated word. Moreover, the majority – arguably all – of the expressions used in Yélî do not exclusively denote colour information. For instance, the expression *yi kuu yââ*, which might be translated as "tree fresh leaves", is used by Yélî-speakers to refer to 'green'. But is doesn't exclusively mean green – it relates to young leaves growing on the tree. Moreover, and as Levinson points out, none of the expressions used by the Rossel islanders appears to have psychological salience as a colour term. Accordingly, it is difficult to make the case for Yélî having any basic colour terms at all.

As for claim 2, the tradition deriving from the work of Berlin and Kay came to assume that, due to the perceptual salience of colour, the basic colour terms of any language are adequate to describe colour space exhaustively. Writing in 1999, Paul Kay makes this claim crystal clear: "every language contains a small set of words – the basic colour terms – each of whose signification jointly partitions the psychological color space".[39] But when Levinson replicated the tests involving the Munsell colour chart used by Berlin and Kay, he found the following. Based on judgements by seven native speakers of Yélî Dnye, 40 per cent of the entire colour space was left undescribed, on average. At one extreme, one speaker declined to name 72 per cent of the coloured chips. And even the subject who attempted to name the most Munsell coloured chips left 24 per cent of colour space unnamed.

Indeed, other studies have underlined that speakers typically cannot name 100 per cent of the colour space. For instance, speakers of English who were shown sixty-five coloured Munsell chips could name 95 per cent of them. In contrast, speakers of Setswana – a language spoken in southern Africa – were only able to name 25 per cent of the same array of colours.[40] What these findings illustrate is that languages, and speakers, do not inevitably have the linguistic resources to name the entire colour space – and speakers of some languages can only name up to about a quarter of it. Moreover, there is quite considerable cross-cultural variation in how adept people are at naming the Munsell colour space.

The third claim relates to the presumption that colour expressions in a language will have an ideal or focal hue in the colour spectrum, even when the term can be deployed to describe a wider range of colours. As noted earlier, Berlin and Kay found that a focal hue is seldom "displaced by more than two adjacent chips".[41] But, again, Levinson found that the Rossel language "apart from uniform 'black' and 'white' appears to show a far wider intralinguistic spread than reported" by Berlin and Kay.[42] For instance, some Yélî disagreed with each other on the range of coloured chips that the terms for 'red' related to – there are two terms for 'red' in Yélî. And those that did not disagree felt that the terms could equally well apply to colours ranging from light orange to crimson, without them necessarily having a best exemplar. The finding relating to 'red' is typical of the situation in Yélî.

Finally, Yélî appears not to conform to the pattern predicted on the basis of Berlin and Kay's evolutionary sequence. The three most highly conventionalised terms in Yélî relate to 'white', 'black' and 'red'. According to basic colour terms theory, this places the Rossel language at the second stage on the evolutionary sequence. But this being so, the theory predicts that the black and red terms should be able to apply to a wider range of the colour spectrum: green or blue, for black, and in the yellow range for red. But this is not the case in Yélî. The Rossel language also has other putative 'basic' colour terms at various stages of conventionalisation. But these also deviate in startling ways from the putative universal focal hues that they are supposed to be anchored to.

What Levinson did find, based on his fieldwork, was that the degree of conventionalisation associated with colour expressions matched the sequence proposed by Berlin and Kay. The pattern in Yélî, with most conventionalised expressions on the left, and least conventionalised on the right, is as follows (where 'conventionalised' means the degree to which speakers agree on which colours the terms relate to):

white > black > red > green > yellow > blue

In the final analysis, what this all illustrates is that there is a broad commonality – an implicational scale – in the approximate order in which colour terms emerge across languages. But evidence from Rossel Island undermines the idea of strict semantic universals in the domain of colour.

What, then, is the alternative explanation? While colour terms and their emergence in language must surely be constrained by neurobiological factors, the evidence from Yélî Dnye suggests that it is usage-based *and* cultural pressures that determine *how* the colour expressions derive, rather than absolute semantic universals.

The Yélî language and culture appear to be at a point where colour terms are emerging. But they don't exclusively designate colour: colour 'terms' are not yet fully separated from the object and surface properties from which they derive. Indeed, in Yélî, the colour foci that the emerging terms refer to still largely relate to the salient hues of the objects from whose names the terms derive. For instance, terms for 'red' are saliently associated with the hue of the bird that the expressions derive from. As such, in Yélî, the specific shade that a given colour 'term' designates is drawn away from the putative 'universals' based on neurobiological constraints. This leads to an emerging conventionalisation for the terms, one that is at odds with the pattern predicted by Berlin and Kay.

More generally, the language-as-use thesis contends that colour terms emerge from objects and surface properties, with the colour category emerging over time, once the colour terms become dissociated from their original source objects. For this to happen, the colour terms must become conceptualised as relating to a visual quality independent of any given object. And once that has happened, the focal range to which the term is applicable can come to be constrained by neurobiological factors, rather than salient cultural prototypes – for example, the particular hue of red associated with a species of parrot – as in the case of Yélî. And, over time, the linguistic construction of colour will give rise to a system allowing other terms to move in to occupy parts of the colour space not otherwise accounted for.

Evidence for this usage-based version of events comes from other languages, both living and dead. For instance, in Sanskrit, the cognate term for English *red*, and proto-Gemanic *rauthaz*, was *rudhira*. In Sanskrit this term applied equally to the colour 'red' and blood, suggesting that the colour term, if the language-as-use thesis is correct, emerged from the term for blood. And today, in the Inuit languages of the Canadian Arctic, the term for 'red' literally means "like blood", clearly demonstrating the path of derivation.

Colour through the eyes of a child

To be sure that Berlin and Kay's approach to colour, and to linguistic relativity, is incorrect, we still require further, converging evidence, to support the language-as-use thesis. One additional line of support comes from the way in which children acquire colour expressions. If Berlin and Kay are correct, then we would expect children to acquire colour terms in the order stipulated by the evolutionary pattern, which is to say: 'white', 'black', followed by the four primary colours 'red', 'blue', 'green' and 'yellow', followed by the remaining colours. After all, the evolutionary order in the emergence of basic colour terms is supposed to reflect the neurobiological priority of the colour 'atoms' that make up our innate colour sense. Hence, it stands to reason that the emergence, in language acquisition, of basic colour terms should follow the relative priority of our putative semantic universals for colour. Psychologists Debi Roberson and Jules Davidoff, in a series of studies, sought to test exactly this.

In one study, Roberson, Davidoff and colleagues examined the sequence in which children acquiring Himba, a language spoken in South-West Africa, and English acquire their presumed basic colour terms.[43] While English has, according to Berlin and Kay, eleven basic colour terms, on the basis of the same criteria Himba has five. The study followed twenty-eight English and sixty-three Himba children for three years. The children were first tested prior to acquisition of colour terms. They were subsequently then tested at 6-month intervals. At each testing point, the children underwent a series of tests. For instance, they were asked to name all the colours that they knew, and were shown coloured Aid

Matte stimuli (similar to the Munsell coloured chips) and asked to name the colours they were exposed to.

The striking finding to emerge was this. There was no fixed order exhibited by children from either language. And individuals in both groups exhibited considerable variation. For instance, 'brown' and 'grey' emerged very early for some children – Berlin and Kay predict these colours should be acquired late – whilst for others they did arrive later. Ultimately, this study supports the view that linguistic colour categories are not due to semantic universals.[44] If they were, we would expect clear cross-linguistic and within-language patterns to be evident in terms of colour term acquisition.[45]

Pinker's broadside

In his 2007 book, *The Stuff of Thought*, Steven Pinker aims a broadside at the approach taken by neo-Whorfians – Lucy, Roberson, Davidoff and others. He takes particular issue with some of Levinson's research on the linguistic relativity of space – aspects of which we'll get to below. While the details of Pinker's argument need not distract us here, his conclusion is important. Pinker claims that, for all their bluster, the neo-Whorfians have not demonstrated that the language one speaks restructures cognition. And this follows because languages will inevitably have biases that are language-specific. Just because languages express ideas in different ways – or even express ideas that other languages haven't thought of expressing – it doesn't follow that language influences, and moreover fundamentally affects, thought and perception.

As we shall see below, when we move on from colour and start to look at linguistic relativity in other domains, like time and space, neo-Whorfians have used tasks in the psychology lab to try and tap into the different ways in which the language one speaks results in a restructuring of cognition. Pinker's complaint is that the sorts of tasks that neo-Whorfians have required their subjects to perform unduly influence language users: it looks like there are Whorfian effects – but, according to Pinker, there aren't! The tasks themselves artificially induce subjects to behave in particular ways. In short, and as Pinker puts it: "speakers of different languages tilt in different directions in a woolly task, rather than having differently structured minds".[46]

His point is that the mere fact that different groups of speakers *behave* in different ways from others, and also, coincidentally, *speak* a language that is organised in a different way, doesn't mean language has *caused* the behaviour. Pinker's objection to the entire neo-Whorfian programme is that "it depends on a dubious leap from correlation to causation".[47] For instance – and as we shall see below – an Aboriginal tribe has a language that encodes spatial relationships using cardinal points. They say that "the cup is south of the jug", rather than "the cup is left of the jug" as English would. And if you blindfold them and spin them so that they're dizzy, they can still tell you that the cup is "south" rather than, say, "east" of the jug. Stephen Levinson has claimed that this ability to dead-reckon is induced by language: a Whorfian effect. Pinker's response would be: "Humbug! Correlation is *not* causation."

So how might neo-Whorfians convince a sceptic like Pinker? Well, they have to move away from merely observing correlations, which is all that behavioural tasks in the psychology lab and in the field can show. They need to demonstrate causation. Behavioural tasks, those that get subjects to do something, whose responses are then observed – merely *inferring* an underlying cause – have to be supplemented with other methods. And such methods must directly investigate cognitive processes without utilising language, which might unduly influence a subject, as it can "tilt in different directions".

To settle the question, we require methods that demonstrate that systematic differences between two languages influence their speakers at the automatic level of perceptual processing, before language comes on line, and before, even, subjects are consciously aware of what they are perceiving. This means we need to investigate the way cognition is working in the brain, at time intervals of a fraction of a second, before perceptual experience percolates up to conscious awareness.

Greek Blues

In a recent, remarkable study, two of my colleagues, neuroscientist Guillaume Thierry and psycholinguist Panos Athanasopoulos, together with their research assistants, investigated the effect of language on colour perception at this unconscious level.[48] Their research directly addressed Pinker's broadside: that language cannot affect automatic, low-level and unconscious perceptual processing – and thus, language cannot influence thought in a fundamental way.

Thierry and Athanasopoulos directly investigated how the brain perceives colour in a time range – a fraction of a second – prior to the perceptual experience becoming available to conscious awareness, and so before the subject was 'aware' of what he or she was seeing. They did this by measuring electric signals produced by the brain when it processes perceptual stimuli. Brain activity of this sort can be detected by electrodes being placed on the scalp of a human subject. The method is non-invasive: subjects wear what looks like a swimming cap, with electrodes fitted at various points in the cap. The electrodes are then hooked up to machines that can record the brain's electrical activity. And when subjects see hues of different colours, the parts of the brain that process visual experience produce electrical impulses, within specific temporal windows. These impulses, and the intervals at which they are produced, can be measured down to tiny fractions of a second, allowing the experimenters to assess how individuals are processing colour stimuli even before the perceptual hue registers in the participant's conscious awareness.

If Whorf was right, then different languages should differentially influence how we perceive colour at this automatic, pre-conscious level: differences in language should restructure how we perceive, prior to our colour experience bubbling up into our conscious awareness. To investigate this, Thierry and Athanasopoulos took advantage of the way specific colours are encoded in Greek and in English. While English has a single word, *blue*, that covers the blue range of the colour spectrum, Greek has two terms: *ble*, which covers the dark blue range, and *ghalazio* which covers the light blue range. In the experiment, subjects watched sequences of different coloured shapes on a computer screen. They were asked to press a button when the shape was a square – about 20 per cent of the time – which provided subjects with a focus which was actually irrelevant to the investigators' real aim: rather than focusing on shape, the experimenters were in fact interested in brain activity when different shades of blue were being perceived. In order to provide a reference point, subjects were also exposed to shades of light and dark green. Both English and Greek have a single word to cover the green range.

This is what the experimenters found: the brain activity of Greek speakers was sensitive to differences in the blue range, but not the different shades of green. In contrast, brain activity of English speakers was not sensitive to the different shades in either the blue or the green categories. The conclusion that emerges from this is that there is clear relationship between a linguistic distinction in a speaker's native language – Greek divides blue colour space whilst English doesn't – and the low-level, automatic perception of colour. Before subjects become conscious of the colour they are seeing, the brains of Greek-speakers are responding in a different way from English speakers to the blue colour range. And the only plausible conclusion is that relativistic differences in how Greek, versus English, encodes the blue colour category have indeed restructured Greek cognition.

This experiment avoids the criticism levelled by Pinker: that speakers are, somehow, responding to the vagaries of the task through conscious reflection, thereby distorting findings. After all, the subjects thought the purpose of the task was to spot shapes (squares), rather than focusing on colour. Moreover, brain activity was being measured at fractions of a second, prior to the perceptual experience coming into conscious awareness.[49]

In a further study, my colleague Bastien Boutonnet, in collaboration with Thierry and their research assistants, followed up on the Greek Blues experiment.[50] Using the same methodology – measuring brain electrical impulses – Boutonnet and colleagues investigated not colour, but the relativistic effects across languages on how people categorise physical objects. For instance, English distinguishes between *cup* and *mug*, while Spanish has a single word, *taza*, that covers both. Boutonnet found, just as in the case of the Greek Blues, that language-specific differences make speakers more sensitive to how they perceive and categorise physical objects. English speakers are more sensitive to the shape of drinking vessels than Spanish speakers. And, as before, as the researchers were examining low-level perceptual phenomena, before the categorisation judgements entered the conscious awareness of human subjects, this demonstrates a clear Whorfian effect. Different languages, which label physical objects in different ways, give rise to a restructuring effect on cognition: speakers of different languages perceive those objects in language-specific ways.[51]

Tellingly, Paul Kay, writing – with a colleague, psychologist Terry Regier – in 2009, grudgingly concedes that Whorf may have been partly right, after all. Faced with the mounting welter of evidence that I've been discussing, Kay and Regier accept that: "the Whorf hypothesis is half right, in two different ways: (1) language influences color perception primarily in half the visual field, and (2) color naming across languages is shaped by both universal and language-specific forces".[52] In other words, Kay acknowledges that language does play a role in influencing colour perception and categorisation after all.

All about sex

Thus far, in this chapter, I have been focusing on the human experience and representation of colour, both in language and in the mind. And there is a good reason for this: colour has been the traditional test bed for investigating linguistic relativity, going back to initial investigations conducted by psychologists Eric Lenneberg and Roger Brown in the 1950s.

However, since the 1990s, a range of other domains have been investigated in order to test the principle of linguistic relativity. In language, sex is encoded by grammatical gender – French has masculine and feminine, while German adds a third 'sex': neuter. And while grammatical gender is sometimes strikingly at odds with reality – the French word for *vagina* is masculine, *le vagin* – the patterns are typically consistent with biological realities; in languages that have grammatical gender, male things tend to be grammatically masculine and female things tend to be grammatically feminine – although in German the word for young girl is famously without a sex, being neuter: *das Mädchen*.

Neo-Whorfian researchers have explored whether grammatical gender influences the way in which speakers of languages with gender perceive the world. While a language broadly patterns following biological norms, it is not clear what the sex of some objects is. For instance, take the quotidian example of an apple. If English were to encode grammatical gender, it is not at all obvious whether the word *apple* should be masculine or feminine. And in those languages that do encode gender – for objects like an apple, for instance – the gender is fixed by convention: speakers of a particular language simply agree what the gender will be, absent a clear biological basis for an object such as an apple having a sex. And in this case, *apple* is masculine in German but feminine in Spanish.

The psychologist Lera Boroditsky, and her research assistants, took advantage of discrepancies such as this between languages in order to establish whether grammatical gender gives rise to differences in the way speakers of Spanish and German think.[53] In one study, German and Spanish native speakers were taught, through the medium of English, proper names for objects which didn't correspond with the objects' grammatical genders in their languages. For instance, speakers might have been taught that a particular apple was named Patrick, or Patricia. Subjects were then tested to see how well they could remember the names they had learned for the objects. Boroditsky found that speakers were better able to recall the names correctly when the sex of the name matched the grammatical gender of the word in their respective language.[54] This, again, is a demonstration of linguistic relativity: grammatical gender influences a memory task, in language-specific ways.

In another study, Boroditsky and colleagues asked German- and Spanish-speakers to describe qualities associated with objects which just happened to have opposing grammatical genders in those languages, such as 'key' and 'bridge', which didn't have an obvious biological sex.[55] Based on a comparison of twenty-four words, they found that speakers of both languages consistently described objects in terms of qualities that matched gender-specific stereotypes. For instance, in German 'key' is masculine, whilst it's feminine in Spanish. Boroditsky and colleagues report that German speakers describe keys as being 'hard, heavy, jagged, metal, serrated, and useful'. In contrast, Spanish speakers describe the same object as being 'golden, intricate, little, lovely, shiny and tiny'.

On the reverse pattern, 'bridge' is feminine in German and masculine in Spanish. German speakers ascribed the following qualities to bridges: 'beautiful, elegant, fragile, peaceful, pretty and slender'. In contrast, Spanish speakers describe bridges as: 'big, dangerous, long, strong, sturdy, and towering'.[56] This appears to show that speakers *do* analyse grammatical gender as having a basis in biological sex. And this then influences how native speakers categorise, and otherwise think about, objects, even when they don't have a clear biological sex.

But recall that Pinker's objection to these sorts of behavioural tasks is to label them as "woolly", with the task itself biasing speakers of particular languages to "tilt in different directions".[57] And admittedly, in ordinary life, speakers of German and Spanish don't usually go around spontaneously thinking about bridges and keys in terms of male and female properties: this is, after all, a somewhat artificial task, an artefact of the psychology lab.

To be certain that grammatical gender really does give rise to linguistic relativity, and a real Whorfian effect, we need direct evidence of how the brain is behaving.

This was investigated, again, by my colleagues Bastien Boutonnet, Panos Athanasopoulos and Guillaume Thierry.[58] Using the same methodology as I described earlier for examining Greek Blues, Boutonnet and colleagues recruited speakers of English – which doesn't have grammatical gender – and native speakers of Spanish who had learned English as a second language. If grammatical gender influences non-linguistic thought, then we would expect to see differential patterns in brain activity across the English and Spanish groups.

This is what the experimenters did: subjects were presented with images of two objects which had the same grammatical gender in Spanish, one at a time on a computer screen. Subjects were then presented with a third image. Half the time, the third object's grammatical gender was the same as the first two images, in Spanish. And half the time, the grammatical gender was the opposite. Crucially, subjects were not told that the experiment related to grammatical gender. Rather, they were instructed to indicate whether the third picture matched the semantic category of the first two pictures. To do this, subjects were asked to press different buttons on a keyboard to signal similarity or dissimilarity.

As in the Greek Blues experiment, the researchers measured electrical activity from the brain, using electrodes situated on the scalps of subjects. For English speakers, they found no effect: as grammatical gender is not marked in English, English-speakers categorised the third picture as similar or dissimilar without regard to grammatical gender. In contrast, in Spanish-speakers, shortly after perceiving the third picture, there was increased brain activity just in those cases where the third image was of a different grammatical gender from the first two. Psychologists have established that increased electrical activity – in a brain region and time scale known to reflect grammatical processing – is indicative of information that is more difficult for the brain to integrate. And in this experiment, the findings reveal the following.

Even though subjects were not processing language – the task involved images, and hence visual stimuli – Spanish speakers appeared to be automatically and unconsciously activating grammatical gender – i.e., linguistic information – when categorising the images. The increase in brain activity when the third picture's grammatical gender failed to match is evidence of this. In contrast, English speakers showed no such effect.

This finding provides incontrovertible evidence that language has an impact on a non-linguistic categorisation task in a relativistic way: Spanish-speakers cannot help but use grammatical gender in the task even though the task does not relate to language. In contrast, English-speakers, who have no such thing as grammatical gender, are unable to deploy this information in making categorisation judgements.

Now let's return, for a moment, to the issue of modularity that I explored in Chapter 5. One of the consequences of the relativistic effects of grammatical gender on thought is this: it further undermines the thesis that the mind is modular. After all, if language is a distinct module in the mind, it should not be able to influence non-linguistic categorisation judgements based on visual information: language and vision are claimed to be distinct modules. Yet the very fact that Spanish-speakers are unconsciously accessing grammatical information to help form judgements arising from visual stimuli strongly suggests that visual input is being coerced by linguistic information, even when the grammatical categories were irrelevant for the task at hand. This finding should be impossible, if the modular view of mind were correct. In the final analysis, different brain systems appear to be far more interconnected than the language-as-instinct thesis contends.

On time and space

As a final demonstration, I turn to the domains of time and space, the foundational domains of human experience. Some of the most important work on space in the neo-Whorfian tradition has been carried out by Stephen Levinson and his team at the Max Planck Institute for Psycholinguistics in Nijmegen. Levinson has discovered that the world's languages appear to make use of three broad strategies when locating objects in space.[59] The first involves making use of inherent properties of a landmark to locate the object in question. For instance, when I say *The cat is sitting in front of the window cleaner's house*, you know in which region around the house you might expect to find the cat, precisely because you know that houses have backs, fronts and sides.

In contrast, when I say *The cat is sitting in front of the tree*, you can't use the spatial properties of the tree to help: after all, a tree, being round, is perfectly symmetrical, and unlike a house has no internal properties that can help you figure out on which 'side' of the tree to look for the cat – trees just don't have sides, or fronts and backs, unlike houses. In situations like this, a language such as English allows us to project our own human vantage point onto the tree, in order to assign it 'our' spatial coordinates. For instance, when I say *The cat is in front of the tree*, you now know where to go and look for the cat. But, notice, a tree doesn't have a left – or a right for that matter. Only humans do! And we make use of this aspect of our bodies to project our human perspective, allowing us to locate objects even when landmarks such as trees don't inherently have a left or a right. This is illustrated in the diagram below.

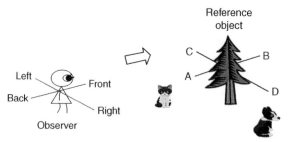

Projecting human spatial co-ordinates onto a tree

Projecting human spatial co-ordinates onto a tree. Adapted from Shinohara and Matsunaka (2010: 296)

In the diagram, the human observer's bodily axis is projected onto the tree. Hence, the observer's front is aligned with the tree's A axis, back aligns with the B axis, right aligns with C, and left with D. And on this view, the tree is now 'facing' the observer.

Finally, our physical environment provides us with a reference system that allows us to locate objects in space. The points of the compass, for instance, take their reference from the Earth's magnetic core. And, in so doing, they provide us with a fixed or absolute frame of reference, allowing us to identify objects, as when I say *The mountain range is north of the tree.* The location of the mountain range, in this case, is guaranteed by my compass, which takes its reference from the Earth's cardinal points.

Intriguingly, not all languages make use of all three of these strategies for locating objects in space. One, now well-studied, example is the Aboriginal language Guugu Yimithirr – an indigenous language of North Queensland, Australia. What's interesting about Guugu Yimithirr is this: it makes exclusive use of an absolute reference frame – the points of the compass. While English only uses cardinal points – north, south, east and west – to describe large-scale geographical distances – e.g., *Africa is south of Europe* – this is the only linguistic strategy available to speakers of Guugu Yimithirr. In this language, and as the linguistic anthropologist William Foley describes, "the sun doesn't go down, it goes west; the fork isn't at my left, it lies south; the tide doesn't go out, it goes east."[60]

An important consequence of this is that speakers of Guugu Yimithirr must be able to figure out their location with respect to the cardinal points of their system, wherever they are in space. After all, in order to be able to know whether a pen is 'to the east', a speaker of this language has to be able to dead-reckon, based on salient landmarks in their visual field, to figure out which way is east.

In order to investigate this further, Levinson compared native speakers of both Guugu Yimithirr and Dutch, in terms of their dead-reckoning abilities: their ability to tell which way is north, south, east and west without the aid of a compass. Like English,

Dutch makes use of all three spatial reference strategies. If Whorf were correct, then we would expect to find that speakers of Guugu Yimithirr are more adept at dead-reckoning than speakers of Dutch; after all, reliance on just one spatial reference strategy – one that requires dead-reckoning – is likely to have enhanced this aspect of their non-linguistic wayfinding.[61]

Levinson found that, when Guugu Yimithirr speakers were taken to an unfamiliar terrain with restricted visibility, such as a dense rainforest, they were still able to work out their location, identifying particular directions such as north and south, east and west, with an error rate of less than 4 per cent. This contrasted with a comparable experiment involving Dutch speakers, who were much less accurate. What this suggests, then, is a real Whorfian effect in the domain of space: the nature of spatial representation in language has consequences for speakers' non-linguistic abilities, here the ability to dead-reckon.

Whorfian effects have also been found in the domain of time. The psychologist Lera Boroditsky investigated the distinctions in English and Mandarin, and their consequences for how speakers of these two languages reason about time.[62] In English, and most other Indo-European languages, temporal sequences involving earlier and later times are metaphorically represented in terms of a horizontal axis in space. For instance, when describing two events, *The transistor came before the microchip*, English conceptualises the relationship as if it were a sequence, such that the earlier event precedes and the later event follows. While Mandarin also exhibits this pattern, it additionally encodes temporal events as being sequenced on the vertical axis. This would correspond to the following hypothetical English sentence: *The transistor is higher than the microchip*.

In Mandarin, the word for 'morning' is *shang-ban-tian*, which literally means 'upper-half-day', while the later event, afternoon, is *xia-ban-tian*, literally 'lower-half-day'.[63] Conceptualising earlier and later events as being sequenced in vertical space is odd from an English-speaker's perspective. Yet, it's nevertheless a fairly common way of expressing temporal sequence relationships in many languages. And this pattern appears to be motivated by experience: when an object is rolled down a slope, the earlier part of the event is at the top of the slope, while, due to the force of gravity, the later part of the event is lower down. I've captured this idea in the diagram below.

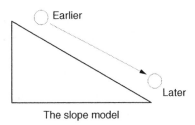

The slope model

The slope model. Adapted from Shinohara (2000: 5).

Boroditsky and colleagues took advantage of the distinction between English and Mandarin to investigate whether this linguistic difference impacts on how speakers of those languages interact with the domain of time in non-linguistic contexts.[64] To do this, they presented English and Mandarin speakers with two photos of Woody Allen, as a young and old man respectively. Subjects were required to indicate whether the second photo was earlier or later than the first by pressing one of two keys, which were coloured white ('earlier') and black ('later'). The experimenters manipulated the keyboard keys such that for some subjects the keys were sequenced next to each other on a horizontal axis. In a second condition, the keys were sequenced vertically. And within each condition (horizontal versus vertical), the sequence of keys was switched: for some subjects in the horizontal condition, the 'earlier' key was to the right of the 'later' key, and for others it was on the 'left'. In horizontal space, both Mandarin and English speakers sequence earlier events as being located on the left and later events on the right, which mirrors the writing direction in both languages. The experimenters then measured how long it took subjects to press the correct button.

Both English and Mandarin speakers were quicker to press the correct key on the horizontal axis when the 'earlier'/'later' keys were sequenced in the order consistent with both languages. They were slower to select the correct key when the order was inconsistent. This indicates that, for both groups, language appears to have an effect in a non-linguistic manual task. Participants were slowed down when the physical placement of the keys was at odds with how their languages encode earlier and later events.

Interestingly, in the vertical condition, English speakers showed no difference in how quickly they pressed the buttons, regardless of whether the correct key was located below or above. However, for Mandarin-speakers, subjects were consistently faster when the keys were sequenced in a way consistent with the way Mandarin encodes 'earlier' (higher), and 'later' (lower) relations. This clearly demonstrates a Whorfian effect: English- and Mandarin-speakers diverge in a manual task, apparently influenced by the way in which these languages systematically encode temporal sequential relationships.

Of course, Pinker's objection to the claims made by Levinson and Boroditsky would be that these findings amount to correlation, *not* causation! But, in conjunction with the rest of the evidence I've reviewed in this chapter, it would be odd if time and space did *not* behave much like colour and gender. Having demonstrated the principle of linguistic relativity in the domains of colour and sex, we would expect to find it in other domains too. And it is only a matter of time before researchers turn their attention to direct demonstrations of Whorfian relativity at the level of pre-attentive perceptual processing in the domains of time and space.

What is linguistic relativity anyway?

In the foregoing, I've sampled some of the findings from the neo-Whorfian tradition. These appear to demonstrate that Whorf's thesis of linguistic relativity is very much on the right lines.

In particular, in this chapter, I've considered structural aspects of language, and how they shape, in a fundamental way, the nature of habitual patterns of thought, especially at the pre-attentive level. I've considered the number and nature of colour terms a language has, how it structures and conceptualises time and space, and how it encodes grammatical gender. Moreover, I've reviewed the concomitant restructuring that takes place in thought, and, especially, in automatic and unconscious aspects of mental function, such as the perception of colour, or the categorisation of objects based on the perception of visual stimuli, as in the research undertaken by Boutonnet and colleagues. In these sorts of examples, the way cognitive processes apply to perception, prior to conscious awareness coming on-line, appears to correlate with fundamental distinctions in different languages.

In the final analysis, linguistic relativity seems not to relate to how we influence the thoughts of others – no one disputes this as a significant function of language: we aim to persuade, prevaricate, request, seduce, all using language. Rather, linguistic relativity is, ultimately, a phenomenon that impacts on the cognitive apparatus of the language user – a consequence of the language one uses: by virtue of using English, rather than, say, Greek, my habitual patterns of thought, in terms of the colour domain, are structured – or restructured – in a relativistic way. I perceive colours in somewhat different terms, whether I like it or not. The psychologist Gary Lupyan has described this process as language augmenting thought.[65] The language I speak does this to me: we have slightly different minds as a consequence of the language(s) we use.[66] Linguistic relativity concerns, then, not what we convince others to do by virtue of our word play; rather, it relates to what happens to our minds because of the language(s) we happen to grow up speaking. And, as such, linguistic relativity is, ultimately, a usage-based phenomenon.

The structural properties associated with a language, as a semiotic system – a language, any language, is made up of stable semantic and grammatical knowledge units – appears to make certain types of thought more likely. And a particular language, as a consequence, inhibits others sorts of patterns of thought.[67] In the final analysis, what this chapter – and indeed this book – has revealed is that human languages and human minds are inexorably interconnected; and, even more significant: they are symbiotic. Moreover, both are largely shaped by experience and use.

8   Language and mind regained

In this book I've been considering the myth of the language instinct: the 'language myth'. The language myth is made up of six component myths. These include the myth that language is a singularity, unrelated to any other animal communication system (Chapter 2); the myth that all languages are underwritten by language universals, a detailed Universal Grammar (Chapter 3); the myth that this Universal Grammar is innate, prescribed by our DNA (Chapter 4); the myth that Universal Grammar is a distinct, informationally encapsulated module in the mind (Chapter 5); the myth that natural languages are learnable because there is an innate Mentalese: the language of thought (Chapter 6); and finally, the myth that habitual patterns of thought can't be influenced by the structure and organisation of different languages, which refutes the principle of linguistic relativity (Chapter 7).

While I've presented my alternative to each of the myths as we've gone along, we still need to round out the language-as-use thesis. And in this final chapter, I examine several outstanding issues.

First up, if language is related to other animal communication systems, why is it that no other species appears to have anything that closely approaches human language? I argue that what makes humans special is our cultural intelligence, leading to pro-social and cooperative behaviour. While other species are social, the nature of the cultural intelligence exhibited by *Homo sapiens* stands out in comparison to any other species, and has facilitated the development of advanced symbolic behaviours, language being the paradigmatic example.

But the fact that we, alone, possess a species-specific cultural intelligence still begs the question: how did language arise? I argue that cultural intelligence gave rise, at some point in our forebears' evolutionary trajectory, to an additional mental competence: an interactional intelligence. And this paved the way for language.

I then examine the nature of our mental grammar: if language is not made up of learned words, and innate rules – the words and rules approach of the language-as-instinct thesis – what does our mental grammar actually look like? I spell out what I think the language-as-use thesis commits us to, sketching my view of our mental grammar.

But if there are no absolute language universals, why are there, nevertheless, commonalities across languages? Most languages appear to have nouns and verbs. Many languages have word order or case systems or both, to indicate relationships between linguistic elements. And there are commonalities in terms of how grammars emerge, develop and change. In lieu of linguistic universals, I claim that there are universal scenes of experience; and these serve as a constraint on the design space of human language.

And in the light of all this, I also ask why there is so much diversity: why are there so many damn languages? I present some of the cutting-edge research from evolutionary biology which sheds light on how language has evolved, and why. I also consider the ever-expanding envelope of human linguistic diversity.

And finally, I offer one valedictory reflection on the language myth: the language-as-instinct thesis. But first things first. Let's begin with what sets us apart from other species.

Cultural intelligence and the ratchet effect

Despite the range of communicative systems evident in the animal kingdom, the complexity of human language – the nature and type of messages it allows us to signal, how it is acquired and, crucially, the range of functions it facilitates – is both of a different quality and on a different level from any other. Given the broad similarities between human intelligence and that of other apes, especially chimpanzees and orang-utans, what then might account for this difference? Michael Tomasello, a psychologist and primatologist, suggests the difference relates to what might be termed 'cultural intelligence'.[1] The social behaviour of animals, including other apes, is for the most part individualistic: it's based on competition. And the various behaviours and intelligences they demonstrate have developed to enable success in competition for food, resources and sexual reproduction. Humans, too, have developed cognitive abilities that facilitate success in competing for resources.

However, our species has also developed skills geared towards cooperation – often despite appearances to the contrary. We have the ability to work together in order to facilitate solutions to problems and challenges that can't be solved individually. And this bestows significant evolutionary advantages. Cooperation in *Homo sapiens* arises from a sophisticated form of cultural intelligence, one that has evolved for participating in a group.[2] It is this cultural intelligence, it would seem, that sets us apart from all other species on our planet.

While apes show remarkable cognitive similarity to the abilities of pre-school children, human infants exhibit more sophisticated cultural intelligence.[3] Pre-literate children are more adept than chimps in terms of intention-reading – which, you'll recall, is the ability to draw inferences about the mental states of others based on, for instance, visual cues.[4] Our cultural intelligence means that human children come into the world especially attuned to adult teaching. The trust placed in adult instruction is based on cooperative motives. For instance, in one experiment, children who observed a puppet playing a game objected strenuously if the game was subsequently played according to rules that differed from the ones they had been taught. Moreover, the formal schooling system in place in many cultures, which occupies much of the formative period of a child's life, is a manifestation of cooperation. Adults intentionally teach children things, give up their time and energy in doing so, and assume that this is in the best interests of the child.[5]

Indeed, human language stands out as an example of cooperative behaviour *par excellence*. We cooperatively agree upon

symbols and their meanings in our social groups, thereby establishing linguistic conventions: language emerges in and through
use, with humans agreeing what the meaning of an arbitrary
symbol should be – rather than through instinct. Many cultures
even have bodies that safeguard and rule on linguistic conventions,
such as the Académie française, established in 1635.

The British philosopher Paul Grice observed that, when humans
engage in linguistic communication, we each assume other speakers
are behaving cooperatively. Grice observed that when people
communicate, they appear to follow several unspoken maxims
guided by this principle of cooperation.[6] For instance, when we
ask someone a question, we presume the truthfulness and relevance of our conversationalist in making their response. And even
contravening cooperativeness is perceived as being cooperative.
I once knew someone who feigned a gluten allergy in order to
have an excuse to decline her great-aunt's notorious homemade
Welsh cakes – otherwise referred to by family members as "bake
stones": but only when out of the great-aunt's earshot. The
response, on the face of it – "I have a gluten allergy" – clearly flouts
the maxim of relevance. In offering her great-niece a "bake stone",
great-aunt Margaret wasn't enquiring after allergies – the more
relevant response would have been: "No thank you". Yet, the actual
response is still cooperative. The young woman is attempting to
spare her great-aunt's feelings.

Humans have brains that are, on average, about three times
larger than that of chimpanzees. But it is not brain size, per se,
that gives you and me our cognitive advantage. Tomasello claims
that it is cultural intelligence that sets humans apart from other
species. Cultural intelligence allows us to enhance other cognitive
skills in a general way. For instance, human children can boot-
strap skills of physical cognition by imitating others. And we
imitate others because we understand they are showing us how
to do things. We intuitively recognise, understand and reciprocate
cooperative behaviour. This allows pre-linguistic children to imitate tool use, and so learn how to use artefacts such as knives

and forks, and even the TV remote control – much to their parents' annoyance: my daughter, even before she could string two words together, would invariably find the remote and switch off the TV in the middle of a gripping episode of *Dr Who*, one of the few programmes I regularly watch on TV.

Children also learn to use linguistic symbols through imitation, as we saw in Chapter 4. Indeed, human cultural intelligence ensures that humans have a suite of skills that allow the cognitive abilities shared with other apes to be harnessed for collaboration and communication, and for cultural learning and transmission. Cultural intelligence means that specific institutions come into being because, and *only* because, everyone in the group believes *and* behaves as if they do. Money, marriage, monarchs and Prime Ministers are all created by our shared cultural intelligence; they are constructed and modified in use, in our cultural milieu, by virtue of our pro-social intelligence through cooperative behaviour and practice.

In addition, by bootstrapping other cognitive abilities, cultural intelligence allows the entities created by our cooperative behaviour to accumulate modifications over time. For instance, through cooperative activities, human culture has produced complex technologies which future generations build upon, ratcheting up their complexity.[7] One consequence of this ratchet effect is that complexity develops exponentially, leading to an increase in complexity over time – indeed, over relatively short periods of time.

For instance, the Old Stone Age (the Paleolithic era) spanned a period running roughly from 2.5 million years ago to around 12,000 years ago. During this period, tools used by hominins – initially Australopithecines, and later *Homo habilis*, and then *Homo erectus* – evolved from simple pebble technology to the more sophisticated flake technology of the Middle Stone Age. From around 300,000 to 50,000 years ago, when the Neanderthals were roaming Europe, stone technology allowed various species of the genus *Homo* to manufacture stone-tipped spears, by hafting stone flakes onto wooden poles. This greatly enhanced success at hunting. During the later part of the Old Stone Age, from 50,000 years ago, new technologies began to burgeon, giving rise to jewellery, cave painting, and the construction of dwellings manufactured by sophisticated tools made from carving stone, bone and wood.

The New Stone Age (the Neolithic era), from somewhere in the region of 10,000 BCE to around 4,000 years or so BCE, saw an explosion in technology, with the invention of pottery, the lever, and the use of fire in metalwork. Around this time, vehicles began to be constructed expressly for transportation, including canoes and sledges. In later ages, bronze, iron and steel came to be manufactured, and the range and complexity of the inventions ratcheted up in complexity. In the twentieth century, for instance, technology advanced at a dizzying rate. The century began with the first manned flight, and the first automobile, and took in airliners, hovercraft, nuclear energy, computers, jet aircraft, rockets and organ transplants. We can expect the ratchet effect to deliver even greater jumps in technology over the next 100 years.

Phases of technological development and the ratchet effect over the last 12,000 years

Age	Technology
The New Stone Age 10,000–4000 BCE	Fire for metalworking, pottery, the lever, stone weapons, transportation by canoe and sledge, agriculture
The Bronze Age 4000–1200 BCE	The wheel, writing, farming, transport by horses and carts, metal-tipped weapons, bows and arrows, leather armour
The Iron Age 1200 BCE – 500 CE	Keystone arch, use of saddles for riding horses, seafaring galleys, scale armour
The Age of Steel 500–1450 CE	Steel weapons, mathematics with zero, saddles with stirrups, sailing ships, crossbows and chainmail
The Renaissance 1450–1700 CE	Printing, gunpowder, muskets, full-rigged ships
The Industrial Revolution 1700–1900 CE	Mass production factories, steam power, railways, dynamite, repeating guns, electricity

(cont.)

Age	Technology
The World Wars 1900–45	Cars, planes, radio, ocean liners, submarines, tanks, machine guns, fission bombs, hydroelectricity
The Modern Era 1945 – the present	Nuclear energy, computers, manned space-flight, hovercraft, fusion missiles, nuclear power, organ transplants, ballistic airliners, cloning, the genesis of nano-technology

The human interaction engine

But while cultural intelligence has enabled a pro-social bias in human behaviour, this still doesn't quite explain how humans have come by language. Stephen Levinson has proposed that humans have, additionally, an interactional intelligence: a predisposition to engage in interaction with one another in communicative settings for specific ends.[8] Interaction is a specific type of cooperative behaviour; as such, it most likely emerged as a consequence of our cultural intelligence. Crucially, however, our ability to interact with one another is independent of language: it seems reasonable to suppose it was the key evolutionary development that allowed language to emerge.

To illustrate, Levinson recounts an anecdote from his time on Rossel Island conducting fieldwork – recall that Rossel Island is a remote island in Papua New Guinea. One day, when Levinson was on his own, Kpémuwó, a 28-year-old deaf man passed by. Kpémuwó was the only deaf person in his village, and a 3-hour walk away from the nearest other deaf person. Even though Levinson and Kpémuwó shared no language, and little culture, they engaged in a 'conversation': Kpémuwó recounted the story of a woman who was dying of cancer in his village. Levinson was amazed that he could understand what Kpémuwó was 'saying', communicating using pointings and iconic gestures.

Another example of our seemingly universal interactional intelligence is the party game Charades: players must guess a word using the clues being provided. But the clues involve the miming of actions and gestures in response to the guesses of others. Charades is a paradigmatic example of our shared interactional intelligence – it depends upon it, as is deliciously illustrated in the cartoon below.

Despite Eric's best efforts, no-one guessed 'Bangkok'.

'Charades' by Tim Whyatt. Reprinted with permission. Copyright Tim Whyatt (whyatt.com.au).

And interactional intelligence seems to be deeply embedded in our species. Infants exhibit an early awareness of the give and take of interaction. Try 'speaking' to a pre-linguistic baby: a baby younger than 9 months of age. You'll find that the baby babbles in response, taking its turn to respond before becoming silent, awaiting the caregiver's response. And, moreover, the duration and intensity of babbling closely correlates with the duration and intensity of the speech produced by the adult. And, depending on the measure, infants can engage in communicative interaction as early as 48 hours after birth.[9]

Even adults who have lost the ability to produce language, as in Broca's aphasia, can still interact and communicate.[10] For all this to be so, Levinson concludes, "there has to be some powerful meaning-making mystery that we all share". It isn't that language makes interaction possible, "it is interactional intelligence that made language possible as a means of communication".[11]

There are a number of properties that are universal to human interaction. First, we respond to communicative intentions, rather than behaviours. For instance, a cough can be a reflex action to choking on food: a behaviour. Or we can interpret it as a surreptitious signal to stay quiet, in a tricky situation: an intentional action.

In addition, the intentional actions are transparent to the recipient: they are designed with the recipient in mind. In one famous case, Major Charles Ingram, a contestant on the quiz show *Who Wants to be a Millionaire?*, was convicted of deception while winning the £1,000,000 jackpot. He was aided by a member of the audience, who coughed just as the correct answers were read out, helping the Major to his jackpot win.

Next, and as I've already intimated, interaction for communicative ends is independent of language. In Chapter 3, I considered Goldin-Meadow's remarkable 'home-sign' children: deaf children who were not taught a sign language. I described how these children developed their own communicative system by developing gestures – iconic pointings and hand-shapes – in order to communicate. What this reveals is that the ability to communicate in humans is a property of our minds, arising from our interactional intelligence: it is independent of language, "language just enormously amplifies its potential."[12]

Moreover, interaction is cooperative. This doesn't mean we all get on with each other. It simply means that, whenever we communicate, we cooperate for purposes of the interaction. The eminent psychologist Herbert Clark has described this aspect of human interaction as 'joint activities'.[13] For instance, when we go to a store to buy the pair of John Wayne boots I discussed in Chapter 1, the interaction between the customer and sales assistant is cooperative: the sales assistant indicates their availability to 'serve' the customer with a customary greeting such as "Do you need any help?", or simply by wearing a uniform and a badge, allowing the customer to do the approach work. And the entire service encounter is geared towards a specific goal, the purchase of the pair of boots. Even less staid interactions are goal-oriented.

Gossiping with a neighbour over a garden-fence can serve to provide useful information about goings-on in the neighbourhood, or to maintain a good relationship with someone on whom we may need to rely from time-to-time, such as for feeding the cat when we're on vacation.

And finally, interaction has a structure to it. This arises not from rules, but, rather, from expectations. For instance, a question demands an answer, giving rise to a turn-taking sequence. A telephone caller awaits the 'Hello' from the recipient of the call, to signal the channel for communication is open – even unsolicited, recorded phone calls trying to sell us something have a slight pause allowing the caller to say "Hello", before the recording begins.

In the case of joint activities, such as the cowboy boots purchase, the sequence of events goes something like this. A sales assistant approaches you and offers to help; you interact with the assistant in order to have your feet measured; the assistant fetches the required boots from the stock room for you to try on; you agree the purchase, making payment; and the assistant boxes or wraps the boots. Joint activities consist of many different kinds, but they have a common set of features, which I've summarised in the table below.

Features of joint activities[14]

Feature of joint activity	Examples
Scriptedness	While some joint activities are highly scripted, such as a marriage ceremony, others, such as a chance meeting in a supermarket, are unscripted. There are other activities which lie between these two poles of scriptedness.
Formality	Joint activities also vary in terms of formality between two extremes; while some activities can be highly formal, such as a court hearing, the other extreme is that of complete informality, such as a gossip session between friends over a cup of tea or a drink in the pub.
Use of language	This concerns the degree to which language is integral to a given activity. Again, there are extremes and

(*cont.*)

Feature of joint activity	Examples
	event types in-between. For instance, a telephone call is constituted solely by language, while a football match is primarily not linguistic in nature.
Cooperative vs adversarial	Joint activities range from those that are wholly cooperative to those that are adversarial in nature. For instance, making a purchase in a shop is cooperative as it relies on both the customer and the shop assistant working cooperatively in order to effect the purchase. In contrast, a tennis match, at least in one sense, is adversarial, rather than cooperative, as the players seek to cause their opponent(s) to lose.
Degree of symmetry of participant roles	Different participants have distinct roles in the joint activity, as in the case of the customer and the sales assistant in the shoe shop joint activity. Importantly, these roles can be symmetric or asymmetric: this concerns whether their roles are equally balanced or not in terms of significance and contribution towards realising the goal of the joint activity. For instance, making a purchase in a shop involves a degree of equality or symmetry: both participants, the customer and the shopkeeper, must work equally in order to effect the sale. In contrast, in some activities one participant is especially dominant, as in the case of a public speech by a politician, where the speaker is far more dominant than the audience. In this case, the participant roles are asymmetric, with respect to the goal of the joint activity: the delivery of the speech.

The properties of human interaction that I have been describing appear to be supported by a common cognitive infrastructure that makes communication possible.[15] Levinson dubs this our "interaction engine": a toolkit of knowledge and behaviours that allows us to communicate with one another. The toolkit consists of a number of ingredients that enable interaction.[16] First, we must be able to recognise others in our species as having thoughts, wishes and beliefs – this is what philosophers refer to as a theory of mind: we must be aware that others have minds, like our own. We must also be able to simulate what others are thinking and feeling, and what they would do in particular contexts. In short, we must be able to anticipate the thoughts, and behaviours, of others. We must also be able to recognise the communicative intentions of others, for instance that a cough has a particular significance, rather than simply being a behavioural reflex. And finally, we must understand, and be aware of, the natural structure of interactions – question–answer turn-taking sequences being a salient example. These ingredients enable interaction, and give grist to the interaction engine: by understanding that others have minds, in the same way that you and I do, and having thoughts and feelings which we can anticipate, we can attempt to influence others by signalling our communicative intentions.

My claim, then, is that our species has a special kind of cultural intelligence, which leads us to cooperative patterns of behaviour. Cultural intelligence has given rise to a further more specialised interactional intelligence. And so, language arises in our species not because we have a dedicated grammar gene, as claimed by the language myth. Rather, language arises because our species has specialised types of intelligences – cultural and interactional – qualitatively different from those seen in other species.

But a caveat is in order here: these 'intelligences' are not modules of mind. They are not the result of specialised and dedicated neural structures. They most likely arise from an amalgam of various mental competences, a consequence of the ecological niche to which our bipedal hominin forebears adapted.

The rise of language

So how might our interaction engine have enabled us to evolve language? Given that interaction, upon which language depends, is a specialised type of cultural intelligence, one plausible scenario is that it arose in social contexts – in the words of Daniel Everett, language is the paradigm example of a "cultural tool".[17]

The comparative psychologist Robin Dunbar suggests that language arose in contexts which took on the role that non-linguistic interaction played in the social interaction of our non-linguistic forebears. In particular, he has proposed it arose in order to facilitate gossip. Gossip is an archetypal form of social interaction. Dunbar thinks that language may have arisen in ancestral humans to functionally replicate the role of grooming in other ape species. In one study, Dunbar found that the Kapanora tribe from New Guinea spend around a third of their daylight interactions engaged in social interaction (or gossip). This compares with Gelada baboons, who spend around 20 per cent of their time in grooming – which fulfils a similar function to gossiping.[18]

In western society, one estimate maintains – setting aside solo pastimes such as fishing – that, whether at work or play, we may spend up to as much as 70 per cent of our time engaged in social interaction.[19] It seems, then, that, with the advent of cultural intelligence – intelligence that enabled us and our ancestors to thrive in a group – the next step was to hone this intelligence to facilitate sophisticated interaction, to further enhance the group life-style that is the human way.[20] Our groupings have become ever larger over time, facilitated by our cultural and interactional intelligences: from small communities, to the city-states of antiquity, to modern nation states. And with the advent of new economic and political unions, the EU being a case in point, further enlargements of the groupings in which we live appear to be on the cards.

And there *is* evidence to support the view that language has enabled the rise in the size of communities in which humans can effectively live. Robin Dunbar has found a correlation between brain size and the average size of groups in which primates live.[21] In the modern world, increasingly dominated, over the last decade or so, by new media such as Facebook, we may be tempted to think that we have friendships that might number in the thousands. And the number of Twitter followers of the latest teen pop idols can even reach hundreds of thousands. But in reality, an individual person can only maintain up to 150 stable relationships. And this number corresponds closely to the average size of the first permanent human settlements from around 12,000 years ago. The first villages consisted of no more than 150 people. So the point is that language provides a relatively 'cheap' means of facilitating social interaction, enabling us to maintain far larger – albeit looser – social relationships, with a larger number of people. Traditional and new media, driven by language, and underwritten by our collective interaction engine, have enabled the size of our social groupings to rise in a way that remains impossible for our near primate cousins. What this all reveals is that language enables us to maintain relationships that would be otherwise impossible: a far higher number than what we would otherwise expect, given our brain size. Cultural intelligence has facilitated our ability to interact in social contexts. And language has emerged, replicating and massively enhancing our interactional intelligence.

While Dunbar's account of language – as having evolved to facilitate gossip – may not be exactly right – and some experts disagree with Dunbar on the details – it is surely the case that social interaction has played an important function in the development of language.

What does our mental grammar look like?

So, if language emerged in order to facilitate and enhance social interaction, how is it made up? In this section, I consider what the language-as-use thesis has to say about our mental grammar, which underpins human language.[22]

Our grammar is made up of linguistic units. These units are conventional pairings of form and meaning. For instance, a prototypical linguistic unit is a word, such as *cat, bra* or *jealousy*. Words involve a sequence of one or more mental sound units, or phonemes – the form – and a concept – the meaning – that is conventionally associated with that sequence. By way of example, let's take the English word *cat*. This involves three sound segments, in a specific order, which are associated, in the minds of English-language-speakers, with a particular type of meaning, namely a four-legged animal, with whiskers and tail that is the pet of choice for many households in the western world. I have diagrammed this relationship in the figure below.

A linguistic unit: *cat*. Adapted from Evans and Green (2006).

As linguistic units, like the word *cat*, are constructed from elements of form and meaning – brought together as a single paired unit – they are referred to as 'constructions'. And, in fact, our mental grammar is essentially an inventory of constructions.

Of course, not all constructions are word-like. Many are more complex, or more abstract. For instance, fixed phrases such as idioms are also constructions. An idiom like *He kicked the bucket* involves a sequence of words which appear in a fixed order, and which obtain a meaning that is not the result of the combination of the words. After all, this idiomatic expression does not – normally – relate to a frustrated janitor who kicked the bucket in a fit of pique. Nor can any of the component words such as *kick* or *bucket* be altered without radically altering the meaning. For instance, the expression *He kicked the mop* would, presumably, indeed signal that the frustrated janitor was angry. It certainly couldn't mean 'He died', which is the conventional meaning associated with *He kicked the bucket.*

In terms of meaning, an idiom such as *He kicked the bucket* is more abstract than a word such as *cat*, in the following sense. The meaning relates to the idiom as a whole, rather than residing in the individual words in a part–whole relationship. Put another way, we don't understand what the expression means by adding the meanings of the words together. Rather, we simply have to know what the expression means as a unit. In terms of form, the idiom is abstract in the sense that not all the words are fully specified. For instance, while *kicked* and the *bucket* are obligatory elements, the pronoun *he* is not obligatory, nor even the fact that it should be a pronoun. We might just as easily say: *John/ Jane/she kicked the bucket.* Moreover, *kicked*, at least in the past tense form, is not obligatory; although the verb stem must be *kick* – unless we wish to radically change the meaning.

That said, we could say, *Jane will / is going to / might kick the bucket.* What this shows is that the subject of the phrase is not fully specified. This tells us that, in our mental grammars, we list a volitional subject as part of the construction – an inanimate entity such as a rock can't 'kick the bucket'. But the precise details of the subject, whether it be Tom, Dick or Harry, or indeed someone or something else, is not recorded. We fill that in later, during language use, and as required by our communicative intention. In similar fashion, tense is not fully specified. Again, the construction records that there must be tense – a point in time relative to which the 'kicking of the bucket' – the dying event – takes place.

In short, part of our knowledge of this idiom, which we must therefore hold in long-term memory, is that there is a subject, which can be populated by a delimited set of subject types – including proper names (*John*, *Jane* and so on) and pronouns (*he*, *she* and so on) – as well as permutations on tense and modality that apply to the verb *kick*. This is an impressive amount of information that native speakers have, *just* for a single idiomatic construction.

Other types of construction are more abstract still, in terms both of form and of meaning. One example of such a construction is the sentence-level grammatical pattern exemplified by the following sentence: *The window cleaner gave the supermodel his heart.* We can break down this sentence into the entities affected in differing ways by the verb. For instance, *the window cleaner* is the doer of the action described by the verb. *The supermodel* is the recipient of the action described by the verb. And *the heart,* representing the window cleaner's love, is the entity transferred to *the supermodel* as a consequence of the action the verb describes. Crucially, however, we have to know which entity is which: we must know that there is an entity that is the doer of the transfer event, that there is a transfer event, that there is a recipient of the transfer, and an object of transfer. All of this information is unique to this particular construction.

What I am saying, then, is that there is an abstract 'doer' role, an abstract 'recipient of the transfer' role and so on, that underlie the specific words that make up this particular sentence: *The window cleaner gave the supermodel his heart.* The construction that underlies this example sentence contains these components in abstract form.

This idea is important, and perhaps not obvious, so let's look at it in a bit more detail to show you what I mean. In the sentence I've been discussing – *The window cleaner gave the supermodel his heart* – the abstract form of the sentence can be represented as X CAUSES Y TO RECEIVE Z, where X, Y and Z represent, respectively, the doer, the recipient and the object of transfer. The order of each is obligatory, but other than that, there is a great deal of flexibility. Indeed, the verb doesn't need to be one that ordinarily implies transfer. While a verb such as *give* entails transfer, consider a verb like *bake,* as in *The window cleaner baked a cake.* *To bake* relates to an activity in which an item is created by virtue of being heated in an oven, e.g., the cake is created from cake mix by virtue of the baking process. Baking does not normally imply transfer. But when we put *bake* into the X CAUSES Y TO RECEIVE Z construction, the verb *bake* now has its meaning massaged, so that transfer – or at least the intention to cause transfer – *is* caused by the baking, for instance: *The window cleaner baked the supermodel a cake (on their first anniversary).*

This reveals that there is an underlying meaning associated with the sentence that is relatively abstract: X CAUSES Y TO RECEIVE Z. It is abstract in the sense that it is not tied to the words that populate the sentence, but must exist in the mind of a native speaker, independently of specific words. This then enables speakers to be able to slot particular words into the X, Y and Z positions.

But what of the form of the construction? Like the meaning, X CAUSES Y TO RECEIVE Z, this is also abstract. There are no obligatory word forms required. In our mental grammar, we must know that there is a slot for a noun phrase (NP) that corresponds to X. There is a verb that entails, or at least can be interpreted as relating to, transfer. And this is paired with the 'cause to receive' component. And there must be NPs that correspond to the Y and Z slots. We can therefore represent the abstract construction as follows:

Meaning: X CAUSES Y TO RECEIVE Z
Form: NP1 VERB OF TRANSFER NP2 NP3

And this basic construction allows us to convey a host of quite different scenes of transfer; here are some example sentences:

The window cleaner gave the supermodel a bouquet of roses.
The supermodel threw the window cleaner an evil look.
The window cleaner offered the supermodel his hand in
    marriage.
The supermodel passed the window cleaner anti-balding hair
    treatment.

In short, these sentences, and countless others, are made possible because we have an abstract X CAUSES Y TO RECEIVE Z construction in our mental grammars.

The language-as-use view of grammar is, consequently, quite different from the language-as-instinct perspective. Grammar consists of constructions: form–meaning pairs, which vary in abstractness in terms of both meaning and form. And, as a consequence, there is no principled distinction between words (or lexicon) and rules (or syntax). The mental grammar is, essentially, a repository of constructions, ranging from words to idioms to sentence-level constructions; these all vary in the degree to which they are filled by pre-specified sound components. While words are fully specified, idioms such as *kick the bucket* are partially specified. At the extreme, sentence-level constructions such as X CAUSES Y TO RECEIVE Z, and countless others, are fully abstract.

How, then, would such a perspective explain the way in which infants learn the latter sort of constructions, the abstract sentence-level type upon which sentence structure depends? The idea is that sentence-level constructions ('rules') are abstracted from the way in which words are combined in the input to which infants are exposed. When children hear expressions that embody the X CAUSES Y TO RECEIVE Z construction, the pattern is slowly, and painstakingly, abstracted, giving rise to a mental grammatical unit, a 'schema' – the process I described in Chapter 4. By around the age of four, infants have a complex mental corpus,[23] made up of words, fixed patterns of words (e.g., idioms), and more abstract sentence-level constructions, that have been extracted from the language they have been exposed to. These form relatively abstract schemas, or grammatical 'rules'.

But the key point is this: the 'rules' are, in principle, no different from words. They, like words, are constructions, consisting of stable pairings of form and meaning. The only difference is a qualitative one, relating to levels of abstractness in terms of the form and meaning that are coupled in the construction.

So how does this mental corpus of constructions allow us to communicate? In essence, when we combine words, what we are in fact doing is integrating them into the larger, more abstract, sentence-level constructions. Sometimes larger, more encompassing constructions restrict what sorts of words can be integrated. Such constructions include idioms, such as *kick the bucket*. An idiom is essentially a highly restrictive construction: it is highly selective as to what sorts of words can be integrated with it. For instance, the *kick the bucket* idiom already specifies that *kick the bucket* must appear in the construction. But, as I observed earlier, it leaves open possibilities for other elements, such as the subject. In contrast, a more abstract construction such as X CAUSES Y TO RECEIVE Z allows a wider range of words to be integrated with it.

In the final analysis, language provides a repertoire of constructions with varying levels of complexity and abstractness. Language use involves the combination of these, so that words, the most concrete type of construction, are combined with more over-arching constructions in building up phrases and larger sentence-like utterances. When we use language to produce novel sentences, what we are in fact doing is integrating words with these abstract sentence-level constructions.[24]

One consequence of this view – that both words and more abstract sentence-level schemas are constructions – is that the mental grammar exhibits a lot of redundancy. For instance, while a specific expression such as *girls* is predictable from the word *girl*, plus the plural schema [NOUN-s], the word *girls* is nevertheless stored in our mental grammar along with the singular form *girl*, as well as the plural schema [NOUN-s]. And the reason for this redundancy derives from the way we learn language: constructions arise due to frequency and repetition. Both *girl* and *girls* are highly frequent in the language input we are exposed to.

As I observed in Chapter 4, the consequence of frequency and repetition in language acquisition is that language is learned as chunks. The linguist Joan Bybee says that "Chunking is the process behind the formation and use of formulaic or prefabricated sequences of words such as *take a break, break a habit, pick and choose*."[25] In the early stages of language learning, these chunks are learned as entire units due to their repetition in language use, which explains why *girl* and *girls* both appear in our mental grammars. And later, schemas are abstracted, giving rise to the 'rules' of grammar. Hence, the plural schema [NOUN-s] is extracted from multiple instances of the *-s* suffix being found on nouns, giving rise to a plural meaning.

But this situation contrasts with a plural noun like *portcullises*, which is unlikely to be stored, because this expression has low frequency. Instead, this form would be constructed by combination of the plural schema [NOUN-(e)s] and the singular form *portcullis*.

Finally, the language-as-use thesis claims that linguistic units – constructions – are organised in an individual's mind as a network, with more abstract schemas being related to more specific instances of language. In this way, each of us carries around with us, in our heads, a grammar that has considerable internal hierarchical organisation: less abstract schemas are instances of more abstract schemas. For example, consider prepositions (P) like *for*, *on* and *in*, which are combined with a noun phrase (NP) to form a preposition phrase (PP). In the following examples, the NP is bracketed:

to [me]
on [the floor]
in [the garage]

The expressions *to me*, *on the floor* and *in the garage* are common phrases that are probably sufficiently frequently used for them to be stored as chunks for most speakers of English. However, there is another schema related to these constructions, which has the highly schematic form [P [NP]] and the highly schematic meaning DIRECTION OR LOCATION WITH RESPECT TO SOME PHYSICAL ENTITY. The specific expressions, *to me*, *on the floor*, and so on, are instances of the more abstract schema [P [NP]]. I have illustrated this relationship in the diagram below, showing the relationship between the more abstract and more specific schemas.

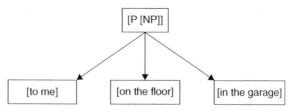

An example of the hierarchical organisation of mental grammar.

Universal scenes of experience

In Chapter 3, I showed that the notion of absolute linguistic universals is a myth. Yet while languages often surprise us in their diversity, all languages appear to have the means of conveying the basic scenes of human experience. Each day, no matter whether you are a speaker of English, Malay, Wolof or Guugu Yimithirr, you move objects from one location to another, you give someone something, and perform countless other sorts of mundane tasks. Moreover, these everyday scenes are performed many times a day, no matter where you come from or what culture you are embedded in. These sorts of everyday scenes are common to all of us: they are universal. And it turns out that these everyday scenes from human experience are encoded across all the world's languages. This doesn't mean that languages encode universal scenes in the same way – it simply means that they have conventional linguistic resources for doing so.

In the previous section I described the X CAUSES Y TO RECEIVE Z construction. This sentence-level construction exemplifies one such universal scene of experience. Countless times a day, we give something to someone: I pass a biscuit to a child, I loan money to a friend, I give a book to a student, I pay the shopkeeper, and so on. And English conveniently encodes the essential components of these scenes of object transfer with a sentence-level construction. While the details vary, such as who does the transferring, the nature of the transfer event, what is transferred and to whom, English provides us with a ready-made template that enables us to convey anything ranging from concrete transfer – *The supermodel gave the window cleaner a hanky* – to more abstract scenes of transfer – *The supermodel gave the window cleaner a piece of her mind.*[26]

While scenes of transfer are relatively complex, there are other types of relational scenes which are simpler in nature, but which also appear to be universal. For instance, humans the world over appear to conceptualise certain entities as belonging to others. This notion of possession also appears to be a universal, a relation that is central to human experience. Languages differ, often markedly, in how they express this.[27] Possession can be signalled by genitive case, indicated by the – *'s*, as in *John's shoes*; by prepositions, for instance *of* in *Queen of England*; by dedicated possessive markers; or in a range of other ways. But, to my knowledge, all languages so far discovered encode possession in one way or another.

Other sorts of universals relate to domains of experience, such as time and space. Here I'm not thinking about the relatively abstract ideas about what space and time are. After all, much philosophical ink has been spilt as to whether time is real, or a phantasm created by the human mind.[28] Regardless of the ontological status of these domains, in our everyday lives we are very much creatures that inhabit the here and now: space and time. We all need to be able to distinguish between here and there, and now and then. And the grammatical systems of the world's languages provide a range of lexical and grammatical resources allowing us to distinguish between present and past, and our relative location in space with respect to other aspects of our physical environment.[29] Whether it has a grammatical system for tense or aspect, or signals temporal distinctions in other ways, each language provides its users with resources for speaking and thinking about their egocentric experiences in the spatio-temporal matrix of embodied experience. Even pre-industrial societies, such as the Amondawa – a remote tribe of around 150 Amazonian Indians – which lack indigenous calendar and time-reckoning systems, nevertheless have complex lexical and grammatical resources for conceptualising events, sequences and cycles of events, and their relationship with the agrarian cycle that looms large in their lives.[30]

In the final analysis, any objective researcher would be hard-pressed to identify linguistic universals – beyond the banal. And this is because human 'universals' don't reside *in* language. Universals, such as they are, derive from the sorts of experiences that we share, a consequence of the broadly equivalent physical environment all humans experience, and the common neuro-anatomical structures we all have: our brains and bodies are broadly similar, regardless of the language(s) we speak. And this ensures that there are certain commonalities that all languages must be able to express, regardless of the language-specific strategies for doing so.

Why are there so many languages?

But if there are universal scenes of human experience, why are there so many damn languages? With advances in the study of biological evolution, the way in which languages evolve is becoming clearer. And this sheds light on why there are so many languages, and why they are so very different.

An important idea in biological evolution is that of variation. When there is variation in a species – in terms of the gene pool – this leads to diversification, and in time, evolution: a new species is born. This notion of variation also turns out to be key in understanding why there are so many languages in the world; variation in a language provides the basis for divergence. And with the essential ingredient, time, languages come to be born, slowly diverging from their ancestor languages.

One example of this great diversity is the number of distinct sounds found in the world's languages. Some languages, such as Rotokas, a language spoken in the Pacific, have only a dozen distinct sounds, or phonemes. Others, such as the Khoi-San languages, spoken in Africa, have well over 100.

Our species, *Homo sapiens*, originated in Africa around 170,000 years ago.[31] In a series of diaspora, from around 100,000 years ago, our species has slowly colonised all habitable parts of the planet. But it turns out that genetic diversity is, for the most part, greatest in Africa, and diminishes with increasing distance from Africa. This is an example of what evolutionary biologists call a 'founder effect': as each sub-group moves away from the founding group, it carries less of the genetic variation with it. Hence, successive moves away from Africa, around the globe, have led to less genetic diversity.[32]

A recent study on the sound inventories of human languages has found a remarkably similar founder effect. Languages appear, albeit with exceptions – including a number of indigenous languages from the American northwest coast – to exhibit broadly diminished variation the farther they are from Africa. Whilst languages in Africa exhibit the greatest number of phonemes, the further away you go, languages exhibit increasingly diminished numbers in their sound inventories, with the lowest levels in the Pacific.

This pattern illustrates one way in which language change and diversification closely resemble biological evolution: "when a small sub-population hives off from a larger one, it carries only a small part of the larger population's variation, so further changes start from a different base".[33] What this means, in language terms, is that the new linguistic community will develop in divergent ways from the original group from which it diverged: its lingueme pool – the variation in linguistic material available to its users – is different from that of the founder population.

Another reason for diversification in languages arises from the phenomenon of drift. Changes to isolated communities, including to the sound systems of a language, grammatical innovations and semantic shifts, are sufficient for a language, within just a few hundred years, to change almost beyond recognition. English is very different from German, even though they both evolved from the same group of communities who, 1,500 years ago, inhabited what is now northern Germany, Jutland in modern-day Denmark, and part of Holland. Isolated populations drift apart linguistically, over time, as the changes accumulate, rendering mutual intelligibility impossible in only a few generations.

And this phenomenon of drift evolves in lineage-specific ways. The mother language of European languages is Proto-Indo-European or PIE for short. But PIE probably lacked noun phrases with complex internal structure like *the Queen of England's litter of corgis*.[34] These have emerged, over time, in both Germanic languages (including English) and Romance languages (including French).[35] This is the result not of some underlying innate blueprint for language, but of a process of gradual evolutionary drift: a consequence of a variation that has taken hold in earlier mother languages from which English and French are descended.

That said, the degree to which languages change is highly variable. While English has changed virtually beyond recognition in a little over 1,000 years, over the same period, Icelandic, which is also a Germanic language, has, in comparison, changed barely at all. Many contemporary speakers of Icelandic can, with a little effort, understand the Icelandic Sagas written in Old Icelandic around 800 years ago – Old Icelandic was a western dialect of Old Norse. For contemporary speakers of English, even the Middle English of Chaucer written around 600 years ago remains a foreign language. Moreover, the writing system for Old Icelandic, which was laid down in the early twelfth century in a document called the First Grammatical Treatise, remains remarkably similar to modern Icelandic, and can be more or less straightforwardly read by contemporary speakers.

But while individual languages vary in how quickly they change, the rate of language change is sufficient, in just a few thousand years, for any hint of a common origin to be all but obliterated. As language is a form of social behaviour, and is maintained and evolves in daily interaction and use, geographical separation means that different linguistic communities will change in different ways, following markedly different trajectories. For instance, the modern descendants of Classical Latin are French, Italian, Spanish, Portuguese and Romanian. But each of these languages is quite different, and, moreover, consists of dialects that may even border on mutual unintelligibility. Geographical separation provides the conditions within which a new language can incubate. Languages are reflections of social customs, conventions, institutions, as well as legal, political and educational systems. They mirror (and reinforce) behaviours, beliefs, attitudes and socio-cultural forms of practice. Language reflects all these aspects of its users and the cultural milieu that they cooperatively construct and enact on a daily basis, in part through language. Language is part of the mosaic of social life. The normal process of innovation and propagation of change mirrors cultural divergence, leading, over time, inescapably, to great linguistic diversity.

In addition to the regular processes of language change in distinct social groups, the velocity of diversity receives a burst from the movement of peoples. Whenever people from different socio-cultural groups come into contact, this furthers the rate of diversification in language. Language contact gives rise to often unpredictable alterations in a linguistic system, leading to far-reaching change. Language contact can result from war, invasion, empire building and colonisation, exploration and travel, slavery, transportation and a constellation of other factors.

Finally, languages can also be born without requiring evolution from mother to daughter languages, as when Latin gave rise to Italian, French, Romanian and so on. In the case of home-sign, languages can be created from gestures, due to the human inter-action engine. These factors have all led to a rapid diversification of language. We can, more or less, trace English back to Proto-Germanic, which can, in turn, be traced back to Proto-Indo-European. But this only goes back around several thousand years. We have no idea what human languages sounded like at an earlier point in our lineage.

One thing we can be sure of, however, is that diversification is continuing apace, despite our globalised world, and the seemingly relentless rise of the world's global language: English. Recent advances in the computational modelling of linguistic evolution demonstrate that, rather than putative universals determining language change, languages are evolving based on patterns in their lineages. And, due to evolutionary pressures, language families and the languages that populate them are, in fact, moving further apart: as the time-depth of human language increases, so languages are drifting further apart, in terms of their diversity.[36] And in the future, we can be sure of one thing, if nothing else: languages will continue to evolve, change and diversify, enlarging the design-space for what human language looks like.

One final reflection …

To close, I offer one final reflection on the language-as-instinct thesis. Chomsky was, throughout his career, desperate to separate out language from communication. He consistently argued that language – by which he meant our inborn competence to deploy innate rules of grammar – is distinct from performance – how we use language to communicate with one another. As Daniel Everett has tellingly observed, on the face of it, this is an extremely odd stance to take.[37] Why would one wish to claim that language is not, fundamentally, about communication and meaning? The reason, presumably, is that, if the central purpose of language is to facilitate communication, then at least two people would simultaneously have had to acquire the chance mutation that led to language and put us on a plane far above all other species.[38] But the chances of two individuals simultaneously developing such a mutation are vanishingly remote.

Chomsky reasoned as follows: if language evolved, in hopeful monster fashion, in one sudden leap, and for some purpose other than communication, then the story becomes more plausible. Chomsky appears to assume that language emerged all at once to facilitate thinking – language does, after all, provide a means of encoding and externalising concepts, as we have seen. Writing in 2002, Chomsky claims that "language use is largely to oneself: 'inner speech' for adults, monologue for children".[39] And in this way, perhaps, the evolutionary genesis of language lay not in communication at all. The utility of language for communicative purposes emerged only later, as a friend with benefits, so to speak. Chomsky also reasoned that, once the utility of language – in supporting thinking – had spread through the early human population, it then became co-opted as a means of communication. But in the beginning, language had no communicative function.

In Chapter 2, I observed that Chomsky has argued that language emerged all at once, in a near-perfect form, in one individual as a sudden jump in evolution: a macro-mutation: "roughly 100,000+ years ago ... there were no languages ... [but] ... a rewiring of the brain took place in some individual, call him Prometheus". This rewiring, of course, supposedly instigated language.[40] And once the role of language facilitated the evolutionary advantage of more sophisticated thought, only then did it develop a communicative function, so Chomsky reasons.

But such a hopeful monster account is hard to swallow, even for die-hard language-as-instinct stalwarts: Steven Pinker, to his credit, doesn't buy it.[41] After all, a single, large-scale evolutionary jump – a macro-mutation – is at odds with the modern neo-Darwinian synthesis. Moreover, it is also at odds with what all sensible evolutionary researchers believe. It now seems plausible, if not likely, that human language is far older than the 100,000 years that Chomsky presumed.

In recent research, Dan Dediu and Stephen Levinson claim that *Homo neanderthalensis*, the last surviving species of the genus *Homo*, humans excepted, most likely already had language.[42] Neanderthals may have already been present in Eurasia as early as 600,000 years ago, way before the advent of *Homo sapiens* in Africa. And for Neanderthals to have had language, it must have already been present, at least in proto-language form, prior to that in the common ancestor of both humans and Neanderthals: fossil remains of *Homo heidelbergensis* have been found in both Africa and Europe from around 1.3 million years ago, and would appear to be the common ancestor of both *Homo sapiens* and *Homo neanderthalensis*. In short, linguistic abilities of some kind are

likely to have been present in the genus *Homo* way before 100,000
years ago, and prior to the emergence of humans 170,000 years
ago. As such, this casts yet further doubt on Chomsky's account of
a sudden, unexplained, evolutionary jump: let there be language!
And, at the end of the day, does any sensible person really believe
that language could plausibly have evolved for anything other
than communication?

In the final analysis, the distinctive qualities of human language
point not to a sharp divide between human language and non-
human communicative systems. Rather, they point to a special
kind of cultural intelligence which other species don't have.
Despite frequent evidence to the contrary, we as a species are
inherently cooperative. This allows us to advance and extend the
cognitive abilities, including the communicative systems, that
our ancestors shared with other apes. Language is the paradigmatic example of our cultural intelligence, built upon pro-social
motives, and our interaction engine. Language is the measure of
our lives, and what it means to be human.

Notes

1 Language and mind rethought

1 Mithen (1996).
2 www.nobelprize.org/nobel_prizes/literature/laureates/1993/morrison-lecture.html
3 Although see Dąbrowska and Street (2006) who demonstrate that language is not inevitably blind to socioeconomics: level of education has a bearing on ultimate language attainment.
4 Lakoff (2004).
5 Bolinger (1980).
6 From a letter published in the *Manchester Guardian* on 21 June 1954.
7 "José Mourinho's return rekindles his fling with the English game!", article accessed 5 June 2013 www.guardian.co.uk/football/blog/2013/jun/05/jose-mourinho-chelsea-fling?INTCMP=SRCH.
8 Popper (1959).
9 Tomasello (2003).
10 Dawkins (1986).
11 Everett (2013).
12 Chemero (2009).
13 Fromkin and Rodman (1997: 19).
14 Brinton (2000: Chapter 1).
15 Mithen (1996).
16 Dawkins (2010).
17 Chomsky (2004, 2009).
18 Deacon (1997).
19 Levinson and Gray (2012).
20 Hardcastle (1976).
21 Tomasello and Herrmann (2010).
22 Varela *et al.* (1991).
23 Deacon (1998).
24 Arbib (2012); Pika *et al.* (2005).
25 Hurford (2007, 2012).

2 Is human language unrelated to animal communication systems?

1 http://www.huffingtonpost.com/2012/07/26/tori-smoking-orangutan-_n_1708105.html, date accessed 26 July 2012.
2 Chomsky (2010: 58–9).
3 See Hurford (2007) for details.
4 Hauser, et al. (2002).
5 Everett (2005).
6 Von Frisch (1953).
7 Seyfarth et al. (1980).
8 Hauser et al.(2002).
9 Marcus (2006).
10 Genter et al. (2006).
11 Payne and McVay (1971); Suzuki et al. (2006).
12 Antunes et al. (2011).
13 Antunes et al. (2011).
14 Rendell and Whitehead (2003a, b).
15 Norris et al. (2000).
16 Pika et al. (2005).
17 Searle (1969).
18 Searle (1969).
19 Kellogg and Kellogg (1933).
20 Barney et al. (2012).
21 Nishimura et al. (2003).
22 Lieberman et al. (1969, 1972).
23 Gardner and Gardner (1969, 1974).
24 Fouts et al. (1978).
25 Premack (1974, 1986); Premack and Premack (1983).
26 Lovgren (2005).
27 Pika et al. (2005); Tomasello (2011).
28 Terrace (1979).
29 Pinker (1994: 337–9).
30 Hurford (2007, 2012).
31 Hurford (2012: x).
32 Hockett (1966).
33 Emmorey (2002); Goldin-Meadow and Mylander (1990); Klima and Bellugi (1979).
34 Pepperberg (1983, 2000).

35 MacNeilage (2008).
36 Arbib (2012); Mukamel *et al.* (2010).
37 Arbib (2010); Corballis (2003); Tomasello (1999).
38 Corballis (2003).
39 Rizzolatti and Craighero (2004).
40 Herman *et al.* (1984).
41 Herman *et al.* (1984).
42 Gardner and Gardner (1969).
43 Savage-Rumbaugh and Lewin (1996).
44 Arnold and Zuberbühler (2006); Yip (2006).
45 Ouattara *et al.* (2009).
46 Rumbaugh (1977).
47 Lana's awareness of word order was not, however, mirrored by Sarah, who seemed not to grasp syntax at all (Premack and Premack 1983).
48 Sandler *et al.* (2011).
49 Hillix *et al.* (2004).
50 Mulcahy and Call (2006).
51 Byrne and Whiten (1988).
52 Call and Tomasello (2008); Lurz (2011); Pika *et al.* (2005); Schmelz *et al.* (2012); Tomasello and Call (1997).
53 Crockford *et al.* (2011).
54 Patterson and Linden (1985).
55 Clayton *et al.* (2001); Clayton *et al.* (2007).
56 Heinrich and Pepper. (1998).
57 Terrace (1979); Terrace *et al.* (1979).
58 Lieberman (1984).
59 Savage-Rumbaugh *et al.* (1986: 305).
60 Byrne and Whiten (1988).
61 Tomasello (2008).
62 Pika *et al.* (2005).
63 Gerhardt (1994).
64 Tomasello (2008).

3 Are there language universals?

1 Chomsky (1980a: 48).
2 Chomsky (1965).
3 *Ethnologue*: www.ethnologue.com.

4 Crystal (2002).
5 Fishman (2000); Nettle and Romaine (2002).
6 Evans and Levinson (2009).
7 Evans and Levinson (2009: 438).
8 Austin and Bresnan (1996).
9 Levinson (1996:133).
10 Chomsky (1965).
11 Pinker (1994: 238).
12 See Givon (1984) for a detailed critique.
13 Evans and Levinson (2009).
14 Sandler *et al.* (2011); see also the special issue of *Language &*
   Cognition, 2012 (4/4), which focuses on duality of patterning.
15 Jakobson and Halle (1956).
16 Ladefoged and Maddieson (1996).
17 Pierrehumbert (2000: 12).
18 Evans and Levinson (2009).
19 Enfield (2004).
20 Jelinek (1995).
21 See Evans and Green (2006: Chapter 2), for review and discussion.
22 That said, in some contexts it may be possible to use a formulation
   of this sort, for instance if someone is totting up how much
   someone owes.
23 Matthews (1981: 255).
24 Dryer and Haspelmath (2011): http://wals.info/.
25 After Dryer and Haspelmath (2011: Chapter 81).
26 Van Valin and La Polla (1997).
27 Greenberg (1986: 14).
28 Evans and Levinson (2009).
29 Chomsky (1981).
30 Jackendoff (2002).
31 See discussion in Sampson (2001).
32 See Popper (1959).
33 Dryer (1998).
34 Pederson (1993).
35 Croft (2000).
36 Croft's inspiration is specifically David Hull's (1989) Generalised
   Theory of Selection.
37 Dawkins (1976).

38 Croft (2000); Keller (1994).
39 LePage and Tabouret-Keller (1985).
40 Croft (2000: 75).
41 Labov (1994).
42 Jesperson (1909).
43 This corresponds to a well-known tendency in vowel shifts for long vowels to rise, while short vowels fall.
44 For discussion see Evans (2009); Evans and Green (2006); and Tyler and Evans (2003).
45 Trask (1996).
46 Campbell (2010); Trask (1996).
47 Trask (1996).
48 Renfrew (1990).
49 Bouckaert *et al.* (2012).
50 Campbell (2010: 8).
51 Smith (1997).
52 Goldin-Meadow (2003).
53 Senghas (2005).
54 Sandler *et al.* (2005).
55 Marsaja (2008).
56 Evans and Levinson (2009); Goldin-Meadow (2003).
57 Sandler *et al.* (2005).
58 Chomsky (1980b: 48).
59 Dunn *et al.* (2011).

4 Is language innate?

1 Tomasello (2003: 19)
2 Chomsky (1975: 4).
3 Tomasello (2003).
4 McNeill (1966: 69).
5 Chomsky (2002: 41).
6 Chomsky (1975: 11).
7 Gallistel (2007).
8 Chomsky (1980a: 110).
9 Pinker (1994:12).
10 See recent discussion of poverty of stimulus arguments provided by Berwick *et al.* (2011).

11 Crain (1991); Crain and Nakayama (1986).
12 Prinz (2002: 210).
13 Boyd and Goldberg (2011); Goldberg (2011); Suttle and Goldberg (2011).
14 Gold (1967).
15 Bates *et al.* (1999: 599).
16 For a detailed critique of the poverty of the stimulus argument, see Pullum and Scholz (2002).
17 Azevedo *et al.* (2009); Herculano-Houzel (2009).
18 Drachman (2005).
19 Alonso-Nanclares *et al.* (2008).
20 Churchland (1995).
21 Bates *et al.* (1999: 593).
22 Wills (1991).
23 Edelman (1987); Wills (1991).
24 Bates *et al.* (1999); Elman *et al.* (1996).
25 Sur, Pallas and Roe (1990).
26 Stanfield and O'Leary (1985).
27 Bruno *et al.* (2012); Greenough *et al.* (1993); Merzenich (1995); Pons *et al.* (1991).
28 Edelman (1987).
29 Deacon (1997).
30 Rakic (1995).
31 Bates *et al.* (1997).
32 Bates *et al.* (1999).
33 Elman *et al.* (1996).
34 Radford (1990: 61).
35 Chomsky (1981); Chomsky and Lasnik (1993).
36 Tomasello (1992, 2003).
37 Bloom (1973).
38 Braine (1963).
39 Examples are drawn from Braine (1963).
40 Ambridge and Lieven (2011); Tomasello (2003).
41 Bates *et al.* (1984); Bates and MacWhinney (1989); De Villiers and De Villiers (1973).
42 Tomasello (1992).
43 Brooks and Tomasello (1999).

44 See Tomasello (2003) for a review of the relevant literature.
45 Naigles and Hoff-Ginsberg (1998).
46 Theakston *et al.* (2004).
47 Huttenlocher *et al.* (2002).
48 Tomasello (2003: 110).
49 Lieven *et al.* (2003).
50 Saffran *et al.* (1996).
51 See Tomasello (2003) for a review.
52 Tomasello (2003).
53 See Tomasello (2003, 2008).
54 Fantz (1963).
55 Legerstee (1991).
56 Trevarthen (1979).
57 Meltzoff (1995).
58 Carpenter *et al.* (1998).
59 Bybee (e.g., 2001, 2006, 2010).
60 See also the work of Ellis (e.g., 2006) who has explored the roles that salience and contingency play in language acquisition.
61 Boyd and Goldberg (2011); Goldberg (2011); Suttle and Goldberg (2011).
62 Bickerton (1981, 1984).
63 Maratsos (1984); Samarin (1984); Seuren (1984).
64 Goldin-Meadow and Mylander (1990); see also Goldin-Meadow (2003).
65 Casasanto (2013).
66 Goldin-Meadow (2003); Kendon (2004); McNeill (1992).
67 Arbib (2012, 2013); Arbib *et al.* (2008).
68 Casasanto (2013: 373).
69 Langacker (2002: 2); see also Langacker (2000).
70 Bybee (2010).
71 See Tomasello (2003) for detailed discussion of the evidence for the usage-based approach to language acquisition. See Ambridge and Lieven (2011) which nicely compares and contrasts the language-as-instinct versus language-as-use approaches to child language acquisition.
72 Scholz and Pullum (2006).
73 See Ibbotson (2013) for an excellent overview of the scope of the language-as-use thesis.

5 Is language a distinct module in the mind?

1 Fodor (1983); see also Chomsky (1980a), and Gardner (1985).
2 Pinker (1994: 45); see also Smith and Tsimpli (1995).
3 Pinker (1994: 46).
4 Broca (1877; translated in Harrington 1987: 65–66).
5 Chance and Crow (2007).
6 Caplan (2006).
7 Pinker (1994:46).
8 Gardner (1974: 60–1).
9 Lai *et al.* (2001).
10 Pinker (1994: 49).
11 Chomsky (2011).
12 Smith (1999: 26).
13 Grodzinsky and Santi (2008).
14 Maess *et al.* (2001).
15 Plaza *et al.* (2009).
16 Plaza *et al.* (2009).
17 Dronkers *et al.* (2007).
18 Corballis (2003); Fadiga *et al.* (2005); Skipper *et al.* (2007).
19 Corballis (2003); cf. Arbib (2012).
20 Uttal (2001).
21 Pulvermüller (1999).
22 Dąbrowska (2004).
23 Vargha-Khadem *et al.* (1995).
24 Enard *et al.* (2002).
25 Dąbrowska (2004: 75).
26 Bellugi *et al.* (1992); Karmiloff-Smith *et al.* (1995); Mervis and Bertrand (1993).
27 Bates and Goodman (1999).
28 Capirici *et al.* (1996).
29 Singer Harris *et al.*(1997).
30 Bellugi *et al.* (1994).
31 Karmiloff-Smith (2001: 50–1).
32 Bishop (1997, 2006); Leonard (1998).
33 Johnston (1994).
34 Thal and Katich (1996).
35 Townsend *et al.* 1995).
36 Bishop (1997); Leonard (1998); Tallal *et al.* (1996).

37 Mody *et al.* (1997).
38 Bates *et al.* (1995); Dale (1991); Dale *et al.* (1989); Fenson *et al.* (1993); Fenson *et al.* (1994); Marchman and Bates (1994).
39 Bates and Goodman (1999).
40 Bates and Goodman (1999).
41 Caselli *et al.* (1995).
42 Bates and Goodman (1999).
43 Jahn-Samilo *et al.* (2000).
44 Bates and Goodman (1997, 1999); Tomasello and Slobin (2004).
45 Pinker (1994: 97).
46 Pinker (1994: 437).
47 Pinker (1997).
48 Prinz (2006).
49 Machery (2007: 827).
50 Prinz (2006); Wallace (2010).
51 Carruthers (2006).
52 Cosmides (1989).
53 Stone *et al.* (2002).
54 Prinz (2006); Wallace (2010).
55 Tooby and Cosmides (1992). See also Carruthers (2006).
56 See also Jackendoff (1987, 1992).
57 McGurk and McDonald (1976)
58 Hötting and Roder (2004).
59 Pinker (2002: 238).
60 Dawkins (2010).
61 See papers and references in Rose and Rose (2001).
62 Quartz (2002).
63 Finlay and Darlington (1995).
64 Gibbs and Van Orden (2010: 149).
65 Machery (2007: 827).
66 See the telling critique of massive modularity in Gibbs and Van Orden (2010).
67 Prinz (2006).
68 Deacon (1997).
69 Varela *et al.* (1991).
70 Gibbs and Van Orden (2010).
71 Mahmoudzadeha *et al.* (2012).
72 Varela *et al.* (1991).

73 Karmiloff-Smith (1994).
74 Fromkin *et al.* (2013: 479).

6 Is there a universal Mentalese?

 1 Fodor (1975, 1998, 2008).
 2 Hurford (2007).
 3 Prinz (2002: 1).
 4 Fodor (1975: 68).
 5 Pinker (1994: 82).
 6 Fodor (1975, 2008); Pinker (1997).
 7 Jackendoff (1987, 1992).
 8 Wynn (1992, 1995).
 9 McGonigle and Chalmers (1977).
10 Bond *et al.* (2003).
11 Hobbes ([1651] 2012: part I, Chapter 5).
12 Fodor (1975: 27).
13 Harnad (1990).
14 Maslin (2001).
15 Pinker (1997: 79).
16 Pinker (1997: 79).
17 Pinker (1997: 79).
18 Pinker (1997: 79).
19 See Wallace (2010) for detailed discussion.
20 Chomsky (1957).
21 Wallace (2010: 103).
22 James Pustejovsky (1995) refers to this as 'semanticality'.
23 Fodor (2008).
24 Fodor (2008).
25 Fodor (2008: 143).
26 Sinha (1988).
27 Clark (1997).
28 Chemero (2009).
29 Thelen (1995); Thelen and Smith (1994).
30 Churchland (2002); Grush (1997, 2004).
31 Clark (1997).
32 Lakoff and Johnson (1980, 1999).
33 Examples derived from Lakoff and Johnson (1980).

34 Dahan and Tanenhaus (2004).
35 Isenberg *et al.* (1999); Martin and Chao (2001); Pulvermüller (1999); see also Buccino *et al.* (2005). For a review, see Taylor and Zwaan (2009).
36 Dahan and Tanenhaus (2004); Stanfield and Zwaan (2001); Zwaan and Yaxley (2003).
37 Büchel *et al.* (1998); Martin and Chao (2001).
38 Isenberg *et al.* (1999).
39 LeDoux (1995).
40 Glenberg and Kaschak (2002); Klatzky *et al.* (1989); Spivey *et al.* (2000).
41 Zwaan (2004: 36); see also Clark (1997).
42 Glenberg and Kashak (2002).
43 Lakoff and Johnson (1980).
44 Casasanto and Dijkstra (2010).
45 Lakoff and Johnson (1999).
46 See Jackendoff (1983, 1992) for related views.
47 Li and Gleitman (2002: 266).
48 Scholz and Pullum (2006).

7 Is thought independent of language?

1 Bloom and Keil (2001: 354).
2 Whorf (1956: 213).
3 Pinker (1994: 51).
4 Pinker (1994: 58–9).
5 Lupyan (2012a, b).
6 Casasanto (2008).
7 Fodor (1985: 5).
8 Fodor (1985: 5).
9 Fodor (1985: 5).
10 Pinker (1994, 2007).
11 Pourcel (2005).
12 Sapir (1985: 159).
13 Whorf (1956: 221).
14 Lee (1996).
15 Lee (1996); see also Pourcel (2005).
16 Pourcel (2005: 14).
17 Brown (1976: 128); Brown and Lenneberg (1954); Lenneberg (1953); see also Brown (1957, 1958).

18 Whorf (1956: 239).
19 Levinson (2000: 3).
20 Rosch (1977: 519).
21 Lumsden and Wilson (1981); Shepherd (1991); Thompson (1995).
22 Berlin and Kay (1969: 109).
23 Saunders (2000: 82).
24 Kay and McDaniel (1978: 630).
25 Rosch Heider (1972).
26 Rosch Heider (1972).
27 Berlin and Kay (1969: 13). See also Kay et al. (2009).
28 Hurvich and Jameson (1957).
29 De Valois and De Valois (1993).
30 Bornstein et al. (1976).
31 Lucy (1992a, b, 1997). See also Saunders (2000).
32 See, for instance, Saunders (2000).
33 In addition to the work of John Lucy, see also papers in the following
    collections: Gentner and Goldin-Meadow (2003); Gumperz and
    Levinson (1996).
34 Lyons (1995); Wierzbicka (1996).
35 Lucy (1997).
36 For critiques of the physiological basis for colour terms, see D'An-
    drade (1989), and Saunders and van Brakel (1997). For critiques of
    the proposed evolutionary sequence, see Casson (1997), Lyons
    (1995) and MacLaury (1992). For critiques of the definition of basic
    colour terms, see Crawford (1982), Davies and Corbett (1995), Maffi
    (1990), and Moss (1989). For a critique of the biasing effect of using
    the Munsell colour system, see Lucy and Schweder (1979).
37 See, for instance, the following: Kay and Berlin (1997); Kay and
    Kempton (1984); Kay and MacDaniel (1978); Kay et al. (2009).
38 Levinson (2000).
39 Kay (1999). Note that this idea is distinct from the claim relating to
    the evolutionary sequence whereby a language obtains its basic
    colour terms. A language can, on this view, use its basic colour terms
    to designate the full colour spectrum without having a full set of
    basic colour terms.
40 Davies and Corbett (1995); Davies et al. (1992).
41 Berlin and Kay (1969: 13).
42 Levinson (2000: 26).

43 Roberson *et al.* (2004).

44 A wide array of cross-linguistic studies have now concluded that language influences how language users categorise and perceive colour categories. See, in particular, Daoutis *et al.* (2006); Davidoff *et al.* (1999); Davies and Corbett (1998); Roberson *et al.* (2005); Roberson *et al.* (2008); and Winawer *et al.* (2007).

45 The finding on Himba and English is consistent with findings reported by other studies (e.g., Macario 1991; Mervis *et al.*, 1975; Pitchford and Mullen 2002; Shatz *et al.*, 1996).

46 Pinker (2007: 148).

47 Pinker (2007: 139, citing Daniel Casasanto).

48 Thierry *et al.* (2009).

49 Thierry *et al.* (2009).

50 Boutonnet *et al.* (2013).

51 See also Lupyan (2012a).

52 Regier and Kay (2009: 439).

53 Boroditsky *et al.* (2003).

54 Boroditsky *et al.* (2003).

55 Boroditsky *et al.* (2003).

56 See Boroditsky *et al.* (2003).

57 Pinker (1997: 148).

58 Boutonnet *et al.* (2012).

59 Levinson (2003).

60 Foley (1997: 217).

61 Levinson (2003).

62 Boroditsky (2001); Boroditsky *et al.* (2011).

63 Yu (1998).

64 Boroditsky *et al.* (2011).

65 Lupyan (2012a, b).

66 See Evans (2009).

67 Deutscher (2011: 151).

8 Language and mind regained

1 Tomasello (1999, 2008).

2 Dunbar (1996).

3 Tomasello (2008, 2011).

4 Tomasello (2011).

5 Pika *et al.* (2005); Tomasello (2011).
6 Grice (1989).
7 Tomasello (1999).
8 Levinson (2006).
9 Melzoff and Moore (1977); see also Bruner (1976); Trevarthen (1979).
10 Goodwin (2003).
11 Levinson (2006: 43).
12 Levinson (2006: 45).
13 Clark (1996).
14 Adapted from Clark (1996).
15 Levinson (2006); Tomasello (2008).
16 Levinson (2006).
17 Everett (2012).
18 Dunbar (1996).
19 Levinson (2006).
20 Dunbar (1996).
21 Dunbar (1992).
22 See Evans (2009) for detailed discussion, and Evans and Green (2006) for an overview. Also see Goldberg (1995, 2006) and Langacker (2008).
23 Taylor (2012).
24 For a fairly accessible overview of the language-as-use approach to grammar see Evans and Green (2006, especially Chapter 14). For more technical overviews, see Goldberg (1995) and Langacker (2008).
25 Bybee (2010: 34).
26 See Goldberg's (1995) scene-encoding hypothesis – the idea that sentence-level constructions encode specific scenes from human experience.
27 See, for instance, Aikhenvald and Dixon (2013); Börjars *et al.* (2013); and Nichols and Bickel (2005).
28 See discussion in Evans (2013).
29 See Talmy (2000) for detailed discussion.
30 Sinha *et al.* (2011).
31 Mithen (1996).
32 Levinson and Gray (2012).
33 Levinson and Gray (2012: 170).
34 Van de Velde (2009a, b, 2010, 2011)
35 Faarlund (2001: 1713); Himmelmann (1997); Ledgeway (2011, 2012); Luraghi (2010); and Perridon and Sleeman (2011).

36 Levinson and Gray (2012).
37 Everett (2012, 2013).
38 Paul Ibbotson (personal communication).
39 Chomsky (2002: 76–7).
40 Chomsky (2010: 58–9).
41 In *The Language Instinct*, Pinker acknowledges that "Chomsky has puzzled many readers with his skepticism about whether Darwinian natural selection . . . can explain the origins of the language organ he argues for" (1994: 24).
42 Dediu and Levinson (2013).

References

Aikhenvald, A., and R. Dixon. (2013). *Possession and Ownership: A Cross-linguistic Typology.* Oxford University Press.

Alonso-Nanclares, L., J. Gonzalez-Soriano, J. R. Rodriguez and J. DeFelipe. (2008). Gender differences in human cortical synaptic density. *Proceedings of the National Academy of Sciences, USA,* 105/38: 14615–19.

Ambridge, B., and E. V. M. Lieven. (2011). *Child Language Acquisition: Contrasting Theoretical Approaches.* Cambridge University Press.

Antunes, R., T. Schulz, S. Gero, H. Whitehead, J. Gordon and L. Rendell. (2011). Individually distinctive acoustic features in sperm whale codas. *Animal Behaviour* 81/4: 723–30.

Arbib, M. A. (2013). Précis of how the brain got language. *Language and Cognition,* 5/2–3: 107–32, plus comments 133–272.

   (2012). *How the Brain Got Language: The Mirror System Hypothesis.* Oxford University Press.

Arbib, M. A. (2010). Mirror system activity for action and language is embedded in the integration of dorsal and ventral pathways. *Brain and Language,* 112/1: 12–24.

Arbib, M. A., K. Liebal and S. Pika. (2008). Primate vocalization, gesture, and the evolution of human language. *Current Anthropology,* 49/6: 1053–63.

Arnold, K., and K. Zuberbühler. (2006). The alarm-calling system of adult male putty nosed monkeys, *Cercopithecus nictitans martini. Animal Behavior,* 72: 643–53.

Austin, P., and J. Bresnan. (1996). Non-configurationality in Australian Aboriginal languages. *Natural Language and Linguistic Theory,* 14: 215–68.

Azevedo, F., L. Carvalho, L. Grinberg, J. Farfel, R. Ferretti, R. Leite, W. Filho, R. Lent *et al.* (2009). Equal numbers of neuronal and nonneuronal cells make the human brain an isometrically scaled-up primate brain. *The Journal of Comparative Neurology,* 513/5: 532–41.

Barney, A., S. Martelli, A. Serrurier and J. Steele. (2012). Articulatory capacity of Neanderthals, a very recent and human-like fossil hominin. *Philosophical Transactions of the Royal Society B*, 367/ 1585: 88–102.

Bates, E., P. Dale and D. Thal. (1995). Individual differences and their implications for theories of language development. In P. Fletcher and B. MacWhinney (eds.), *Handbook of Child Language* (pp. 96–151). Oxford: Basil Blackwell.

Bates, E., J. Elman, M. H. Johnson, A. Karmiloff-Smith, D. Parisi and K. Plunkett. (1999). Innateness and emergentism. In W. Bechtel and G. Graham (eds.), *A Companion to Cognitive Science* (pp. 590–601). Oxford: Blackwell.

Bates, E., and J. Goodman. (1999). On the emergence of grammar from the lexicon. In B. MacWhinney (ed.), *The Emergence of Language* (pp. 29–79). Mahwah, NJ: Lawrence Erlbaum.

Bates, E., and J. Goodman. (1997). On the inseparability of grammar and the lexicon: evidence from acquisition, aphasia and real-time processing. *Language and Cognitive Processes*, 12/5–6: 507–84.

Bates, E., and B. MacWhinney. (1989). Functionalism and the competition model. In B. MacWhinney and E. Bates (eds.), *The Crosslinguistic Study of Sentence Processing* (pp. 3–73). Cambridge University Press.

Bates, E., B. MacWhinney, C. Caselli, A. Devescovi, F. Natale and V. Venza. (1984). A cross-linguistic study of the development of sentence interpretation strategies. *Child Development*, 55: 341–54.

Bates, E., D. Thal, D. Trauner, D. Aram, J. Eisele and R. Nass. (1997). From first words to grammar in children with focal brain injury. In D. Thal and J. Reilly (eds.), Special issue on the origins of communication disorders. *Developmental Neuropsychology*, 13/3: 275–343.

Bellugi, U., A. Bihrle, H. Neville, T. Jernigan and S. Doherty. (1992). Language, cognition, and brain organization in a neurodevelopmental disorder. In M. Gunnar and C. Nelson (eds.), *Developmental Behavioral Neuroscience* (pp. 201–32). Hillsdale, NJ: Lawrence Erlbaum.

Bellugi, U., P. Wang and T. L. Jernigan. (1994). Williams syndrome: an unusual neuropsychological profile. In S. Broman and J. Grafman (eds.,), *Atypical Cognitive Deficits in Developmental Disorders: Implications for Brain Function* (pp. 23–56). Hillsdale, NJ: Lawrence Erlbaum.

Berlin, B., and P. Kay. (1969). *Basic Color Terms: Their Universality and Evolution*. Cambridge University Press.

Berwick, R. C., P. Pietroski, B. Yankama and N. Chomsky. (2011). Poverty of the stimulus revisited. *Cognitive Science*, 35: 1207–42.

Bickerton, D. (1984). The language bioprogram hypothesis. *Behavioral and Brain Sciences*, 7: 173–221.

—— (1981). *Roots of Language*. Ann Arbor, MI: Karoma Publishers.

Bishop, D. V. (2006). What causes specific language impairment in children? *Current Directions in Psychological Science*, 15/5: 217–21.

—— (1997). *Uncommon Understanding: Development and Disorders of Language Comprehension in Children*. Hove: Psychology Press Limited.

Bloom, L. (1973). *One Word at a Time*. The Hague: Mouton.

Bloom, P., and F. Keil. (2001). Thinking through language. *Mind and Language*, 6: 351–67.

Bolinger, D. (1980). *Language: the Loaded Weapon*. London: Longman.

Bond, A. B., A. C. Kamil and R. P. Balda. (2003). Social complexity and transitive inference in corvids. *Animal Behaviour*, 65: 479–87.

Börjars, K., D. Denison and A. Scott. (2013). *Morphosyntactic Categories and the Expression of Possession*. Amsterdam: John Benjamins.

Bornstein, M. H., W. Kessen and S. Weiskopf. (1976). The categories of hue in infancy. *Science*, 191: 4223.

Boroditsky, L. (2001). Does language shape thought? English and Mandarin speakers' conceptions of time. *Cognitive Psychology*, 43/1: 1–22.

Boroditsky, L., O. Fuhrman and K. McCormick. (2011). Do English and Mandarin speakers think about time differently? *Cognition*, 118/1: 123–9.

Boroditsky, L., L. Schmidt and W. Phillips. (2003). Sex, syntax, and semantics. In D. Gentner and S. Goldin-Meadow (eds.,), *Language in Mind: Advances in the study of Language and Cognition* (pp. 61–80). Cambridge, MA: MIT Press.

Bouckaert, R., P. Lemey, M. Dunn, S. J. Greenhill, A. V. Alekseyenko, A. J. Drummond, R. D. Gray, M. A. Suchard and Q. D. Atkinson (2012). Mapping the origins and expansion of the Indo-European language family. *Science*, 337/6097: 957–960.

Boutonnet, B., P. Athanasopoulos and G. Thierry. (2012). Unconscious effects of grammatical gender during object categorisation. *Brain Research*, 1479: 72–9.

Boutonnet, B., B. Dering, N. Viñas-Gusach and G. Thierry. (2013). Seeing objects through the language glass. *Journal of Cognitive Neuroscience*, 25/10: 1702–10.

Boyd, J. K., and A. E. Goldberg. (2011). Learning what not to say: the role of statistical preemption and categorization in 'a'-adjective production. *Language*, 81/1: 1–29.

Braine, M. D. S. (1963). The ontogeny of English phrase structure: the first phrase. *Language*, 39: 1–14.

Brinton, L. J. (2000). *The Structure of Modern English*. Amsterdam: John Benjamins.

Broca, P. (1877). Sur la circonvolution limbique et la scissure limbique. *Bulletins de la Société d'Anthropologie*, 12/2: 646–57.

Brooks, P., and M. Tomasello. (1999). How children constrain their argument structure constructions. *Language*, 75: 720–38.

Brown, R. W. (1976). Reference: n memorial tribute to Eric Lenneberg. *Cognition*, 4: 125–53.

(1958). *Words and Things*. New York: Macmillian.

(1957). Linguistic determinism and the part of speech. *Journal of Abnormal and Social Psychology*, 55: 1–5.

Brown, R. W., and E. H. Lenneberg. (1954). A study in language and cognition. *Journal of Abnormal and Social Psychology*, 49: 454–62.

Bruner, J. (1976). From communication to language – a psychological perspective. *Cognition*, 3: 255–87.

Bruno, R., M. M. Merzenich and R. Nudo. (2012). The fantastic plastic brain. *Advances in Mind Body Medicine*, 26/2: 30–5.

Buccino, G., L. Riggio, G. Melli, F. Binofski, V. Gallese and G. Rizzolatti. (2005). Listening to action-related sentences modulates the activity of the motor system: a combined TMS and behavioral study. *Cognitive Brain Research*, 24: 355–63.

Büchel, C., C. Price and K. Friston. (1998). A multimodal language region in the ventral visual pathway. *Nature*, 394: 274–7.

Bybee, J. (2010). *Language, Usage and Cognition*. Cambridge University Press.

(2006). *Frequency of Use and the Organization of Language*. Oxford University Press.

(2001). *Phonology and Language Use*. Cambridge University Press.

Byrne, R. W., and A. Whiten. (1988). *Machiavellian Intelligence: Social Expertise and the Evolution of Intellect in Monkeys, Apes, and Humans.* Oxford University Press.

Call, J., and M. Tomasello. (2008). Does the chimpanzee have a theory of mind? 30 years later. *Trends in the Cognitive Sciences*, 30: 187–92.

Campbell, L. (2010). Language isolates and their history, or, what's weird, anyway? Paper delivered at the 36th annual meeting of the Berkeley Linguistics Society, Berkeley, CA, 7 February.

Capirici, O., L. Sabbadini and V. Volterra. (1996). Language development in Williams syndrome: a case study. *Cognitive Neuropsychology*, 13/7: 1017–39.

Caplan, D. (2006). Aphasic deficits in syntactic processing. *Cortex*, 42/6: 797–804.

Carpenter, M., N. Akhtar and M. Tomasello. (1998). Fourteen- to 18-month-old infants differentially imitate intentional and accidental actions. *Infant Behavior and Development*, 21: 315–30.

Carruthers, P. (2006). *The Architecture of the Mind: Massive Modularity and the Flexibility of Thought.* Oxford University Press.

Casasanto, D. (2013). Gesture and language processing. In H. Pashler, T. Crane, M. Kinsbourne, F. Ferreira and R. Zemel (eds.), *Encyclopedia of the Mind* (pp. 372–4). Thousand Oaks, CA: Sage Publications.

(2008). Who's afraid of the Big Bad Whorf? Cross-linguistic differences in temporal language and thought. *Language Learning*, 58/1: 63–79.

Casasanto, D., and K. Dijkstra. (2010). Motor action and emotional memory. *Cognition*, 115/1: 179–85.

Caselli, M. C., E. Bates, P. Casadio, L. Fenson, J. Fenson, L. Sanderl and J. Weir (1995). A cross-linguistic study of early lexical development. *Cognitive Development*, 10: 159–99.

Casson, R.W. (1997). Color shift: evolution of English color terms from brightness to hue. In C. L. Hardin and L. Maffi (eds.), *Color Categories in Thought and Language* (pp. 224–39). Cambridge University Press.

Chance S. A., and T. J. Crow. (2007). Distinctively human: Cerebral lateralisation and language in *Homo sapiens. Journal of Anthropological Sciences*, 85: 83–100.

Chemero, A. (2009). *Radical Embodied Cognitive Science.* Cambridge, MA: MIT Press.

Cheney, D. L., and R. M. Seyfarth. (1990). *How Monkeys See the World: Inside the Mind of Another Species.* University of Chicago Press.

Chomsky, N. (2011). Language and the cognitive science revolution(s). Lecture given at Carleton University, 8 April.

(2010). Some simple evo-devo theses: how true might they be for language? In R. Larson, V. Déprez and H. Yamakido (eds.), *The Evolution of Human Language* (pp. 54–62). Cambridge University Press.

(2009). *Cartesian Linguistics: A Chapter in the History of Rational Thought (Third Edition).* Cambridge University Press.

(2004). Language and mind: current thoughts on ancient problems. Part I & Part II. In Lyle Jenkins (ed.), *Variation and Universals in Biolinguistics* (pp. 379–405). Amsterdam: Elsevier.

(2002). *On Nature and Language.* Cambridge University Press.

(1981). *Lectures on Government and Binding.* Dordrecht: Foris.

(1980a). *Rules and Representations.* New York: Columbia University Press.

(1980b). On cognitive structures and their development: a reply to Piaget. In M. Piatelli-Palmarini (ed.), *Language and Learning: The Debate between Jean Piaget and Noam Chomsky* (pp. 35–54). Cambridge, MA: MIT Press.

(1975). *Reflections on Language.* New York: Parthenon.

(1965). *Aspects of the Theory of Syntax.* Cambridge, MA: MIT Press.

(1957). *Syntactic Structures.* The Hague: Mouton.

Chomsky, N., and H. Lasnik. (1993). The theory of principles and parameters. In J. Jacobs *et al.* (eds.), *Syntax: An International Handbook of Contemporary Research, Vol. 1* (pp. 506–69). Berlin: Walter de Gruyter.

Churchland, P. M. (1995). *The Engine of Reason, the Seat of the Soul: A Philosophical Journey into the Brain.* Cambridge, MA: MIT Press.

Churchland, P. S. (2002). *Brain-Wise: Studies in Neurophilosophy.* Cambridge, MA: MIT Press.

Corballis, M. (2003). *From Hand to Mouth: The Origins of Language.* Princeton University Press.

Clark, A. (1997). *Being There: Putting Brain, Body and World Together Again.* Cambridge, MA: MIT Press.

Clark, H. (1996). *Using Language.* Cambridge University Press.

Clayton, N. S., J. M. Dally and N. J. Emery. (2007). Social cognition by food-caching corvids: the western scrub-jay as a natural psychologist. *Philosophical Transactions of the Royal Society B*, 362: 507–52.

Clayton, N. S., D. P. Griffiths, N. J., Emery and A. Dickinson. (2001). Elements of episodic-like memory in animals. *Philosophical Transactions of the Royal Society B*, 356: 1483–91.

Cosmides, L. (1989). The logic of social exchange: has natural selection shaped how humans reason? Studies with the Wason selection task. *Cognition*, 31: 187–276.

Crain, S. (1991). Language acquisition in the absence of experience. *Behavioral and Brain Sciences*, 14: 597–650.

Crain, S., and M. Nakayama. (1986). Structure dependence in children's language. *Language*, 62: 522–43.

Crawford, T. D. (1982). Defining 'Basic Color Term'. *Anthropological Linguistics*, 25: 338–43.

Crockford, C., R. M. Wittig, R. Mundry and K. Zuberbühler. (2011). Wild chimpanzees inform ignorant group members of danger. *Current Biology*, 22: 142–6.

Croft, W. (2000). *Explaining Language Change*. London: Longman.

Crystal, D. (2002). *Language Death*. Cambridge University Press.

Dąbrowska, E. (2004). *Language, Mind and Brain: Some Psychological and Neurological Constraints on Theories of Grammar*. Edinburgh University Press.

Dąbrowska, E., and J. Street. (2006). Individual differences in language attainment: Comprehension of passive sentences by native and non-native English speakers. *Language Sciences*, 28: 604–15.

Dahan, D., and M. K. Tanenhaus. (2004). Continuous mapping from sound to meaning in spoken-language comprehension: evidence from immediate effects of verb-based constraints. *Journal of Experimental Psychology: Learning, Memory and Cognition*, 30: 498–513.

Dale, P. S. (1991). The validity of a parent report measure of vocabulary and syntax at 24 months. *Journal of Speech and Hearing Sciences*, 34: 565–71.

Dale, P. S., E. Bates, S. Reznick and C. Morisset. (1989). The validity of a parent report instrument of child language at 20 months. *Journal of Child Language*, 16: 239–49.

D'Andrade, R. G. (1989). Cultural cognition. In M. I. Posner (ed.), *Foundations of Cognitive Science* (pp. 795–830). Cambridge, MA: MIT Press.

Daoutis, C., A. Franklin, A. Riddett, A. Clifford and I. R. L. Davies. (2006). Categorical effects in children's colour search: a cross-linguistic comparison. *British Journal of Developmental Psychology*, 23: 1–29.

Davidoff, J., I. Davies and D. Roberson. (1999). Colour categories of a stone-age tribe. *Nature*, 398: 203–4.

Davies, I., and G. Corbett. (1998). A cross-cultural study of color-grouping: tests of the perceptual-physiology account of color universals. *Ethos*, 26/3: 338–60.

(1995). A practical field method for identifying probable Basic Color Terms. *Languages of the World*, 9/1: 25–36.

Davies, I., I. C. MacDermid, G. Corbett, D. Jerrett, T. Jerrett, H. McGurle and P. T. Snowden. (1992). Color terms in Setswana: a linguistic and perceptual approach. *Linguistics*, 30: 1065–103.

Dawkins, R. (2010). *The Greatest Show on Earth*. London: Black Swan.

(1986). *The Blind Watchmaker*. New York: W. W. Norton and Co.

(1976). *The Selfish Gene*. Oxford University Press.

Deacon, T. (1997). *The Symbolic Species: The Co-evolution of Language and the Brain*. New York: W. W. Norton and Co.

Dediu, D., and S. C. Levinson. (2013). On the antiquity of language: the reinterpretation of Neandertal linguistic capacities and its consequences. *Frontiers in Psychology*, 4: 397.

Deutscher, G. (2011). *Through the Language Glass: Why the World Looks Different in Other Languages*. London: Arrow Books.

De Valois, R .L., and K. K. De Valois. (1993). A multi-stage color model. *Vision Research*, 3: 1053–65.

De Villiers, J. G., and P. A. De Villiers. (1973). A cross-sectional study of the acquisition of grammatical morphemes in child speech. *Journal of Psycholinguistic Research*, 2/3: 267–78.

Drachman, D. (2005). Do we have brain to spare? *Neurology*, 64/12: 2004–5.

Dronkers, N. F., O. Plaisant, M. T. Iba-Zizen and E. A. Cabanis. (2007). Paul Broca's historic cases: high resolution MR imaging of the brains of Leborgne and Lelong. *Brain*, 130/5: 1432–41.

Dryer, M. S. (1998). Why statistical universals are better than absolute universals. *Chicago Linguistic Society 33: The Panels*: 123–45.

Dryer, M. S., and M. Haspelmath. (2011). *The World Atlas of Language Structures Online* (http://wals.info/).

Dunbar, R. I. M. (1999). The social brain hypothesis. *Evolutionary Anthropology*, 6/5: 178–90.

(1996). *Grooming, Gossip and the Evolution of Language*. London: Faber and Faber.

(1992). Neocortex size as a constraint on group size in primates. *Journal of Human Evolution*, 22/6: 469–984.

Dunn, M., S. J. Greenhill, S. C. Levinson, and R. D. Gray. (2011). Evolved structure of language shows lineage-specific trends in word-order universals. *Nature*, 473: 79–82.

Edelman, G. M. (1987). *Neural Darwinism: The Theory of Neuronal Group Selection*. New York: Basic Books.

Ellis, N. (2006). Language acquisition as rational contingency learning. *Applied Linguistics*, 27/1: 1–24.

Elman, J., A. Karmiloff-Smith, E. Bates, M. H. Johnson, D. Parisi and K. Plunkett. (1996). *Rethinking Innateness: A Connectionist Perspective on Development*. Cambridge, MA: MIT Press.

Emmorey, K. (2002). *Language, Cognition, and the Brain: Insights from Sign Language Research*. Hillsdale, NJ: Lawrence Erlbaum.

Enard, W., M. Przeworski, S. E., Fisher, C. S. Lai, V. Wiebe, T. Kitano, A. P. Monaco and S. Pääbo. (2002). Molecular evolution of FOXP2, a gene involved in speech and language. *Nature*, 418/6900: 869–72.

Enfield, N. (2004). Adjectives in Lao. In R. M. W. Dixon and A. Y. Aikhenvald (eds.), *Adjective Classes: A Cross-linguistic Typology* (pp. 323–47). Oxford University Press.

Evans, N., and S. C. Levinson. (2009). The myth of language universals: language diversity and its importance for cognitive science. *Behavioral and Brain Sciences*, 32/5: 429–48.

Evans, V. (2013). *Language and Time: A Cognitive Linguistics Approach*. Cambridge University Press.

(2009). *How Words Mean: Lexical Concepts, Cognitive Models and Meaning Construction*. Oxford University Press.

(2004). *The Structure of Time: Language, Meaning and Temporal Cognition*. Amsterdam: John Benjamins.

Evans, V., and M. Green. (2006). *Cognitive Linguistics: An Introduction*. Edinburgh University Press.

Everett, D. (2013). 60 years of cognitive science. Lecture given to the British Academy, London, 4 October.

(2012). *Language: The Cultural Tool*. New York: Vintage.

(2005). Cultural constraints on grammar and cognition in Pirahã: another look at the design features of human language. *Current Anthropology*, 46: 621–46.

Faarlund, J. T. (2001). From ancient Germanic to modern Germanic languages. In M. Haspelmath, E. König, W. Österreicher and W. Reible (eds.,), *Language Typology and Language Universals*, Vol. II (pp. 1706-19). Berlin: Mouton de Gruyter.

Fadiga, L., L. Craighero, M. F. Destro, L. Finos, N. Cotillon-Williams, A. T. Smith and U. Castiello. (2005). Language in shadow. *Social Neuroscience*, 1/2: 77-89.

Fantz, R. L. (1963). Pattern vision in newborn infants. *Science*, 140/3564: 296-7.

Fenson, L., P. Dale, J. Reznick, E. Bates, D. Thal and S. Pethick. (1994). *Variability in early communicative development. In Monographs of the Society for Research in Child Development*. University of Chicago Press.

Fenson, L., P. Dale, J. S. Reznick, D. Thal, E. Bates, J. Hartung, S. Pethick and J. Reilly. (1993). *The MacArthur Communicative Development Inventories: User's Guide and Technical Manual*. San Diego: Singular Press.

Finlay, B. L., and R. B. Darlington. (1995). Linked regularities in the development and evolution of mammalian brains. *Science*, 268: 1578-84.

Fishman, J. (2000). *Can Threatened Languages be Saved? Reversing Language Shift, Revisited - A 21st Century Perspective*. Bristol: Multilingual Matters.

Fodor, J. (2008). *LOT2: The Language of Thought Revisited*. Oxford University Press.

—— (1998). *Concepts: Where Cognitive Science Went Wrong*. Oxford University Press.

—— (1985). Précis of 'Modularity of Mind'. *Behavioral and Brain Sciences*, 8: 1-42.

—— (1983). *Modularity of Mind*. Cambridge, MA: MIT Press.

—— (1975). *The Language of Thought*. Cambridge, MA: MIT Press.

Foley, W. A. (1997). *Anthropological Linguistics: An Introduction*. Blackwell.

Fouts, R. S., G. L. Shapiro and C. O'Neil. (1978). Studies of linguistic behavior in apes and children. In P. Cavalieri and P. Singer (eds.), *Understanding Language Through Sign Language Research* (pp. 29-41). New York: Academic Press.

Fromkin, V., and R. Rodman. (1997). *An Introduction to Language (sixth edition)*. New York: Heinle and Heinle Inc.

Fromkin, V., R. Rodman and N. Hyams. (2013). *An Introduction to Language (tenth international edition).* New York: Heinle and Heinle Inc.

Gallistel, C. R. (2007). Learning organs [English original of L'apprentissage de matières distinctes exige des organes distincts]. In J. Bricmont and J. Franc (eds.), *Cahier no 88: Noam Chomsky* (pp. 181–7). Paris: L'Herne.

Gardner, B. T., and R. A. Gardner. (1974). Comparing the early utterances of child and chimpanzee. In A. Pick (ed.), *Minnesota Symposium on Use of Signs by Chimpanzees with Humans: Child Psychology,* Vol. VIII (pp. 3–23). Minneapolis: University of Minnesota Press.

Gardner, H. (1985). *The Mind's New Science: A History of the Cognitive Revolution.* New York: Basic Books.

(1974). *The Shattered Mind.* New York: Vintage.

Gardner, R. A., and B. T. Gardner. (1969). Teaching sign language to a chimpanzee. *Science,* 165: 664–72.

Gentner, D., and S. Goldin-Meadow. (2003). *Language in Mind: Advances in the Study of Language and Thought.* Cambridge, MA: MIT Press.

Genter, T. Q., K. M. Fenn, D. Margoliash and H. C. Nusbaum. (2006). Recursive syntactic pattern learning by songbirds. *Nature* 440: 1204–7.

Gerhardt, H. C. (1994). The evolution of vocalization in frogs and toads. *Annual Review of Ecology and Systematics,* 25: 293–324.

Gibbs, R. W., and G. van Orden (2010). Adaptive cognition without massive modularity. *Language and Cognition,* 2: 149–76.

Givon, T. (1984). *Syntax Volume I.* Amsterdam: John Benjamins.

Glenberg, A. M., and M. P. Kaschak. (2002). Grounding language in action. *Psychonomic Bulletin and Review,* 9: 558–65.

Gold, E. M. (1967) Language identification in the limit. *Information and Control,* 10/5: 447–74.

Goldberg, A. E. (2011). Corpus evidence of the viability of statistical preemption. *Cognitive Linguistics* 22/1: 131–54.

(2006). *Constructions at Work.* Oxford University Press.

(1995). *Constructions: A Construction Grammar Approach to Argument Structure.* University of Chicago Press.

Goldin-Meadow, S. (2003). *Hearing Gesture: How Our Hands Help Us Think.* Cambridge, MA: Harvard University Press.

Goldin-Meadow, S., and C. Mylander. (1990). Beyond the input given: the child's role in the acquisition of language. *Language*, 66/2: 323–55.

Goodwin, C. (2003). *Conversation and Brain Damage*. Oxford University Press.

Greenberg, J. (1986). On being a linguistic anthropologist. *Annual Review of Anthropology*, 15: 1–24.

Greenough, W. T., J. E. Black and C. S. Wallace. (1993). Experience and brain development. In M. H. Johnson (ed.), *Brain Development and Cognition: A Reader* (pp. 290–322). Oxford: Blackwell.

Grice, H. P. (1989). *Studies in the Way of Words*. Harvard: Harvard University Press

Grodzinsky, Y., and A. Santi. (2008). The battle for Broca's region. *Trends in Cognitive Sciences*, 12/12: 474–80.

Grush, R. (2004). The emulation theory of representation: motor control, imagery, and perception. *Behavioral and Brain Sciences*, 27: 377–442.

(1997). The architecture of representation. *Philosophical Psychology*, 10/1: 5–23.

Gumperz, J., and S. C. Levinson. (1996). *Rethinking Linguistic Relativity*. Cambridge University Press.

Hardcastle, W. (1976). *Physiology of Speech Production: Introduction for Speech Scientists*. New York: Academic Press.

Harnad, S. (1990). The symbol grounding problem. *Physica D*, 42: 335–46.

Harrington, A. (1987). *Medicine, Mind and the Double Brain: A Study in Nineteenth-Century Thought*. Princeton University Press.

Hauser, M. D., N. Chomsky and W. T. Fitch. (2002). The faculty of language: what is it, who has it, and how did it evolve? *Science*, 298: 1569–79.

Heinrich, B., and J. Pepper. (1998). Influence of competitors on caching behaviour in the common raven (*Corvus corax*). *Animal Behavior*, 56: 1083–90.

Herculano-Houzel, S. (2009). The human brain in numbers: a linearly scaled-up primate brain. *Frontiers in Human Neuroscience*, 09.031.

Herman, L. M., D. G. Richards and J. P. Wolz. (1984). Comprehension of sentences by bottlenosed dolphins. *Cognition*, 16: 129–219.

Hillix, W. A., and D. P. Rumbaugh. (2004). *Animal Bodies, Human Minds: Ape, Dolphin and Parrot Language Skills*. New York: Kluwer Academic.

Himmelmann, N. P. (1997). *Deiktikon, Artikel, Nominalphrase: Zur Emergenz syntaktischer Struktur*. Tübingen: Max Niemeyer Verlag.

Hobbes, Thomas. ([1651] 2012). *Leviathan*. Critical edition by N. Malcolm (3 volumes). Oxford University Press.

Hockett, C. (1966). The problem of universals in language In J. Greenberg (ed.), *Universals of Language* (pp. 1–29). Cambridge, MA: MIT Press.

Hötting, K., F. Rösler and B. Röder. (2004). Altered multisensory interaction in congenitally blind humans: an event-related potential study. *Experimental Brain Research*, 159: 370–81.

Hull, D. (1989). *The Metaphysics of Evolution*. Stony Brook: State University of New York Press.

Hurford, J. (2012). *The Origins of Grammar*. Oxford University Press.

(2007). *The Origins of Meaning*. Oxford University Press.

Hurvich, L. M., and D. Jameson. (1957). An opponent-process theory of color vision. *Psychological Review*, 64/1–6: 384–404.

Huttenlocher, J., M. Vasilyeva and P. Shimpi. (2002). Syntactic priming in young children. *Journal of Memory and Language*, 50: 182–95.

Ibbotson, P. (2013). The scope of usage-based theory. *Frontiers in Psychology*, 4: 255.

Isenberg, N., D. Silbersweig, A. Engelien, S. Emmerich, K. Malavade, B. Beattie, A. C. Leon and E. Stern. (1999). Linguistic threat activates the human amygdala. *Proceedings of the National Academy of Science, USA*, 96: 10456–9.

Jackendoff, R. (2002). *Foundations of Language: Brain, Meaning, Grammar, Evolution*. Oxford University Press.

(1992). *Languages of the Mind: Essays on Mental Representation*. Oxford University Press.

(1987). *Consciousness and the Computational Mind*. Cambridge, MA: MIT Press.

(1983). *Semantics and Cognition*. Cambridge, MA: MIT Press.

Jahn-Samilo, J., J. C. Goodman, E. Bates, M. Appelbaum and M. Sweet. (2000). *Vocabulary Learning in Children from 8 to 30 Months of Age: A Comparison of Parental Report and Laboratory Measures. Project in Cognitive and Neural Development, Technical Report #00–06*. La Jolla: University of California, San Diego.

Jakobson, J., and M. Halle (1956). *Fundamentals of Language*. Amsterdam: Mouton.

Jelinek, E. (1995). Quantification in Straits Salish. In E. Bach, E. Jelinek, A. Kratzer and B. Partee (eds.), *Quantification in Natural Languages* (pp. 487–540). New York: Kluwer Academic.

Jesperson, O. (1909). *A Modern English Grammar on Historical Principles (Volume I)*. Heidelberg: Carl Winter.

Johnston, J. R. (1994). Cognitive abilities of children with language impairment. In R. V. Watkins and M. L. Rice (eds.), *Specific Language Impairments in Children* (pp. 107–21). Baltimore, MD: Paul H. Brookes.

Karmiloff-Smith, A. (2001). Research into Williams syndrome: the state of the art. In C. A. Nelson and M. Luciana (eds.), *Handbook of Developmental Cognitive Neuroscience* (pp. 691–700). Cambridge, MA: MIT Press.

(1994). *Beyond Modularity: A Developmental Perspective on Cognitive Science*. Cambridge, MA: MIT Press.

Karmiloff-Smith, A., E. Klima, U. Bellugi, J. Grant and S. Baron-Cohen. (1995). Is there a social module? Language, face processing, and theory of mind in individuals with Williams Syndrome. *Journal of Cognitive Neuroscience*, 7/2: 196–208.

Kay, P. (1999). The emergence of Basic Color Lexicons hypothesis: a comment on 'The vocabulary of colour with particular reference to ancient Greek and classical Latin' by John Lyons. In A. Borg (ed.), *The Language of Color in the Mediterranean: An Anthology on Linguistic and Ethnographic Aspects of Color Terms* (pp. 76–90). Stockholm: Almqvist and Wiksell.

Kay, P., and B. Berlin. (1997). Science ≠ imperialism: response to Saunders and van Brakel. *Behavioral and Brain Sciences*, 20/2: 196–201.

Kay, P., B. Berlin, L. Maffi, W. R. Merrifield and R. Cook. (2009). *The World Color Survey*. Stanford, CA: CSLI Publications.

Kay, P., and W. Kempton. (1984). What is the Sapir–Whorf hypothesis? *American Anthropologist*, 86: 65–79.

Kay, P., and C. K. McDaniel. (1978). The linguistic significance of the meanings of Basic Color Terms. *Language*, 54: 610–46.

Keller, R. (1994). *On Language Change: The Invisible Hand in Language*. London: Routledge.

Kellogg, W. N., and L. A. Kellogg. (1933). *The Ape and the Child: A Study of Environmental Influence Upon Early Behavior*. New York: McGraw-Hill.

Kendon, A. (2004). *Gesture: Visible Action as Utterance*. Cambridge University Press.

Klatzky, R. L., J. W. Pellegrino, B. P. McCloskey and S. Doherty. (1989). Can you squeeze a tomato? The role of motor representations in semantic sensibility judgments. *Journal of Memory and Language*, 28: 56–77.

Klima, E. S., and U. Bellugi. (1979). *The Signs of Language*. Cambridge, MA: Harvard University Press.

Labov, W. (1994). *Principles of Linguistic Change*, Vol. I: *Internal Factors*. Oxford: Blackwell.

Ladefoged, P., and I. Maddieson (1996). *The Sounds of the World's Languages*. New York: Academic Press.

Lai, C. S. L., S. E. Fisher, J. A. Hurst, F. Vargha-Khadem and A. P. Monaco. (2001). A fork-head gene is mutated in a severe speech and language disorder. *Nature*, 413: 519–23.

Lakoff, G. (2004). *Don't Think of an Elephant! Know Your Values and Frame the Debate – The Essential Guide for Progressives*. New York: Chelsea Green Publishing.

Lakoff, G., and M. Johnson. (1999). *Philosophy in the Flesh: The Embodied Mind and its Challenge to Western Thought*. New York: Basic Books.

(1980). *Metaphors We Live By*. University of Chicago Press.

Langacker, R. W. (2008). *Cognitive Grammar: A Basic Introduction*. Oxford University Press.

(2002). *Concept, Image and Symbol. Second Edition*. Berlin: Mouton de Gruyter.

(2000). A dynamic usage-based model. In M. Barlow and S. Kemmer (eds.), *Usage-based Models of Language* (pp. 1–63). Stanford, CA: CSLI Publications.

Ledgeway, A. (2012). *From Latin to Romance: Morphosyntactic Typology and Change*. Oxford University Press.

(2011). Syntactic and morphosyntactic typology and change. In A. Ledgeway, M. Maiden and J.-C. Smith (eds.), *The Cambridge History of the Romance Languages* (pp. 382–471). Cambridge University Press.

LeDoux, J. E. (1995). Emotion: clues from the brain. *Annual Review of Psychology*, 46: 209–35.

Lee, P. (1996). *The Whorf Theory Complex: A Critical Reconstruction*. Amsterdam: John Benjamins.

Legerstee, M. (1991). The role of person and object in eliciting early imitation. *Journal of Experimental Child Psychology*, 51:423–33.

Lenneberg, E. H. (1953). Cognition in ethnolinguistics. *Language*, 29: 463–71.

Leonard, L. B. (1998). *Children with Specific Language Impairment*. Cambridge, MA: MIT Press.

LePage, R. B., and A. Tabouret-Keller. (1985). *Acts of Identity: Creole-based Approaches to Ethnicity*. Cambridge University Press.

Levinson, S. C. (2006). On the human 'interaction engine'. In N. J. Enfield and S. C. Levinson (eds.), *Roots of Human Sociality: Culture, Cognition and Interaction* (pp. 39–69). Oxford: Berg.

— (2003). *Space in Language and Cognition: Explorations in Cultural Diversity*. Cambridge University Press.

— (2000). Yélî Dnye and the theory of basic color terms. *Journal of Linguistic Anthropology*, 10/1: 3–55.

— (1996). Frames of reference and Molyneux's question: cross-linguistic evidence. In P. Bloom, M. Peterson, L. Nadel and M. Garrett (eds.), *Language and Space* (pp. 109–69). Cambridge, MA: MIT Press.

Levinson, S. C., and R. D. Gray. (2012). Tools from evolutionary biology shed new light on the diversification of languages. *Trends in Cognitive Sciences*, 16/3: 167–173.

Li, P., and L. Gleitman. (2002). Turning the tables: language and spatial reasoning. *Cognition*, 83/3: 265–94.

Lieberman, P. (1984). *The Biology and Evolution of Language*. Cambridge, MA: Harvard University Press.

Lieberman, P., E. S. Crelin and D. H. Klatt. (1972). Phonetic ability and related anatomy of the newborn and adult human, Neanderthal man, and the chimpanzee. In D. Quiatt and J. Itani (eds.), *Hominid Culture in Primate Perspective* (pp. 233–51). Boulder: University Press of Colorado.

Lieberman, P., D. Klatt and W. Wilson. (1969). Vocal tract limitations on the vowel repertoires of rhesus monkeys and other nonhuman primates. *Science*, 64/3884: 1185–7.

Lieven, E. M., T. Cameron-Faulkner and M. Tomasello. (2003). A construction based analysis of child directed speech. *Cognitive Science*, 27: 843–73.

Lovgren, S. (2005). Chimps, humans 96 percent the same, gene study finds. *National Geographic News*, 31 Aug.

Lucy, J. A. (1997). The linguistics of color. In C. L. Hardin and L. Maffi (eds.), *Color Categories in Language and Thought* (pp. 320–46). Cambridge University Press.

(1992a). *Language Diversity and Thought: A Reformulation of the Linguistic Relativity Hypothesis.* Cambridge University Press.

(1992b). *Grammatical Categories and Cognition: A Case Study of the Linguistic Relativity Hypothesis.* Cambridge University Press.

Lucy, J. A., and R. Schweder. (1979). Whorf and his critics. *American Anthropologist,* 81: 581–615.

Lumsden, C., and E. O. Wilson. (1981). *Genes, Mind and Culture: The Co-evolutionary Process.* London: World Scientific Publishing Co.

Lupyan, G. (2012a). Linguistically modulated perception and cognition: the label feedback hypothesis. *Frontiers in Cognition,* 3:54.

(2012b). What do words do? Toward a theory of language-augmented thought. In B. H. Ross (ed.), *The Psychology of Learning and Motivation,* Vol. LVII (pp. 255–97). New York: Academic Press.

Luraghi, S. (2010). The rise (and possible downfall) of configurationality. In S. Luraghi and V. Bubenik (eds.), *A Companion to Historical Linguistics* (pp. 212–29). London: Continuum.

Lurz, R. W. (2011). *Mindreading Animals: The Debate over What Animals Know about Other Minds.* Cambridge, MA: MIT Press.

Lyons, J. (1995). Colour in language. In T. Lamb and J. Bourriau (eds.), *Colour: Art and Science* (pp. 194–224). Cambridge University Press.

Macario, J. F. (1991). Young children's use of colour in classification: foods and canonically coloured objects. *Cognitive Development,* 6: 17–46.

Machery, E. (2007). Massive modularity and brain evolution. *Philosophy of Science,* 74: 825–38.

MacLaury, R. (1992). From brightness to hue. *Current Anthropology,* 33/2: 137–86.

MacNeilage, P. (2008). *The Origin of Speech.* Oxford University Press.

Maess, B., S. Koelsch, T. C. Gunter and A. D. Friederici. (2001). Musical syntax is processed in Broca's area: an MEG study. *Nature Neuroscience,* 4: 540–5.

Maffi, L. (1990). Somali color term evolution: grammatical and semantic evidence. *Anthropological Linguistics,* 33/3–4: 316–34.

Mahmoudzadeha, M., G. Dehaene-Lambertz, M. Fourniera, G. Kongoloa, S. Goudjila, J. Dubois, R. Grebea and F. Walloisa. (2013). Syllabic discrimination in premature human infants prior to complete formation of cortical layers. *PNAS*, 19/110: 4846–51.

Maratsos, M. (1984). How degenerate is the input to Creoles and where do its biases comes from? *Behavioral and Brain Sciences*, 7: 200–201.

Marchman, V., and E. Bates. (1994). Continuity in lexical and morphological development: a test of the critical mass hypothesis. *Journal of Child Language*, 21: 339–66.

Marcus, G. F. (2006). Language: startling starlings. *Nature*, 440: 1117–18.

Marsaja, I. G. (2008). *Desa Kolok - A Deaf Village and its Sign Language in Bali, Indonesia*. Nijmegen: Ishara Press.

Martin, A., and L. L. Chao. (2001). Semantic memory and the brain: structure and processes. *Current Opinion in Neurobiology*, 11: 194–201.

Maslin, K. T. (2001). *An Introduction to the Philosophy of Mind*. Oxford: Blackwell.

Matthews, P. H. (1981). *Syntax*. Cambridge University Press.

McGonigle, B. O., and M. Chalmers. (1977). Are monkeys logical? *Nature*, 267/5613: 694–6.

McGurk, H., and J. MacDonald. (1976). Hearing lips and seeing voices. *Nature*, 264/5588: 746–8.

McNeill, D. (1992). *Hand and Mind: What Gestures Reveal About Thought*. University of Chicago Press.

—— (1966). Developmental psycholinguistics. In F. Smith and G. A. Miller (eds.), *The Genesis of Language* (pp. 15–84). Cambridge, MA: MIT Press.

Meltzoff, A. (1995). Understanding the intentions of others: re-enactment of intended acts by 18-month-old children. *Developmental Psychology*, 31: 838–50.

Meltzoff, A., and M. Moore. (1977). Imitation of facial and manual gestures by human neonates. *Science*, 198: 75–78.

Mervis, C. B., and J. Bertrand. (1993). Acquisition of early object labels: the roles of operating principles and input. In A. Kaiser and D. B. Gray (eds.), *Enhancing Children's Communication: Research Foundations for Intervention* (pp. 287–316). Baltimore: Brookes.

Mervis, C. B., J. Bertrand and J. R. Pani. (1975). Transaction of cognitive linguistic abilities and adult input: a case study of the acquisition of color terms and color-based subordinate object categories. *British Journal of Developmental Psychology*, 13:285–302.

Merzenich, M. M. (1995). Cortical plasticity: shaped, distributed representations of learned behaviors. In B. Julesz and I. Kovacs (eds.), *Maturational Windows and Cortical Plasticity in Human Development: Is There a Reason for an Optimistic View?* (pp. 73–86). Reading, MA: Addison Wesley.

Mithen, S. (1996). *The Prehistory of the Mind: A Search for the Origins of Art, Science and Religion.* London: Phoenix.

Mody, M., M. Studdert-Kennedy and S. Brady. (1997). Speech perception deficits in poor readers: auditory processing or phonological coding? *Journal of Experimental Child Psychology,* 64: 199–231.

Moss, A. E. (1989). Basic Color Terms. *Lingua,* 78: 313–20.

Mukamel, R., A. D. Ekstrom, J. Kaplan, M. Iacoboni and I. Fried. (2010). Single-neuron responses in humans during execution and observation of actions. *Current Biology,* 20: 750–6.

Mulcahy, N. J., and J. Call. (2006). Apes save tools for future use. *Science,* 312/5776: 1038–40.

Naigles, L. R., and E. Hoff-Ginsberg. (1998). Why are some verbs learned before other verbs? Effects of input frequency and structure on children's early verb use. *Journal of Child Language,* 25: 95–120.

Nettle, D., and S. Romaine. (2002). *Vanishing Voices.* Oxford University Press.

Nichols, J., and B. Bickel. (2005). Possessive classification and obligatory possessive inflection. In M. Haspelmath, M. S. Dryer, D. Gil and B. Comrie (eds.), *The World Atlas of Language Structures* (pp. 242–5). Oxford University Press.

Nishimura, T., A. Mikami, J. Suzuki and T. Matsuzawa. (2003). Descent of the larynx in chimpanzee infants. *Proceedings of the National Academy of Science, USA,* 100/12: 6930–3.

Norris, T., J. Jacobsen and S. Cerchio. (2000). *A Comparative Analysis of Humpback Whale Songs Recorded in Pelagic Waters of the Eastern North Pacific: Preliminary Findings and Implications for Discerning Migratory Routes and Assessing Breeding Stock Identity.* NOAA Technical Memorandum, N0 AA-TM-NMFS-S W FSC-295. US Department of Commerce, National Oceanic and Atmospheric Administration, National Marine Fisheries Service, Southwest Fisheries Science Center.

Ouattara K., A. Lemasson and K. Zuberbühler. (2009). Campbell's monkeys use affixation to alter call meaning. *PLoS ONE*, 4/11: e7808.

Patterson, F., and E. Linden. (1985). *The Education of Koko*. New York: Holt.

Payne, R. S., and S. McVay (1971). Songs of humpback whales. *Science*, 173/ 3997: 585–97.

Pederson, E. (1993). Geographic and manipulable space in two Tamil linguistic systems. In A. U. Frank and I. Campari (eds.), *Spatial Information Theory* (pp. 294–311). Berlin: Springer-Verlag.

Pepperberg, I. M. (2000). *The Alex Studies: Cognitive and Communicative Abilities of Grey Parrots*. Cambridge, MA: Harvard University Press.

(1983). Cognition in the African Grey parrot: preliminary evidence for auditory/vocal comprehension of the class concept. *Animal Learning Behavior*, 11: 179–85.

Perridon, H., and P. Sleeman. (2011). The noun phrase in Germanic and Romance: common developments and differences. In P. Sleeman and H. Perridon (eds.), *The Noun Phrase in Romance and Germanic: Structure, Variation, and Change* (pp. 1–21). Amsterdam: John Benjamins.

Pierrehumbert, J. (2000). The phonetic grounding of phonology. *Bulletin de la Communication Parlée*, 5: 7–23.

Pika, S., K. Liebal, J. Call and M. Tomasello. (2005). Gestural communication of apes. *Gesture*, 5/1–2: 41–56.

Pinker, S. (2007). *The Stuff of Thought*. New York: Viking Press.

(2002). *The Blank Slate*. New York: Penguin.

(2001). *Words and Rules*. London: Phoenix.

(1997). *How the Mind Works*. New York: W. W. Norton and Co.

(1994). *The Language Instinct*. New York: William Morrow.

Pitchford, N. J., and K. T. Mullen. (2002). Is the acquisition of Basic Colour Terms in young children constrained? *Perception*, 31: 1349–70.

Plaza, M., P. Gatignol, M. Leroy and H. Duffau. (2009). Speaking without Broca's area after tumor resection. *Neurocase*, 15/4: 294–310.

Pons, T. P., P. E. Garraghty, A. K. Ommaya, J. H. Kaas, E. Taub and M. Mishkin (1991). Massive cortical reorganization after sensory deafferentation in adult macaques. *Science*, 252/5014: 1857–60.

Popper, K. (1959). *The Logic of Scientific Discovery*. London: Routledge.

Pourcel, S. (2005). Relativism in the linguistic and cognitive conceptualisation of motion events across verb-framed and satellite-framed languages. Unpublished Ph.D. thesis: Department of Linguistics, University of Durham.

Premack, D. (1986). *Gavagai! Or the Future History of the Animal Language Controversy*. Cambridge, MA: MIT Press.

(1974). *Intelligence in Ape and Man*. Hillsdale, NJ: Lawrence Erlbaum.

Premack, D., and A. J. Premack. (1983). *The Mind of an Ape*. New York: Norton.

Prinz, J. (2006). Is the mind really modular? In R. J. Stainton (ed.), *Contemporary Debates in Cognitive Science* (pp. 22–36). Malden, MA: Blackwell Publishing.

(2002). *Furnishing the Mind*. Cambridge, MA: MIT Press.

Pullum, G. K., and B. C. Scholz. (2002). Empirical assessment of stimulus of poverty arguments. *The Linguistic Review*, 19: 9–50.

Pulvermüller, F. (1999). Words in the brain's languages. *Behavioral and Brain Sciences*, 22: 253–336.

Pustejovsky, J. (1995). *The Generative Lexicon*. Cambridge, MA: MIT Press.

Quartz, S. R. (2002). Toward a developmental evolutionary psychology: genes, development, and the evolution of the human cognitive architecture. In S. Scher and M. Rauscher (eds.), *Evolutionary Psychology: Alternative Approaches* (pp. 1–35). Dordrecht: Kluwer.

Radford, A. (1990). *Syntactic Theory and the Acquisition of English Syntax: The Nature of Early Child Grammars of English*. Oxford: Blackwell.

Rakic, P. (1995). A small step for the cell, a giant leap for mankind: a hypothesis of neocortical expansion during evolution. *Trends in Neuroscience*, 18: 383–8.

Regier, T., and P. Kay. (2009). Language, thought and color: Whorf was half right. *Trends in Cognitive Sciences*, 13/10: 439–46.

Rendell, L. E., and H. Whitehead (2003a). Vocal clans in sperm whales. *Proceedings of the Royal Society of London Series B: Biological Sciences*, 270: 225–31.

(2003b). Comparing repertoires of sperm whale codas: a multiple methods approach. *Bioacoustics*, 14: 61–81.

Renfrew, C. (1990). *Archaeology and Language: The Puzzle of Indo-European Origins*. Oxford University Press.

Rizzolatti, G., and L. Craighero. (2004). The mirror-neuron system. *Annual Review of Neuroscience*, 27: 169–92.

Roberson, D., J. Davidoff, I. R. L. Davies and L. R. Shapiro. (2004). The development of color categories in two languages: a longitudinal study. *Journal of Experimental Psychology: General*, 133: 554–71.

Roberson, D., I. R. L. Davies, G. Corbett and M. Vandervyver. (2005). Freesorting of colors across cultures: are there universal grounds for grouping? *Journal of Cognition and Culture*, 5: 349–86.

Roberson, D., H. S. Pak and J. R. Hanley. (2008). Categorical perception of colour in the left and right visual field is verbally mediated: evidence from Korean. *Cognition*, 107: 752–62.

Rosch, E. (1977). Human categorization. In N. Warren (ed.), *Advances in Cross-cultural Psychology*, Vol. I (pp. 1–49). New York: Academic Press.

Rosch Heider, E. (1972). Probabilities, sampling, and ethnographic method: the case of Dani colour names. *Man*, 7: 448–66.

Rose, H., and S. Rose. (2001). *Alas Poor Darwin: Arguments Against Evolutionary Psychology*. New York: Vintage.

Rumbaugh, D. M. (1977). *Language Learning by a Chimpanzee: The Lana Project*. New York: Academic Press.

Saffran, J., R. Aslin and E. L. Newport. (1996). Statistical learning by 8-month-old infants. *Science*, 274/5294: 1926–8.

Samarin, W. (1984). Socioprogrammed linguistics. *Behavioral and Brain Sciences*, 7: 206–7.

Sampson, G. (2001). *The 'Language Instinct' Debate (revised edition)*. London: Continuum.

Sandler, W., M. Aronoff, I. Meir and C. Padden. (2011). The gradual emergence of phonological form in a new language. *Natural Language and Linguistic Theory*, 29/2: 503–43.

Sandler, W., I. Meir, C. Padden and M. Aronoff. (2005). The Emergence of Grammar in a New Sign Language. *Proceedings of the National Academy of Sciences* 102/7: 2661–2665.

Sapir, E. (1985). *Selected Writings in Language, Culture, and Personality*. Edited by D. G. Mandelbaum. Berkeley: University of California Press.

Saunders, B. (2000). Revisiting basic color terms. *Journal of the Royal Anthropological Institute*, 6: 81–99.

Saunders, B., and J. von Brakel. (1997). Are there nontrivial constraints on colour categorization? *Behavioral and Brain Sciences*, 20: 167–228.

Saussure, F. de. (2013). *Course in General Linguistics*. (New edition.) Translated and annotated by R. Harris. London: Bloomsbury.

Savage-Rumbaugh, S., and R. Lewin. (1996). *Kanzi: The Ape at the Brink of the Human Mind*. New York: John Wiley.

Savage-Rumbaugh, S., K. McDonald, R. A. Sevcik, W. D. Hopkins and E. Rubert. (1986). Spontaneous symbol acquisition and communicative use by pygmy chimpanzees (*pan paniscus*). *Journal of Experimental Psychology: General*, 115/3: 211–35.

Schmelz, M., J. Call and M. Tomasello. (2012). Chimpanzees predict that a competitor's preference will match their own. *Biology Letters*, 9: 20120829.

Scholz, B. C., and G. K. Pullum. (2006). Irrational nativist exuberance. In R. Stainton (ed.), *Contemporary Debates in Cognitive Science* (pp. 59–80). Oxford: Blackwell.

Searle, J. (1969). *Speech Acts: An Essay in the Philosophy of Language*. Cambridge University Press.

Senghas, A. (2005). Language emergence: clues from a new Bedouin sign language. *Current Biology*, 15/12: 463–5.

Seuren, P. (1984). The bioprogam hypothesis: fact and fancy. *Behavioural and Brain Sciences*, 7: 208–9.

Seyfarth, R. M., D. L. Cheney and P. Marler. (1980). Monkey responses to three different alarm calls: evidence of predator classification and semantic communication. *Science*, 210: 801–3.

Shatz, M., D. Behrend, S. A. Gelman and K. S. Ebeling. (1996). Colour term knowledge in two-year olds: evidence for early competence. *Journal of Child Language*, 23: 177–99.

Shepherd, R. H. (1991). The perceptual organization of colors: an adaptation to regularities of the terrestrial world? In J. Barkow, L. Cosmides and J. Tooby (eds.), *The Adapted Mind* (pp. 495–532). Oxford University Press.

Shinohara, K. (2000). *Up–down orientation in time metaphors: analysis of English and Japanese*. Manuscript, Tokyo University of Agriculture and Technology.

Shinohara, K., and Y. Matsunaka. (2010). Frames of reference, effects of motion, and lexical meanings of Japanese front/back terms. In V. Evans and P. Chilton (eds.), *Language, Cognition and Space: The State of the Art and New Directions* (pp. 293–315). London: Equinox.

Singer Harris, N. G., U. Bellugi, E. Bates, W. Jones and M. J. Rosen. (1997). Contrasting profiles of language development in children with Williams and Down syndromes. In D. J. Thal and J. S. Reilly (eds.), Special issue on origins of language disorders. *Developmental Neuropsychology*, 13/3: 345–70.

Sinha, C. (1988). *Language and Representation: A Socio-Naturalistic Approach to Human Development*. Brighton: Harvester Press.

Sinha, C., V. da Silva Sinha, J. Zinken and W. Sampaio. (2011). When time is not space: the social and linguistic construction of time intervals and temporal event relations in an Amazonian culture. *Language and Cognition*, 3/1: 137–69.

Skipper, J. I., S. Goldin-Meadow, H. C. Nusbaum and S. L. Small. (2007). Speech-associated gestures, Broca's Area, and the human mirror system. *Brain and Language*, 101/3: 260–77.

Smith, C. (1997). *Sign Language Companion: A Handbook of British Signs*. London: Human Horizons.

Smith, N. (1999). *Chomsky: Ideas and Ideals*. Cambridge University Press.

Smith, N., and I.-M. Tsimpli. (1995). *The Mind of a Savant*. Oxford: Blackwell.

Spivey, M. J., M. Tyler, D. C. Richardson and E. Young. (2000). Eye movements during comprehension of spoken scene descriptions. In L. R. Gleitman and K. R. Joshi (eds.), *Proceedings of the Twenty-second Annual Meeting of the Cognitive Science Society* (pp. 487–92). Mahwah, NJ: Erlbaum.

Stanfield, B. B., and D. D. O'Leary. (1985). Fetal occipital cortical neurones transplanted to the rostral cortex can extend and maintain a pyramidal tract axon. *Nature*, 313/5998: 135–7.

Stanfield, R. A., and R. A. Zwaan. (2001). The effect of implied orientation derived from verbal context on picture recognition. *Psychological Science*, 12: 153–16.

Stone, V. E., L. Cosmides, J. Tooby, N. Kroll and R. T. Knight. (2002). Selective impairment of reasoning about social exchange in a patient with bilateral limbic system damage. *PNAS*, 99/17: 11531–6.

Sur, M., S. L. Pallas and A. W. Roe. (1990). Cross-modal plasticity in cortical development: differentiation and specification of sensory neocortex. *Trends in Neuroscience*, 13: 227–33.

Suttle, L., and E. Goldberg. (2011). Partial productivity of constructions as induction. *Linguistics*, 49/6: 1237–69.

Suzuki, R., J. R. Buck and P. L. Tyack. (2006). Information entropy of humpback whale songs. *Journal of the Acoustical Society of America*, 119/3: 1849–66.

Tallal, P., S. Miller, G. Bedi, G. Byma, X. Wang, S. Nagarajan, C. Schreiner, W. Jenkins and M. Merzenich. (1996). Language comprehension in learning impaired children improved with acoustically modified speech. *Science*, 271: 81–4.

Talmy, Leonard. (2000). *Toward a Cognitive Semantics* (2 volumes). Cambridge, MA: MIT Press.

Taylor, J. A. (2012). *The Mental Corpus: How Language is Represented in the Mind*. Oxford University Press.

Taylor, L. J., and R. A. Zwaan. (2009). Action in cognition: the case of language. *Language and Cognition*, 1: 45–58.

Terrace, H. (1979). *Nim*. New York: Kopf.

Terrace, H., L. A. Petitto, R. J. Sanders and T. G. Bever. (1979). Can an ape create a sentence? *Science*, 206/4421: 891–902.

Thal, D. J., and J. Katich. (1996). Predicaments in early identification of specific language impairment: does the early bird always catch the worm? In D. J. Thal, K. N. Cole and D. Phillip (eds.), *Assessment of Communication and Language* (pp. 1–28). Baltimore, MD: Brookes Publishing Company.

Theakston A. L., E. V. Lieven, J. Pine and C. Rowland. (2004). Semantic generality, input frequency and the acquisition of syntax. *Journal of Child Language*, 31: 61–99.

Thelen, E. (1995). Motor development: a new synthesis. *The American Psychologist*, 50/2: 79–95.

Thelen, E., and L. B. Smith. (1994). *A Dynamic Systems Approach to the Development of Cognition and Action*. Cambridge, MA: MIT Press.

Thierry, G., P. Athanasopoulos, A. Wiggett, B. Dering and J.-R. Kuipers. (2009). Unconscious effects of language-specific terminology on preattentive color perception. *Proceedings of the National Academy of Science, USA*, 106/11: 4567–70.

Thompson, E. (1995). *Colour Vision. A Study in Cognitive Science and the Philosophy of Perception*. London: Routledge.

Tomasello, M. (2011). Human culture in evolutionary perspective. In M. Gelfand (ed.), *Advances in Culture and Psychology* (pp. 5–51). Oxford University Press.